Contributions to Jungian Psychology
by
The Psychology Club Zurich

Series Editors
Andreas Schweizer and Regine Schweizer-Vüllers

Volume 3

Encounters with C. G. Jung.
The Journal of Sabi Tauber (1951–1961)

Including
C. G. Jung
On Feelings and the Shadow.
Winterthur Colloquies

Editing and commentary by Irene and Andreas Gerber

Translated from the German by Marianne Tauber

DAIMON
VERLAG

Contents

Welcome Address

It is due to historical distance that today authentic personal accounts of encounters with C. G. Jung are becoming increasingly rare. Collaborators or successors of this great researcher of the human soul, who supported his scientific studies or experienced him as an analyst, have themselves become historical personalities. The editors of "Contributions to Jungian Psychology by the Psychology Club of Zurich" have all the more gladly decided to include the present document of a young woman's encounter with C. G. Jung during the years 1951 to 1961 as the third volume in the series. *Encounters with C. G. Jung. The Journal of Sabi Tauber* is the title of these very personal and therefore special records.

In their introduction, the editors, Irene and Andreas Gerber, give an impressive account of the development process of the edition of this journal. Sabi Tauber and her husband, Ignaz Tauber, were engaged members of the Club for many years. Because of this affinity it is meaningful to have these records presented in the publication series of the Psychology Club Zurich.

We would like to thank the members of the Tauber family for their permission to publish this book as well as Marianne Tauber for her translation into English. A very big thanks goes to Irene and Andreas Gerber, who, with tireless personal commitment, have made this edition possible. They have proceeded with the utmost competence, care and sensitivity. Their expertise is clearly expressed in the many helpful footnotes.

The editors of "Contributions to Jungian Psychology by the Psychology Club of Zurich"
Andreas Schweizer and Regine Schweizer-Vüllers

Preface

In the years from 1951 to 1961 Sabi Tauber kept a journal of her encounters with C. G. Jung, the result of which is a valuable and rare document.

As it has been 20 years since Sabi Tauber's death in 2001, we take great pleasure in finally presenting her journal entries to the German- and English-speaking public. We edited both issues with great enthusiasm.

Sabi Tauber was a young woman, a mother of five, whose personal encounters with C. G. Jung nourished her spirit and soul, and quite literally carried her through difficult years of her life. Whether she visited him in his tower in Bollingen or consulted him in his office in Küsnacht, she was touched by the whole of his presence and felt a deep psychic closeness.

In her journal, she records in a personal and thoroughly honest tone what she experienced during her conversations with Jung. She notes his answers to her questions and his comments on her dreams (occasionally also on those of her husband Ignaz Tauber) most conscientiously. C. G. Jung, for his part, responds individually to Sabi Tauber's concerns, but always points to the archetypal reality he recognizes behind the respective problem.

Here, Jung speaks in such a natural and utterly human way that his lively spirit touches us with immediacy. His language is spontaneous, at times completely unacademic, but always connected to what is essential, and deeply meaningful. Those who are familiar with Jung from his books might be surprised at the discernibility of his deep insights, as expressed in his everyday language. The stupendous precision of Jung's thoughts are here embedded in an atmosphere that gives a whole other quality of feeling.

On four occasions, between 1955 and 1959, C. G. Jung accepted invitations from the Tauber family to come to Winterthur, in a private setting, to answer questions of the family and their friends. Sabi

Tauber has integrated also the recordings of these evenings of conversation in her journal.

In one of the last dreams that Sabi could recount to Jung before his death in June of 1961, it reads: "We receive a red and golden box from Jung, with something precious and substantial in it." – May the reader of this edition partake in this treasure.

The editors:

Irene Gerber, MSc, Jungian analyst in private praxis

Andreas Gerber, PhD

gerber.editors.tauberjung@gmail.com

Zurich, December 2020

Acknowledgments

We would like to take this opportunity to thank all those who contributed to this publication.

First and foremost, we are deeply thankful to the entire Tauber family for their great trust in us and in our editing work, by name Christian Tauber, Roswith Tauber, Marianne Ludwig-Tauber, and Marianne Tauber. Their memories of Sabi Tauber, some of which still very vivid, were helpful and enriching. They have made it possible to clarify many biographical details.

Marianne Tauber deserves our greatest thanks. She is the translator of Sabi Tauber's journal into English, including the Winterthur Colloquies. With personal commitment, she contributed significantly to this edition. For many years, the journal records of Sabi, Marianne Tauber's friend and mother of her late husband Jürg, has been close to her heart. With their agreement to include the English translation in this edition, we can now happily present the edition in two languages.

We would like to thank the Foundation of the Works of C. G. Jung for reclaiming the rights of the no longer available publication, C. G. Jung, *Über Gefühle und den Schatten. Winterthurer Fragestunden* (*On Feelings and the Shadow. Winterthur Colloquies*) from the Patmos Verlag, Düsseldorf. This made its republication possible. The *Winterthur Colloquies* appear in a new form, but the content remains unchanged. This is the first time it is being released in English. We thank the members of the board of the Foundation of the Works of C. G. Jung for trusting our editing efforts. Managing director Thomas Fischer and Bettina Kaufmann have accompanied this project with beneficial momentum.

We would like to express our warmest thank to Regine Schweizer-Vüllers and Andreas Schweizer for their immediate, spontaneous agreement to include Sabi Tauber's journal in the publication series of the Psychology Club Zurich. With much personal and professional sensitivity they contributed from the background and provided various valuable suggestions. They explicitly stressed that a proper edition needed notes and comments to help the understanding of those readers who have only limited knowledge of C.G. Jung's psychology.

A heartfelt thankyou also to the people who helped correct the manuscripts from mistakes and have drawn attention to some bumpy spots, in particular to Regine Schweizer-Vüllers and Ursula Stüssi for the German volume, and to Judith Dowling for the English volume. Thanks to Marion Meister for her support in translating our introduction into English.

For his interest and his commitment to publish a special work like this one we deeply thank Robert Hinshaw, Daimon Verlag, Einsiedeln.

Finally, we gratefully acknowledge the financial support of various institutions and foundations interested in Jungian psychology.

Introduction

About this Edition

"I am handing you my journal," Sabi Tauber is reported to have said to her son Christian in the spring of 1984. "Do with it whatever you please. You can burn it or, if you think it could be valuable for others, you can publish it after my death." Obviously she had no objection to publication; on the contrary, she simply did not want to burden anyone with it. Burning was certainly never an option. Sabi also left a copy of her journal to her daughter-in-law, Marianne Tauber, who resides in the USA; she might translate it into English and then, if she should wish, have it published someday.

As trustingly as Sabi handed over her journal to her son, Christian Tauber handed it to us in 2016, asking whether we could imagine doing the editing. He saw it as a continuation of the transcription work we had done on *Winterthur Colloquies* published in 1999.

A brief, initial glance at the densely typewritten pages was enough to realize that the document held real pearls – many eternally authentic teachings of C. G. Jung. These teachings had not only been helpful to the journal's author. They would also be an inspiration to a wider public, who, with the help of Jung's knowledge of the unconscious, is tracing the great questions of humanity. What Jung has to say, for example, about the meaning of the shadow for the continuity of our culture, should not concern us less today than it did then.

The document is extremely valuable, not least because fewer and fewer people remain that can still give such an authentic account of Jung *as a human being, as a man*.

The pathway from the raw typescript to this book, however, would turn out to be long and challenging. It seemed sensible to us to coordinate the German and English editions, since at that point, the English translation by Marianne Tauber was already well on the way.

As soon as the idea of a bilingual edition was welcomed by the entire Tauber family as well as by the Foundation of the Works of C. G. Jung, the project could really take off.

Sabi Tauber's journal integrates the recordings of the aforementioned discussion evenings, where C. G. Jung answered questions within a relatively small circle of the Tauber family's friends. Parts of these recordings were already published in 1999 under the title, C. G. Jung, *Über Gefühle und den Schatten. Winterthurer Fragestunden (On Feelings and the Shadow. Winterthur Colloquies)*. At that time, the text was accompanied by three CDs with the original audio recording. However, the publication had been out of print for some time. In November 1998, in the foreword of the textbook of the abovementioned publication, Christian Tauber wrote:

> "In October 1955, C. G. Jung visited Sabi and Ignaz Tauber-Scheitlin in Winterthur for the first time. Within the family circle, each of us five children was allowed to ask Jung a personal question. When he returned, on May 26, 1956, the circle of attendees had been extended by three couples, with whom they were friends. During his third visit, on May 29, 1957, ten more acquaintances and relatives joined, and someone recorded Jung's answers on tape; unfortunately, the recordings were incomplete. It was not until his fourth visit, on June 27, 1957, that I was in possession of my own tape recorder, and, with Jung's explicit consent, I was able to record all the questions and answers. On March 3, 1961, Jung's state of health no longer allowed him to travel to Winterthur, so the last question and answer session took place at his home in Küsnacht – without a tape recorder.
>
> An initial question would be presented to Jung in the car, as the hosts were picking him up in Küsnacht or Bollingen. All other questions developed in the moment during the course of the evening. [...]"

The *Winterthur Colloquies* are being republished here; and for the first time they now appear in English. A revision wasn't considered necessary, even if, after today's editorial review, perhaps minor linguistic corrections would be made and a few more comments added in footnotes.

The division into chapters and titles (On Feelings, On Redemption, On New Symbols, On Projections, On the Shadow, On Psychological Insights) were added at the time by Walter-Verlag. They remain unchanged to help the reader recognize the identity of the recordings. They reappear here in their original chronology.

The question of what form Jung's statements should take was a bit of a challenge for the present volume. At times, Sabi Tauber wrote her notes during a discussion with Jung. Probably more often, however, she made them immediately afterward, so they can't be regarded as actual quotations. The same applies to Ignaz Tauber's notes, also found in this volume. He made them as a follow-up to a particularly meaningful meeting with Jung. Consequently, where no audio recordings exist, quotes in quotation marks seemed inappropriate and illegitimate.

In the English translation, Sabi's quotation marks were kept in place, which can be justified as far as every translation of a text into another language is a subjective judgement call. Importantly, what Jung said to Sabi shall not be understood as literal quotations. This does not mean that we found any reason whatsoever to doubt the accuracy of the recorded content of Jung's statements. We decided to distinguish Jung's words from Sabi's questions, either by offsetting them visually or by marking them as "commentary." Sometimes we used indirect speech, and other times we appealed to the reader's feeling to apprehend who is speaking.

Because Sabi – an abbreviation of Elisabeth – carried her affectionate pet name throughout her life, we would like to refer to her that way as well.

Preserving the atmosphere of Sabi Tauber's journal entries was particularly important to us. They naturally reflect her own personal way of experiencing, which we would like to honor with the utmost respect. This also includes the fact that we have only made compelling linguistic improvements. Of course, the dialogues in Swiss dialect were noted by Sabi in High German; nevertheless, the colloquial language cannot be ignored. In order to preserve the character of journal entries, we have only very cautiously adapted them to High German. We find it, especially in the case of Jung, quite refreshing to hear his own way of speaking.

At times, considering today's understanding, Jung's wording is not politically correct. However, we need to keep in mind that he lived in a time when people spoke in a certain way, and that it was one of his outstanding qualities to call things directly by their name. Terms like "negro," "primitive," or "archaic" are examples of what was considered acceptable use of language at the time. When we look contextually it becomes obvious that far be it from Jung to make derogatory or racist remarks. Jung's writings, letters, seminars, and even this publication give ample demonstration of his high esteem for those we now respectfully refer to as indigenous peoples. So, for the sake of historical accuracy, we abstained from adjusting his wording.

We have added numerous comments in footnotes, many of which establish the connection of C. G. Jung's spontaneous utterances to his collected works. Some simply provide the reader with useful additional information. The footnotes of the two editions are naturally not completely identical, but rather have been aligned to the extent that the German- and English-speaking reader now hold essentially the same book in their hands.

We have placed particular emphasis on treating the private matters of all persons addressed as sensitively as possible.

Biographical Notes

Sabi lived from 1913 to 2001. She was born Elisabeth Scheitlin, in Winterthur, on August 27, 1913. She had two sisters, seven and thirteen years older. She spent most of her life in the small, proud industrial city of Winterthur.

Her mother, Emma Scheitlin-Steinbrüchel, was a devoted housewife and an excellent cook. She loved the arts and cultivated her talents in embroidery and sewing. She enabled her daughter Sabi to take lessons in music theater and rhythmics with the then-famous Mimi Scheiblauer in Zurich, who was one of the pioneers in introducing rhythmics as a learning tool in remedial education. Later on, Sabi placed great emphasis on musicality and body movement in the education of her own children. All of her five children learned to play an instrument, and daily practice was just as much part of everyday life as brushing their teeth. Sabi loved playing the piano. When she played Bach's Italian Concerto, for example, and her children danced to it, she was thoroughly delighted. Music gave her a lightness that helped her endure hardship.

Sabi's father, Emil Scheitlin, held a significant position as a mechanical engineer at Sulzer AG in Winterthur. In 1936, he received an honorary doctorate from the ETH Zurich (Swiss Federal Institute of Technology) for his significant inventions. He was the inventor of the so-called Sulzer steam turbine. When Sabi was one year old, he took on an attractive job in Petrograd (St. Petersburg). The family moved with him to Russia, where they experienced challenging years from 1913 to 1917. When the outbreak of the revolution forced them to return to Switzerland, the mother and the three girls traveled ahead. On the way home from Petrograd, via Finland and Sweden, Sabi fell ill with scarlet fever and had to spend several months in the hospital in Stockholm. As a result, she suffered from a heart valve disease that wasn't recognized until she was about forty years old.

The original title of Sabi's journal was "Wind in My Face." The title referred to an unforgettable childhood experience that connected her to her father: On several occasions she had the opportunity to experience with him the inauguration of a new steamboat on one of the Swiss lakes. She used to love to sit on the ship bow and watch how the water parted. She loved to feel the wind blowing in her face.

Much later in life she remembered feeling the same fresh breeze in her face whenever she met C. G. Jung.

Sabi was thirty-two years old when she first met Jung in Rapperswil, in 1945, at a lecture for the Medical Society of the Canton of Zurich. It was in the coat room. Jung's hat had fallen to the ground. When she leaned forward to pick it up, Jung did the same, so their heads bumped together. Jung said, laughing: "Wow, you have a hard head!" Sabi replied: "And so do you!" Maybe it was during the lecture that Sabi felt the desire to talk to Jung in person?

Sabi was burdened by family tensions from the time her father got involved in an extramarital relationship. The much younger woman lived with the family: the marital couple and their three daughters. In the beginning, at least, her father's mistress was appreciated by everyone, but later was ostracized as "the temptress." After Sabi's mother passed away, the mistress became the wife of the 80-year-old. At the time, Sabi was without doubt friendly towards her father's second wife, and she may have always possessed a conciliatory eros. Yet, her eros was seriously put to the test once more in her own marriage.

At a young age she swore to herself to never start a family, to never get married and have children. Fortunately, fate had other plans. Right at the beginning of her medical studies she met Ignaz, who radiated vitality. Ignaz dreamt of having at least twelve children, and soon his life-spark also ignited Sabi.

Ignaz was born in Alexandria, Egypt, on December 28, 1907. He was the son of Bernhard and Amelia Tauber-Luzzatto. He had a twin sister and five other siblings. His paternal ancestors were Jews and came from Czernowitz, today's Chernivtsi, in Western Ukraine. His father Bernhard completed a successful military career before turning to a career in diplomacy. As consulate councilor of the Austro-Hungarian Empire, he was sent off to Alexandria, a vivid and cosmopolitan city at the time. Ignaz would have lasting memories of the Arab nannies that punished him and his siblings with horrific stories of demons. And even though he suffered from nightmares, his soul felt a deep, lifelong connection to the Egypt of his childhood days as well as the country's ancient mythology. His wish or urge to write a research paper on Egyptian mythology is mentioned several times in Sabi's journal. – During World War I the family had to leave Alexandria. After yearlong stays in Rome and Cologne, the Taubers were finally able to settle in Switzerland. The once wealthy family had suffered great losses. Ignaz had to complete an apprenticeship as a commercial clerk. Later he took evening classes to attain the qualification for university entrance (matura), before he could finally begin studies in medicine.

Sabi for her part wanted to become a medical doctor in order to help poor families in India. When registering at the University of Zurich, she met Ignaz – though it wasn't their first encounter: the

Tauber and Scheitlin families had previously met in 1923 during their vacations in the mountains. After their engagement, she gave up her own career aspirations. They married in 1935, and throughout Ignaz' time as an assistant doctor she went along with him to various destinations.

Their children were born between 1937 and 1950: Roswith in 1937, Jürg in 1938, Christian in 1942, Lotti in 1944, and Marianne in 1950.

Sabi took the initiative to find a home for the expanding family. She succeeded, and in 1942 they were able to move into their house on Salstrasse 37 in Winterthur. It offered enough space for the large family, and for Ignaz's medical practice on the ground floor.

A little anecdote from that time, the early 1940s: A bookseller friend of theirs from Winterthur sent a new book release to Dr. Tauber for review: *The Psychology of C.G. Jung*, by Jolande Jacobi. Sabi returned it immediately: no interest. The book was sent to them twice more, the third time it sat around the house until it was too late to send it back. Ignaz became strangely fascinated by the book and began reading it, until Sabi took notice and threw it in the trash. Ignaz bought another copy and secretly continued reading it at night. One day, Sabi's curiosity was finally aroused, and she began to read it as well. They were both hooked. Ignaz began an analysis with Jolande Jacobi, and Sabi with C.A. Meier.

After that, the Taubers bought C.G. Jung's books and together discussed what they had read – for Sabi it had been something like a "daily service." When a painful episode broke out in the marriage relationship, necessitating a deeper examination of the unconscious, Sabi wrote to Jung asking if he would take her and her husband into analysis. Jung had to decline, saying he could no longer take new analysands, but sent Sabi to Barbara Hannah and Ignaz to Marie-Louise von Franz. For both of them, this was the best thing that could have happened.

In the early 1950s, Sabi and Ignaz started attending the Psychology Club in Zurich, founded by C.G. Jung in 1916. Jung was often present and gave frequent lectures. In 1952, with a warm recommendation by Jung himself, the couple became regular members. From 1977 to 1984 Ignaz Tauber was president of the Psychology Club Zurich.

Here we close our biographical notes on Sabi and her husband Ignaz. Out of the many recollections of their descendants, we have noted mainly those events that contribute to the understanding of the journal records. There are still many anecdotes yet to be told, many historical details to be revealed, joys and tragedies to be recalled from this life rich with memorable events.

Let us call to mind that the very biography of an individual is essentially created by the self.

Thunderclouds Over the Marriage

With the help of metaphors such as "stormy clouds" and "a dark cloud from which thunder rolled and lightning flashed," Sabi confides in her journal that her marriage suffers deep turmoil. She experiences that archetypal forces can interfere in human relationships as powerful natural phenomena. Ignaz had apparently fallen in love with another woman; Sabi suffers for many long years from this tense and humiliating situation.

Many years later, Sabi retitled the typescript of her journal, "Déjà-vu," assumedly because she realized that she needed to endure and suffer in her marriage what she had likewise experienced as a child, albeit from a different perspective. This time, however, she could share her dreams with Jung. And Jung recognized that basically, the love entanglements of her husband, which were painful for her, had the potential to set her on her individual path. What happens to an individual human being cannot be rationalized away if it is orchestrated by the self and not by collective moral concepts: at least not without causing psychological damage.

Anima and animus are not mere theoretical terms, but names of the divine figures operating in the background of such drama. In Jung's understanding, the anima of a man or the animus of a woman are determining factors that seek to lead individuals to unknown goals in their creative lives. However, if inadequately comprehended in consciousness, these factors potentially create a disturbance that can develop into an irritating and torturous presence, especially in a marriage. They begin to act autonomously and cause any number of disruptions.

In the case of Ignaz and the way he experienced his anima, Jung's explanations are real eye-openers. Jung advised him to focus, by putting down on paper the *essence* of his work on Egypt, so as not to get lost in intuitions. This would help a great deal in liberating him from his anima problem. Jung recognizes that Ignaz is in the grip of the archetype. However, he does not simply defend him on that account; he also expresses outrage over his tactlessness and cruel lack of feeling towards his wife. He sees Ignaz' inflation as the cause of this insensitivity. He explains to Sabi the significance of anima projections and the effect they have, not least, on sexual life.

Jung also does not mince words in regard to Sabi's pronounced animus problem. She suffers, understandably, from her husband's anima entanglements; nonetheless she *herself* is called upon to pursue a creative activity. Not only he, but she, too, has to take on a creative task, even though she is already occupied with caring for five children. For this reason, he supports her participation in a group he has put together for further research on synchronicity. (See below.) Sabi possibly sensed something of this mystery early on, but had yet to understand, by way of her own suffering, that the conflict is rooted in the self. Sabi is noting here core ideas of Jungian psychology.

Only if we recognize this great arc of psychic reality, that is, if we are aware of the presence of divine figures in marriage, can we understand why Sabi, sometime later in her life, almost feels a kind of gratitude that Ignaz did not spare her such difficulties. The love problem formed the *prima materia* for her individuation process, to put it in alchemical words.

Transference to Jung

Sabi is soon destined to experience for herself what it means to be seized by archetypal forces. Quite obviously, she has a so-called "transference" to Jung. Or, as we like to say: The god Eros has hit her and made his incomprehensible demands on her.

Jung encouraged her not to evade, but to allow herself to be over-whelmed by that which is greater than herself. For, so says Jung, with-out being gripped, a person could have no deep experience coming from such an encounter; there would be no effect and ultimately no value.

Sabi registers Jung's comments and interpretations of her dreams, she writes poems full of longing and makes warm-hearted paintings of her encounters with him. Hardly by chance, Sabi records the words of C.G. Jung on the cover of her journal, from his biography *Memories, Dreams, Reflections* (chapter "Late Thoughts II"):

> "There is no better means of intensifying the treasured feeling of individuality than by the possession of a secret which the individual is pledged to guard."

The mystery of her life – or should we say the myth of her life? – is her soul's encounter with C.G. Jung. Occasionally, in the journal, she calls him the "old wise man" or "guru." While this may sound somewhat effusive to today's ears, it was undoubtedly a truth for her. Sabi indeed experienced in Jung the psychopompos, the guide of her soul. He was a guru for her, that is, the personification of an archetypal figure with superhuman charisma and irresistible appeal. Jung, for his part, explicitly refused to accept the role of guru, as we read in Sabi's journal. But he was clear about the function and effect of this significant projection: The conscious experience and such enduring deep emotion can bestow meaning upon one's entire life.

Due to his enormous experience, Jung was able to keep the door open to Sabi during those tumultuous years, while, at the same time, remain on guard so as not to identify himself with the Old Wise Man. He was acquainted all too well with the dangerous side of any identi-fication with the archetypal reality. When at one point Jung explained to Sabi that, in that specific moment, he was a god to her – which may cause some readers to be appalled, or to shake their heads in dismay – Jung alludes exactly to this numinous quality of a love projection.

Throughout his life, Jung tried to find words for this mystery, al-though he knew that, ultimately, there are no words. Over his lifetime he dared to interpret, although he knew perhaps better than anyone else that there are only hints, only verbalizing aided by analogies. In his book, *The Psychology of Transference*, not published until 1946, C.G. Jung admits that the transference phenomenon is so complicated and various that he lacked the categories for a systematic account. He therefore preferred to draw upon the symbolism of the alchemical opus. Here, he had found an adequate language for the otherwise inexpressible. He concluded that the innermost essence of transference is the uniqueness of a life individually lived. Transference belongs to that kind of processes, which nobody can grasp from outside, but which, on the contrary, holds the individual concerned in its grip.

With a lot of personal courage and self-honesty, Sabi Tauber took upon herself all that was visited upon her – but that she had not sought – by fate. Accompanied carefully by Jung, it was possible for her to experience the transference to him, and thereby sense the meaning-giving dimension encountered in this relationship.

The following words are from Sabi's last journal entries: "*He* has shown all of us the possibility of creating culture out of transference. Not a complete sacrifice is required, but a transformation! [...] Not to the beyond belongs our purest love, but into our living hearts on this Earth."

C.G. Jung's Interest in Oracle Methods

One of the longer passages yet to be mentioned in Sabi's journal, for which a few explanations may make many a reader grateful, addresses Jung's occupation with various oracle or divination methods.

Jung and Sabi discuss several geoscopes as well as tarot card spreads, and often they would add a hexagram of the *I Ching*. We reproduced the sketches photographically to preserve the original character of the material they studied together.

Anyone who makes the effort to understand Jung's resulting comments in detail will be amazed at the astonishing connections he makes and will certainly find them rewarding. However, it is not so easy to find one's way through these passages, and often the reader might wish to learn more from Jung than can be found in the short-hand of Sabi's notes.

The question arises: *Why* and *in what way* did C. G. Jung pay so much attention to divination (to geomancy and the tarot, in addition to astrology and the Chinese oracle of the I Ching)? Our anticipated answer: Apparently, he was interested in "synchronicity." But why? And what does that entail?

Jung refers to synchronicity as a meaningful coincidence or correspondence of two events, which are not causally connected. Or, in other words, as a coincidence of subjective and objective facts which cannot be explained causally, but which convey the feeling that a latent meaning exists. Sabi Tauber quotes Jung in her journal: Synchronicity "doesn't work causally, but meaningfully, and only when deep emotion is involved!"

The terms "meaning" and "meaningful" are important here. In his most relevant essay on this topic, "Synchronicity: An Acausal Connecting Principle," C. G. Jung specifies that "meaning" is the essential criterion of the synchronicity phenomena; but what comprises the meaningful factor is beyond our recognition. Nevertheless, Jung wanted to find suitable methods by which the reality of the collective unconscious could be objectively determined. He postulated the existence of an organizing archetype, the archetype of the self, to which he also ascribed the property of unified psyche and matter.

Jung was engaged in the question of the psychological conditions that he suspected behind synchronistic events. When he came across the Chinese *I Ching*, he encountered, for the first time, an entire religious philosophical system that did not characterize linear relationships by cause-and-effect, as is so prevalent in the West, but rather described synchronistic phenomena. His acquaintance with Richard Wilhelm, translator of *the I Ching: Book of Changes*, must have been one of the most significant in Jung's life. Thanks to Wilhelm, Jung gained access to synchronistic thought, which he understood as complementary to the causal thinking of the West. The classical Chinese way of thinking does not consider the question of why something happens, or which factor causes what effect, but rather, "what likes to happen together in a meaningful way in the same moment," to use Marie-Louise von Franz's terminology in *On Divination and Synchronicity: The Psychology of Meaningful Chance.*

These were the connections that fascinated Jung. He wanted to know if the same kinds of connections were also observable in geomancy, the tarot, and, last but not least, in horoscopes. C.G. Jung had an immense interest in astrology, which is extensively documented in Liz Green's book *Jung's Studies in Astrology. Prophecy, Magic, and the Qualities of Time*, published in 2018. Early in life he had already calculated his birth charts. In his *Red Book* he repeatedly illustrates the signs of the zodiac. Throughout his entire body of work, he constantly refers to his psychology in relation to the Platonic age, notably in the *Visions Seminar*, held from 1930 to 1934 (published in 1998), and in *Aion: Researches into the Phenomenology of the Self*, one of his major works.

Even though Jung had rounded off his book on synchronicity by including a preface in 1950, in no way had he considered his research on the subject to be complete. Synchronicity phenomena continued to preoccupy him, perhaps more than ever. This becomes clear from numerous letters of the 1950s and also from the here present journal records (1951 to 1961).

This is where we learn of a group of people who were asked to collect data for Jung, empirical facts for a research project. This group consisted of Sabi Tauber, Linda Fierz-David, Jung's daughter Gret Baumann, Hanni Binder, the latter two of whom were experienced astrologers, and others. It appears Jung hoped to gather as many synchronistic occurrences as possible; he wanted to present a kind of "proof" to substantiate his hypothesis on the reality of the collective unconscious, and ultimately, the unity of psyche and matter. Basically, he wanted nothing less than to shed light on a still obscure field, which to him was of the greatest philosophical importance, as he writes in the preface to his essay on synchronicity. He sought to appraise modern science of his ideas on the living reality of the archetype. At one point, at a colloquium at the Tauber's in Winterthur, he explains *why* for him astrology had its justification: "… because there exists an objective psyche." To substantiate this was his great concern.

In this context, we can now understand the task Sabi Tauber was given. It consisted of interviewing hospitalized accident patients about how they assessed their psychological state or emotional condition before or during the accident. Did they remember dreams or extra-sensory perceptions or anything of that sort? (According to Christian Tauber, there is an archive of one hundred respective cases still waiting to be processed.) Jung wanted to explore whether a possible synchronistic coincidence could be discerned related to the accident, or, as we might say today, a specific unconscious conditioning factor, a constellating archetype.

When he and Sabi brooded over tarot cards and geoscopes – and although these sections may seem of little use to some readers of the journal – we should be aware that Jung's search centers on the great range of questions surrounding synchronicity. The same holds true for the fact that when he encouraged Sabi to write a paper on the *I Ching* and her astrological research. It was not because Jung was looking for a method to predict the future! It was even his explicit intention to revise the paragraphs on astrological experiments in his publication on synchronicity, because he was always misunderstood. He expresses this, for example, in a letter to Prof. Markus Fierz, February 21, 1950 (*Collected Works*, vol. 18). Jung knew very well that parapsychological phenomena could not be proven by applying probability theory – otherwise such phenomena would be causal. In a letter to Prof. Hans Bender, director of the Institute for Frontier Areas of Psychology and Mental Health, on February 12, 1958, Jung states that his question was aimed at the psychic conditions of their occurrence, and he would abstain from coming up with a semi-physical energetic explanation. Nothing could be explained at all by giving such phenomena names like telepathy, clairvoyance, precognition, psychokinesis etc.

Jung's interest in the connection of psyche and matter goes very far back, in fact all the way to this student days, when from 1895 onward, he participated in spiritualistic séances. Now when, in 1951, Sabi quotes Jung in her journal: "In addition, there was the problem of soul and body," a problem also alluded to in his essay "Synchronicity: An Acausal Connecting Principle," published in 1952, we learn something about the psychological burden brought upon him by these questions. His whole life long he attempted to shed light on a mystery that he later called *unus mundus*, in reference to the alchemist Gerhard Dorn.

A few additional comments need to be made in regard to geomancy, which Jung discussed with Sabi. (For technical details about how to create a geoscope, see the notes in the text.) Here also, Jung is less interested in fortune-telling than in the exploration of the archetypal background. In her book *On Synchronicity and Divination*, in which Marie-Louise von Franz captures the depth of the entire issue, she calls geomancy a "terrestrified astrology." We also refer to her book *Number and Time*, in which she details the geomancy technique and its significance for Jungian psychology.

***

Our account of Jung's work on synchronicity brings our introduction to a close, with one further note. It remains to point out the great distress caused to Sabi by the research assignment given to her by Jung. As hard as she tried, her journal states, she often felt overwhelmed by the complexity of the subject matter. There are differing accounts among her descendants as to whether this was why Sabi plucked up the courage one day to write to Jung and ask for an audience, or whether it was rather the agonizing marital situation that was the motivation.

Whatever the reason, it can be said with certainty that Sabi's journal begins with Jung's answer to her letter, in which he offers her an appointment and describes the way from Bollingen station to his tower. Sabi gained a very private access to Jung, as it were through the back door – metaphorically and quite literally – just through the hidden wooden door of the tower of Bollingen.

Irene and Andreas Gerber
Zurich, December 2020

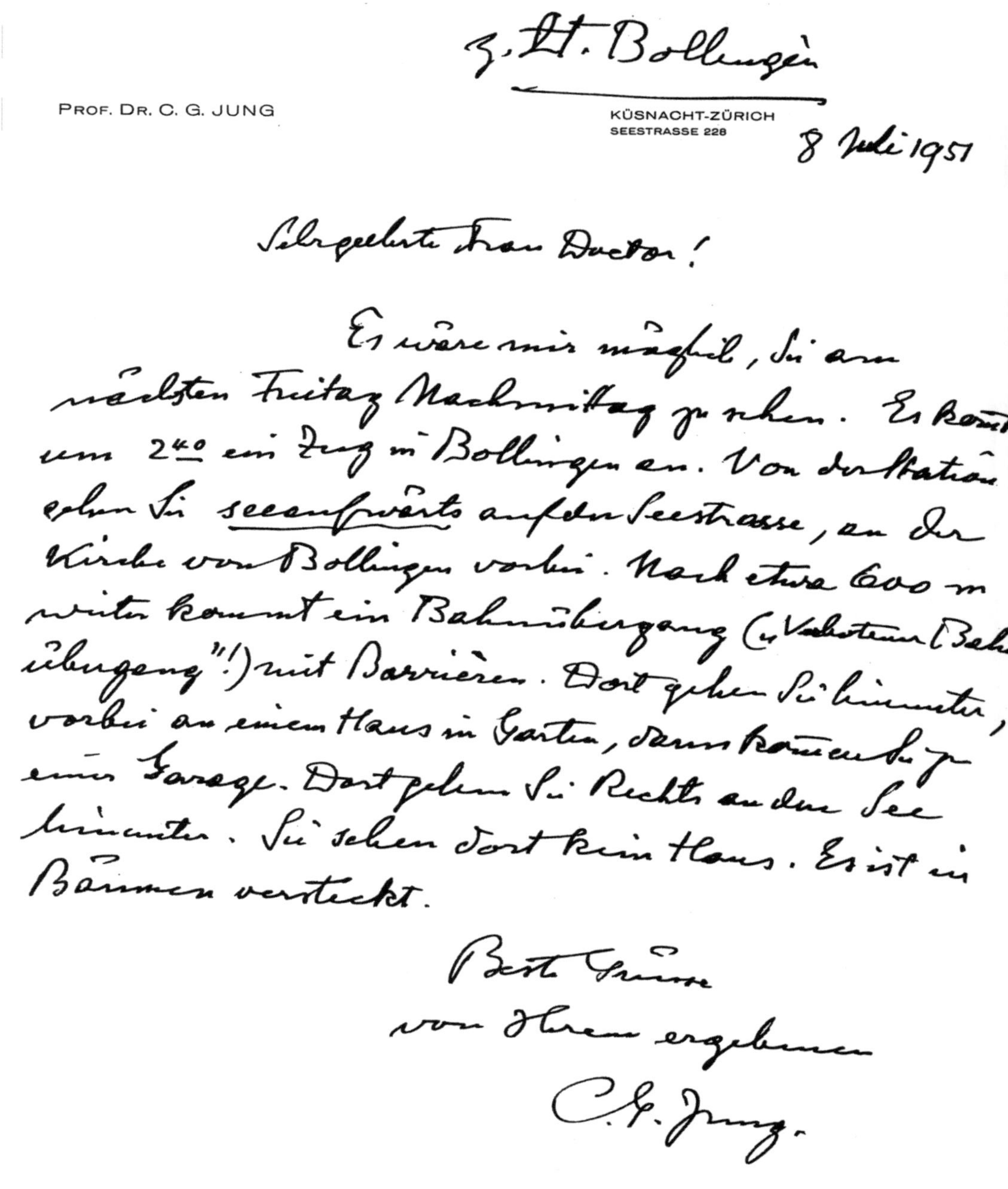

PROF. DR. C. G. JUNG

z. Zt. Bollingen

KÜSNACHT-ZÜRICH
SEESTRASSE 228

8 Juli 1951

Sehrgeehrte Frau Doctor!

Es wäre mir möglich, Sie am nächsten Freitag Nachmittag zu sehen. Es kommt um 2⁴⁰ ein Zug in Bollingen an. Von der Station gehen Sie seeaufwärts auf der Seestrasse, an der Kirche von Bollingen vorbei. Nach etwa 600 m weiter kommt ein Bahnübergang ("Valotimm Bahnübergang"!) mit Barrièren. Dort gehen Sie hinunter, vorbei an einem Haus im Garten, dann kommen Sie zu einer Garage. Dort gehen Sie Rechts an den See hinunter. Sie sehen dort kein Haus. Es ist in Bäumen versteckt.

Beste Grüsse
von Ihrem ergebenen
C. G. Jung.

Fig. 1: Letter of C. G. Jung to Sabi Tauber, July 8, 1951.

1951

Bollingen, July 8, 1951

Dear Frau Doctor!
It would be possible for me to see you next Friday afternoon. There is a train arriving at 2:40 in Bollingen. From the station you walk along the Seestrasse up the lake, past the church of Bollingen. After about another 600 meters there will be a rail-road crossing ("crossing prohibited"!) with barriers. There you cross and go down, past a house in a garden, then you come to a garage. There you go to the right down to the lake. You won't see a house. It is hidden in the trees.

Yours sincerely,
C. G. Jung

I was standing at the lake with this letter in my hot fist, one hour too early. A few meters to the right, between dense green branches, a charming old wooden door was beckoning. I had to clench the other hand into a fist as well. What was the matter with me? After all, I wasn't that young any more, with five children, a beloved husband – and a heavy backpack full of problems. But waiting for a whole hour in front of this door would have been asking too much. By now I knew myself well enough to question the state of mind I would have been in thereafter. *Hic Rhodus, hic salta!*[1] flashed through my mind. I quickly stripped my clothes, hid them behind a bush, and swam out into the wonderfully cool lake. Farther and farther – I had

---

1   An athlete from Rhodes visiting Sparta bragged about his prowess back home, whereupon the Spartans challenged him: Rhodes is right here, jump here! As C.G. Jung writes in *Memories, Dreams, Reflections by C.G. Jung*, recorded and edited by Aniela Jaffé, translated from the German by Richard and Clara Winston (New York: Vintage Books, rev. ed., 1989), p. 189, it was his "watchword." Jung knew that everything he experienced was ultimately directed at this real life of his. He meant to meet its obligations and fulfill its meanings. – *Hic Rhodus, hic salta!* became a favorite maxim of the Tauber family.

a whole hour – just become as cool and light and gray as the water! But I got tired. Turning around, I could see the gray tower at the shore, thick stone walls, and a thicket of shrubbery, but also, to my horror, a sailboat landing exactly at the spot where I had hidden my clothes. I held out for a while longer in the lake, but my strength was vanishing fast, and my conscience was calling time. How utterly silly I felt, slipping hurriedly past a group of men and disappearing in the bushes! I didn't look back, but I could discern very well the one deep, thundering bass among their voices, and that one seemed to come closer. In a mad rush I slipped into my clothes, barely minding the red ants that had crawled in there – a far cry from the serene and quiet countenance with which I had intended to present the many questions I had pondered for so long.

"Ah, so that was you?! Well, there is no more escaping now; please follow me right away!" The voice thundered beside me like the last judgment, but the hand held out for a greeting was thoroughly benevolent, steady and calming to my trembling nerves. The scenery of the strangely-funny "men's group" indulging in an opulent vesper meal within the strong walls of this fort belonged to the image that unfolded in my soul with glowing colors.

"Why didn't you come long ago? Could I have been any nicer to you people? I had to pull you by the hair. One can feel such a thing. After all, we are all connected underneath, and whoever can dive has a felt sense for others in a wide circumference. In the future, see to it that my soul can be at ease within its field of vision and come sooner if things are not going well!"

While lecturing me thus, his eyes nevertheless were resting on me with so much warmth and benevolence that I was completely comfortable, in spite of the felt sense that he knew everything about my soul already, and more than I did myself. It was right for him to know and that now everything, as it were, belonged to him.

Then I remembered my severely ill, dying mother at home, and I told Jung my dream:

> Jung stood tall in front of me and made the sign of the cross with a broad, all-encompassing gesture. Behind him was an

Fig. 2: Outside the door of the tower in Bollingen.

age-old menacing crone, and beside me my husband's anima.[2] Only with Jung's gesture did the two women became visible, and at the same time his gesture protected me against them.

The danger of the dark mother was within me, he said. But I was not to crawl into the dark earth and get stuck in there; rather, I was to wriggle through it cunningly and smartly. That's what one should be able to do! Movement, not paralysis! *Vorwärts ist alles!*[3] Darkness wouldn't want to swallow up the light, otherwise it would cease to exist as well. Right here, on these shores, he once had witnessed a fish jumping out of the water before being swallowed by a snake. But then the fish got stuck in the throat of the snake and both died.[4] Mother cannot swallow father, lest she dies too!

The question arose from within me, "how did you withstand the great darkness?"

Jung's voice was calm when he replied, "I wasn't always able to. But because I surrendered to the darkness, it released me again. You have to be more honest! Pay attention to every movement of the soul, look at it, and be lovingly creative with it. A *noli me tangere*[5] attitude makes one dumb and unrelated. True relationship enriches. To engage in a short-circuited sexual liaison leaves one poor and dumb – one has cheated oneself. If other people's wings are lame, leave them behind; you two are to fly on nevertheless. The true spirit, as it lives for example in the *I Ching*[6] – clear and yet cunning; clever

---

2   According to Sabi's oral communication to her family, it was his practice assistant at the time with whom he had fallen in love.

3   Forging ahead is what matters, a German vernacular.

4   See Barbara Hannah, *Jung. His Life and Work: A Biographical Memoir* (New York: G.P. Putnam's Sons, 1976), p. 236: "He was so much struck by this synchronistic event that he carved the incident on the wall of the courtyard in Bollingen. – Jung's idea was that the serpent represented the pagan spirit, which is emerging so strongly in our times, and that it is trying to eat the Christian spirit, represented by the fish. The new reconciling symbol, for which the alchemists were searching, will be born from these two opposites."

5   *Touch me not*, Jesus' words, to Mary Magdalene after his resurrection (John 20:17). Obviously, the meaning is different here.

6   *The I Ching or Book of Changes*, translated by Cary F. Baynes from the German translation of Richard Wilhelm (Princeton: Princeton University Press, Bollingen Series XIX, 1967).

and wise; open and yet hidden – this spirit helps in dreams and in daily reality to break the spell of the dark mother."

After that, he showed me with great satisfaction the entire fortress he had built with his own hands. In the room up in the tower, however, silence fell upon us; it spoke in its own language, one of the hardest works in the great darkness, of surrender, despair, and of sacred prayer. Heavy steps went ahead of mine, back down the steep, winding staircase. This hunched-over back, how wonderfully strong it must have carried, a lifetime! Jung accompanied me back out into the world, switching to a lighter, conversational tone, as if to cover the deep experience with a silky veil. "Will I succeed with this, my life?" I asked, barely audible. "I certainly would say so!" he thundered, piercing me with his steady gaze. "Only the shock of your own splendor might be too much! But never again are you to swim that far out into the lake. You are in danger, and you must know that."

Jul 13, 1951

He touched me
and brought me to the place
where one takes one's life in hand
and trusts that it may succeed.
He protects me against the power
of the Great Mother,
not overwhelmingly seriously; he even laughed!
Such is the true spirit!
And so that I'll always know
I was allowed to see his best attire:
his humanity.
Please, let me never forget him!
Then, in the great darkness,
I will never drown.

On 11 August, 1951, my mother died. During her last and most difficult days, my youngest, my baby, lay in the cradle next to her bed and made cheerful little noises. It must have appeared like a little angel to my mother, who wouldn't turn her eyes away. Now mother is an angel herself, helping us from the other side.

Mother! Dear!
I pick it up and carry it with joy!
You had to go
and left us
that, which on this earth
still needs to be accomplished.
I hold it sacred and work on it
as much as I can.
Dear God, help me along!
so that, when you will call, it shall be done!

Next to mother's obituary there was a beautiful quote from the poet Hölderlin:

Unser ganzes Leben ist ein nie wiederkehrender Geburtstag der Ewigkeit,
den wir darum freudiger und heiliger begehen sollten.[7]

Summer was warm and imbued with intimacy, especially early morning with the pearls of dew on mother's grave. Planting her gravesite became my innermost, sacred joy. It was as if through this work her essence would open within me like a flower. In my daily life, ever so often I was able to take a tricky emotional situation as a welcome opportunity to live through it fully. Thus, I sometimes would sit at my baby girl's cradle singing softly to her, precisely when the daily workload was heaviest. And my mother seemed to thank me. Or I would play the piano instead of doing the bookkeeping – and life became large and wide.

And yet, by the same measure that time merged with eternity, there was an urgent voice within me: "It's later than you think, make use of your time!" When could I go see the old wise man again? How? Never without having done my work. I forced myself to write down a meditation on the I Ching, # 50 Ting, "The Cauldron," then I asked for another session. Again, there was a gentle smile in his answer, "why not any sooner?" It made me sad, thinking how poorly I was able to

---

7   Our whole life is a never-to-return birthday of eternity, which we, there-fore, should celebrate more joyfully and holier. Presumably by Jean Paul (1763–1825), not Hölderlin.

"dive" and feel the underneath connection. Did he even know how difficult it was for me to live "right"? How much I craved to launch into an inspiring spiritual task – or, just as wonderful and engaging, to simply live according to my feelings, free and unbound like a bird! Against those urges stood everyday life with its many petty chores and obligations. Neglecting those, however, rendered spiritual work and living my feeling impossible.

"Is there a path here?" I asked the Great One faintheartedly, on a gray November evening. Jung answered mildly, telling me matter-of-factly about the almost unbearable challenge of his destiny: For the past 150 years, the ancestors on his mother's side had been ministers, on father's side physicians. He had to take on the issues from both sides and solve them! In addition, there was the problem of the body and soul.

"Often it is the dead ones who are calling on us with their questions and problems. Everything spiritual comes from that realm. Each one takes on his ancestors and passes himself on to the next generation with one's own solution. To find the right way between the calling of our destiny and the tasks of everyday life is very difficult. Weekdays, this is what you do: in the morning you sort out the very urgent from the urgent. The question is: is it better that I do very little for only a few people, or that I die from exhaustion and not be able to do anything for anybody anymore? One has to bear the fact that one cannot do justice to everybody. Then you make a program for the day and hold on to it ritually! By all means, one has to fight every day for one's own free time to restore libido within, otherwise one perishes in today's fast paced, empty rushing. I for one don't go to concerts or the theatre anymore in the evenings. Try to have your kids in bed by 8 pm, and from 8 to 10 pm the time belongs to you and your creativity. Be consistent! But at 10 pm you ritually wrap up and go to bed, otherwise the body gets abused. Discipline makes happy. In your own evening time, you fulfill the demand of your destiny, and thereby think of Confucius' little story:

> A man fell into a torrent and was carried along in the roaring waters. Further down the river became very quiet. There, the man simply climbed on shore again and walked on.

There are times when one has to let oneself be swallowed up by the Great Mother, so that she can spit one out again! That's rebirth and regeneration. People who have a lot of contact with others have to be ready for this sort of regeneration, otherwise they perish!"

I had sent my little essay on the *I Ching* ahead of time and now asked him for his opinion.

"It is good," he said, "because you saw the essence, and you didn't speculate too much. An intuitive has a much more difficult time to cut his wings and stay close to reality. If he doesn't, it's all up in the air, and a depression will surely follow. He ventures into a cave without a light and a rope, and that is too dangerous. Thinking is the light and rope for an intuitive to enter into the cave. Each idea needs scientific validation, and a manuscript has to be read and criticized by ten friends before submitting it for publication. This is intellectual rigor! Because I feel responsible I read all manuscripts that are sent to me, even though the burden of my work almost crushes me."

Winter brought long, dark nights. My dreams became heavy and puzzling. But the Old Wise Man kept his promise about the open door. Shortly before Christmas he enlightened me with his comments to the following dreams:

> (1) Jung secretly whispered a name for me in my ear. Nobody else knew the name; it was sacred.

Jung commented that he, or the Old Wise Man, gives me my name in place of God, which only he and I know, so that I may recognize God and he recognizes me. Consequently, I have become an individual and thus capable of a *Visio Dei*.[8] This is why baptism of newborns is so important, so that they are known by God and have a vision of God if they die early. There are primitives who have two names: an ordinary name and a secret one, only known to the medicine man. Nobody else may know it, lest the person be bewitched! With the name-giving, God bestows his *mana* (numinous power)[9] onto the soul. In an Eskimo

8   Vision of God.
9   C. G. Jung explains how he applies the term *mana*: it can be traced back to the primitive or archaic idea of the "extraordinarily potent", and it still echoes in the Latin *numen* and *genius*. The use of the term *libido* in newer medical psychology has surprising affinities with the primitive *mana*. See for

custom, a louse of the grandfather is put onto the newborn's head; in that way *mana* is being transmitted. The self is being crystallized in the name. One should not give children too exotic, unusual names (parents perhaps indulging a pathological fancy), so that they don't have to be 'hopeless individualists' without real *mana* for this world.

> (2) After an operation to remove my tonsils I was laying on a bed, weak and tired. A monster was sitting on top of me, sucking my blood at the sutures. I was the only one to see the monster, nobody else could. But I was unable to talk, so I wrote onto a piece of paper that only Jung could help me. He came, detected the lesion, and told the doctors exactly where another suture was needed. After that, healing occurred.

Jung: "A tonsillectomy is needed when external poison combined with our own, inner poison becomes one source of poison. Such a monster is very dangerous, for as soon as it is finished with its victim, it goes on to the next one, that is, such a libido-drain into the unconscious 'spreads' and endangers your husband and your children! One becomes the monster, because the libido flows backwards into oneself. The lesion in your case is the inferior, negative intuition. It should lead positively to your feeling, but instead your intuition cuts the feeling off negatively. The blood empties toward the inside and worthlessly seeps away, instead of pouring out into a creative act, full of joy and strength!

For example, a famous, formerly very creative composer came to see me, complaining that he could no longer compose. It turned out that he had a patroness who gifted him much money and a villa.

instance C.G. Jung, "General Considerations and Prospects," in: *The Structure and Dynamics of the Psyche, Collected Works*, vol. 8, par. 441. See also Marie-Louise von Franz, *On Divination and Synchronicity. The Psychology of Meaningful Chance* (Toronto: Inner City Books, 1980), p. 66: The ancient "concept of *energeia* or *mana* can also be understood simply as the extreme impressiveness of something."
The Collected Works of C.G. Jung (referred to as CW), transl. by R.F.C. Hull (except CW 2, 6, and 15), New York: Pantheon Books for Bollingen Foundation, 1953–1960; Bollingen Foundation (distributed by Pantheon Books, a Division of Random House), 1961–1967; London: Routledge & Kegan Paul, 1953–2014; Princeton, New Jersey: Princeton University Press, 1967–2014 (Bollingen Series XX).

Then she stopped, and he could compose again. The money from outside had plugged up his creative source. In your case, the negative intuition is blocking the natural stream of feeling, threatening death. Open the floodgates and pour out your feelings! Venture into life; get a positive attitude!"

It was as if Jung would throw a golden ball into the depth of my 'inner fountain.' Through him I experienced God. He said that he didn't 'believe' – he 'knew.' And I know now firmly through him.

> (3) I wanted to cross a lake together with my youngest child, to go to a chapel on the other side. Suddenly, a high wave ripped my child away and carried it out into the lake. (I woke up horrified.)

Jung: "Well, this is wintertime, when Demeter has to cede her child to Pluto. The Rivergod has kidnapped the child; it's his turn. You have to say yes to that; you have to let it be winter, give yourself to the Rivergod – only then can it be spring again, rebirth. And besides, you don't have to 'endure' it; precisely not to endure, rather, you have to let yourself be overwhelmed, for he is greater than you – he is God! The meaning lies in the wave flooding you. Not that you have to overcome the unconscious; the unconscious has to overcome you. It's an amazing grace to be chosen to become Pluto's mother-in-law, and it is a fabulous honor to be personally called by the Rivergod! God needs the child part-time, because he has to restore its *mana*, renew its divine nature, therefore it is the divine child. The youngest daughter symbolizes one's own future, which one can never fully experience because one dies before that. The other half of the daughter belongs to the Other." (See also the Ishtar-Tammuz legend).

> (4) A timeless wanderer was walking with me through the ages. He showed me ancient carpets and marvels from all over the world, saying that they all belonged to me, for my great-grandfather on mother's side had been a vagabond.

Jung: "We all are pilgrims. We should not be all that attached to this world. A tramp is unbound; he is only a visitor on this earth; his home is in the beyond. The dream tells you: This is what you carry within – know and appreciate it!"

Fig. 3: Rivergod.

(5) The Rivergod emerged from the river and called me.

Jung: "Don't let the Rivergod wait! It is a distinctive honor to be called. A primitive would become chief because of it. With every experience of God our understanding grows, and we become capable of greater things. The self doesn't give us tasks we can't do. One cannot write and speak of everything about God, but between two people one can feel it."

> Wie auch die Welt ihm das Gefühl verteure,
> Ergriffen fühlt er tief das Ungeheure.[10]

Deep down in his eyes I recognized the Rivergod – and drowned in him. "Now I could put a spell on you, since I know your name!" sounded the deep voice. I only nodded, for it had already happened. But he continued, "I'm not so sure, perhaps it's you who are bewitching me at the moment." I burst out laughing, which made him say very earnestly, "See, you'd be delighted!" I was alarmed.

Once again, the experience of the encounter was so big that I could barely tolerate it. Nudging me gently back into reality, he said soberly, "When people are coming to me with red cheeks, bright eyes, and warm hands, then I know that they have put a considerable stream of libido into our meeting and it becomes a deeply meaningful experience, effective and valuable. With averted gaze, a pale face, and cold hands nothing happens; you put nothing into it and get nothing out of it."

The day had started gray and foggy; now the world lay before us in a golden robe of sunlight. It was such a gift.

> The Rivergod, I didn't let him wait,
> he didn't have patience either.
> I danced with him and lived him fully
> and he bestowed on me his wreath divine
> for a new life!

---

10 Faust speaking, "However scarce the world may make this sense / In awe one feels profoundly the immense." J.W. von Goethe: *Faust II*, Act I, Dark Gallery, verses 6273 f., translated by Walter Arndt, edited by Cyrus Hamlin (New York, London: W.W. Norton & Company, 1976, 2001).

No wonder, then, that Maya casts her nets and slings to entangle me in everyday life. It virtually hailed conflicts. They weren't exactly put at my feet; they pierced my heart.

1952

In the new year (February) I went back to see Jung with the following dream:

> I was lying in bed; on my bed cover a beautiful little salamander. Relatives and friends came in to tease and torture it. I stood up to defend it, wanted to protect it, but it shot around in a blind fury, finally hurled itself onto my back and fell onto the floor, dead. I was bleeding in many places and was very sad.

Jung commented, "Don't let your salamander be incited by your relatives! It is a cold-blooded animal that can stand the fire and remains calm through it all. It is the 'stone of wisdom.' Like the snake, it has 'absolute wisdom,' unrelated to the environment. Your relatives can be whatever they want to be, but without you!"

In another dream,

> I laid out a silver snake into the forest to die.

To this, Jung said, "She[11] must not die! She owns the pure spirit! She has a 'spinal soul,' that is, she just does what she does, without reference. For example, she finds warmth, no matter whether in the sun or in a pair of slippers. She moves cold-bloodedly toward her goal. With her silver skin, she is a female moon-snake."

He showed me the ring on his finger that he had brought back from Egypt. (A trip he undertook to get away from the nasty gossip around him, following the powerful motto, One has to let the idiots[12] be the way they are. If one grows angry with them, one becomes one of them.) Engraved into the ring was a snake, rolled up at the bottom, erect at the top, a beam of light around her head like a crown.[13]

---

11 The snake has feminine gender in German, which seems meaningful in this context.
12 Literally, in Swiss German, "the calves."
13 God Abraxas of the Gnostic Basilides, see C. G. Jung, "Septem Sermones ad Mortuos" (Seven Sermons to the Dead), in: *Memories, Dreams, Reflections by C. G. Jung*, pp. 378 ff.; C. G. Jung, *The Red Book: Liber Novus*, ed. by Sonu

Jung continued, "She has both: at the bottom she is embroiled in the world through emotions in the dark; at the top she has light and wisdom. In the future, think of this snake whenever you are involved in a conversation with people of this world who worship the 'God of Reputation' (he owns a vast terrain in this world!), and don't let yourself be tangled up in it. One has to be at home in both domains. Likewise, the Rivergod wants to be flooded by you, not only you by him! (The prostitute wants to be redeemed by the saint; she does not want to seduce him.) You have to become a wave and spread out as a distinct personality with a broad basis. In the ocean you are the mountain; on the mountain, you are water. Both belong to the self. The world infringing upon you is a compensation for the growth of your personality – that's synchronicity!"

In another dream,

> the following mathematica formula was presented to me: $a^2 + 2ab + b^2 = (a^2 + b^2)$

Jung commented: "Now look! The dream shows you the wrong solution, toward which you apparently incline: you are taking the square in, instead of leaving it outside. The right mathematical formula is $a^2 + 2ab + b^2 = (a + b)^2$. Putting the squares into the brackets means that you want to unite (with the brackets) the opposites a and b in their already differentiated and complicated entanglements of the world (in the square). That doesn't work. You want to join two ends that are too far apart. It only works within the archetypal root (a + b)! Only the simplest things can be combined into a union. Exactly such a union of the opposites is expressed in the symbol of the snake that carries the crown of enlightenment above, while below she is curled up on the earth. You have to be mountain and river, earth and water! (a + b) in brackets has the same meaning as the stone of wisdom, or the salamander in the fire – or the Rivergod with the mountain."

Shamdasani (New York, London: W.W. Norton, 2009), p. 205 f.; p. 345, fn 74: "The painting 'Systema munditctius' has a legend at the bottom: 'Abraxas dominus mundi' (Abraxas Master of the World);" and p. 349, fn 93. See also Jung's comment on his ring and Abraxas below p. 165 and in C.G. Jung, *Visions. Notes of the Seminar Given in 1930–1934*, ed. by Claire Douglas (London: Routledge, 1998), vol. 2, pp. 806–808, 1223.

Vast "halls" lit up within me, as if for a splendid feast. From afar I heard his calming voice telling me about the East-Indian delegation that brought him the Om yesterday, a sort of consecration. He had to sit on a square carpet in lotus position; sandalwood incense rose in thick clouds. The delegate from India sat opposite him, pronouncing the Om and a few other words that meant something like, "The truth is the wisdom; in the truth lies the stone of wisdom." He had to eat from a stick made by four young maidens from the juice of forty fruits. A picture was given to him of three women illuminating the path of wisdom with their lights.[14]

At home, I plunged into a project on the I Ching (a comparison between an oracle series and the process of individuation). As soon as I had finished the paper I sent it to Jung. Soon after, he had me come in and declared that it was by no means a scientific work! However, it wasn't a lost effort, for it was valuable in helping me gain terrain in my consciousness. He proceeded by explaining to me exactly what 'scientific work' entailed – until I froze inside. Lastly, he gave me a small, age-old book on geomancy to take home with me and study.[15] He was thinking of a project that I might be able to help him with.

Each time I sat down with this book, the hair stood up on the back of my neck. It was magic, an enigmatic jungle, immensely irrational. Jung was overburdened and had no time for explanations. Every so often I saw him in my dreams, tired and sick. In addition, thick, stormy clouds gathered in our own home,[16] so much so that on an afternoon in the fall I found myself standing in front of that beloved little door at Bollingen, unannounced, desperate. Jung took me in with a wonderful benevolence and understanding, and a week later I was invited for a regular session. Still, he apologized for being so worn out by his heavy correspondence that, unfortunately, he was too tired

14 No reference for this event could be found.
15 Probably the book (in German) Vollenkommene Geomantia ... Punctier-Kunst ... Astrologia terrestris ..., by an anonymous translator (Freystadt, 1703). (Translation of the title: complete geomancy ... dot art ... terrestrial astrology ...) Persistent link to a scan of the copy owned by C. G. Jung: http://dx.doi.org/10.3931/e-rara-5597.
16 Sabi's preferred metaphor for conflict situations, triggered by Ignaz' violent emotional states.

to give any kind of explanation about geomancy[17]. It was my turn, then, to cheer him up by telling him about the various experiences of synchronicity I had had recently. The old man visibly revitalized and new life seemed to pulsate through him. Without quite knowing how it happened, I had my own two geomantic *scuta*[18] laid out on the floor before us, and Jung guided me through them as if following "Ariadne's thread" (fig. 4 and 5):

"The many *populus* here show a rather large unconsciousness within you. In the first house, the unconscious is being presented to you as a task. The *acquisitio* in the third house says that you can master that with which you come into contact. *Fortuna maior* in the fourth house means realization of the self; self-realization in daily reality as basis and foundation. In the fifth house, Mercury plays his ambivalent games and is meddling with your eros and your life-experiments. He

17   The reader will find a few general explanations of geomancy as a method of divination in the introduction to this volume. In the following some details about the technique of this oracle are given. – So-called geomantic figures are being determined. They consist of four lines containing one or two dots (for example ⦂ *cauda draconis*, tail of the dragon). In total there exist sixteen different such figures. In order to obtain a geoscope, sixteen rows of dents are imprinted in quick succession into the sand, or dots are written on paper (hence the term "dot art"). In Arabic, the method, literally translated, was called "sand art", which means "divining from the earth". In a second step, figures are "produced" from the dots. In each row, the points are counted to determine whether it contains an even or odd number – very similar to the I Ching and other oracle techniques. From the results, four geomantic figures are determined, which are assigned to the four "mothers". In several algorithmic steps, twelve further figures are derived from these (for the four "daughters", four "granddaughters", two "witnesses", the "judge" and the "conciliator" / "chief judge"). Finally, in the third step, the judgment is sought and made. For this purpose, the figures are arranged in a certain way. Afterwards, the interpretation and passing of judgment follow, for which there are very comprehensive instructions, which usually establish a link with astrology.

18   *Scutum* (pl. *scuta*, lat. shield) designates a certain shield-shaped order of arrangement of the geomantic figures. However, C.G. Jung and Sabi Tauber used a square arrangement, called *speculum* (lat. mirror). As described above, sixteen figures are determined by counting dots. The first twelve figures (the "mothers", "daughters" and "granddaughters") are arranged counterclockwise all around, corresponding to the twelve astrological houses. The two "witnesses" and the "judge" (*testes* and *iudex*, nos. 13–15) are placed in the middle, while the "conciliator" / "chief judge" (*superiudex*, no 16) is not integrated into the diagram. – Further down, a ring-shaped graphic is used, which links the geoscope and the tarot; there the first twelve figures are placed on the outer circle.

drives you to heights and lets you fall too. He is incomprehensible. You are only half-conscious here. *Albus* in the sixth is the *deus absconditus*, the yet to be experienced, unconscious wisdom – that is your illness (childishness!) and your work. You have a commitment to work, that is, you are called by God, and if you resist, you inevitably fall victim to your illness. And because you are not yet conscious of it, you fall into great sadness, *tristitia*, in the seventh.

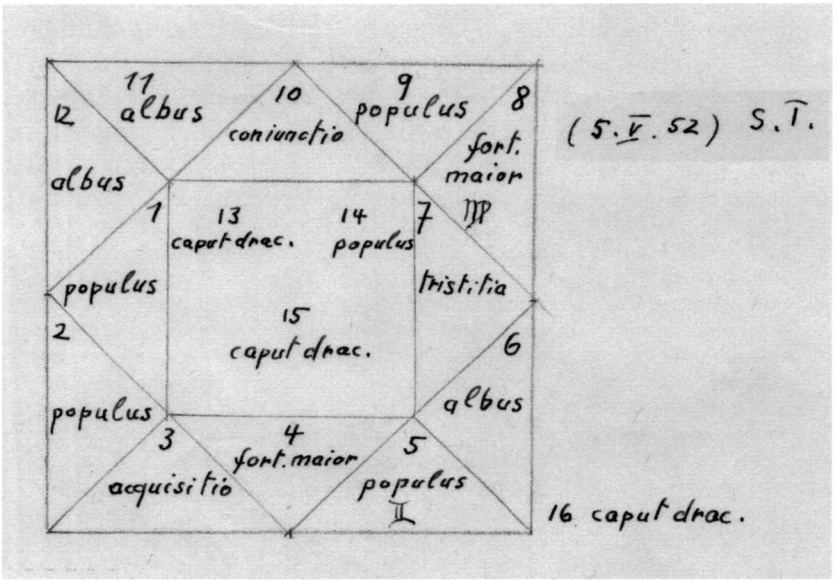

Fig. 4: Geoscope Sabi Tauber, May 5, 1952.

All the difficulties hit you in your marriage and weigh you down heavily. And here, at the end of the seventh house, the end of the first half of life, it always shows whether a neurosis will result, or if one is able to unite the opposites within oneself and to integrate 'life.' The self is illuminating the path in the eighth house (*fortuna maior*, Virgo, Mercury); you can earn it through your work. And this self inevitably will bring you back to your unconscious, *populus* in the ninth, but this time you are armed and prepared through the experience of the self and all of your spiritual, integrative work.[19] In the tenth house we find *coniunctio*, harmony of the opposites, which also has an effect on the outer world. Lastly, God becomes real in the eleventh house, *albus*, a *deus manifestus* (not *absconditus* as in the sixth), that means, you become conscious, which is also indicated in the twelfth."

My second mandala was explicated by Jung three months later:

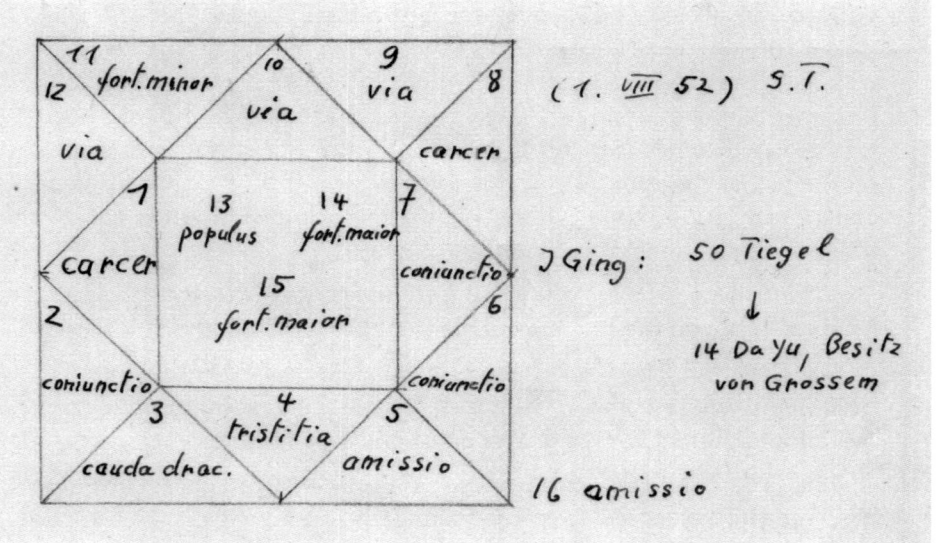

Fig. 5: Geoscope Sabi Tauber, August 1, 1952.
I Ching: 50 *Ting*, "The Cauldron" –
changing to 14 *Ta Yu*, "Possession in Great Measure."

"In the first house is *carcer*, meaning that you are constellated by the *images* of your parents at the moment. But you have the potential to unite those *images* within yourself (second house *coniunctio*). However, a sting from the unconscious is active, in contact with your closest environment (cauda *draconis* in the third house). There you make a projection (summer 1952). In the fourth you fall into a hole that has to do with your innermost disposition (parental images). You therefore miss out on quite a few life experiments (*amissio*, fifth house), but

19 Literally, in German, *geistige Verarbeitung*. "*Geistig*" encompasses both intellectual and spiritual.

through work you will be able to unite the opposites (*coniunctio* in the sixth)! In work and through work you will achieve the same thing for your marriage (*coniunctio* in the seventh). But caution! Whoever has both within, is actually a human god, is dangerous and should be locked up! (*carcer* in the eighth house). A magical circle is necessary and a balancing act: movement! Otherwise the danger of sinking into yourself is too great. You have to imprison the prison (like Paulus)[20]; *vorwärts ist alles!*[21] This is indicated in the ninth house, through *via*, namely the absolute necessity of movement in the spirit. The same is true for outer life (*via* in the tenth), meaning it also shows in how you present yourself (the project on synchronicity). If all is being followed truthfully, *fortuna maior* (in the fifteenth) will manifest, that is the realization of the self. So, you have to engage the unconscious as a collaborator (*populus* in the thirteenth) and acknowledge the self as the goal (*fortuna maior* in the fifteenth)."

Essentially, a) I have to unite the oppositions within me, and b) I have to 'imprison the prison' – movement prevents paralysis!

Oh, that I may find Ariadne's thread again and again! I wouldn't have been able to come up with this interpretation on my own. Once more that autumn, so heavy with emotions, was I granted his help.

This time I laid both the geoscope and the tarot spread[22] of my husband before Jung's eyes [fig. 6 and 7]:

---

20 Psalm 68:18: "Thou hast ascended on high, thou hast led captivity captive..." (King James).
21 Forging ahead is what matters.
22 Tarot is a deck of 78 playing cards used as fortune telling cards. They are divided into 22 trump cards (*le fou, le bateleur, la mort, le diable,* etc. – the fool, the magician, the death, the devil, etc.), called the "great arcana", and the "small arcana", consisting of 56 suit cards: 10 pip cards (Ace to 10) and 4 face cards (here: *valet, cavalier, reine, roi* – jack/ knave/page, knight, queen, king) in 4 suits each (here: *bâton, coupe, denier, épée* – stick, chalice, coin, epee). *Arcanum* (lat.) means secret. Here the cards of the *Tarot de Marseille* are used. On the chart we can recognize: The cards 1–12 are laid out on an outer square – corresponding to the astrological houses in counterclockwise direction. The cards I–IV are laid out clockwise in the corners of an inner square (morning, noon, evening, night), and the cards V–VII in the corners of a triangle in the middle (past, present, future), also clockwise.

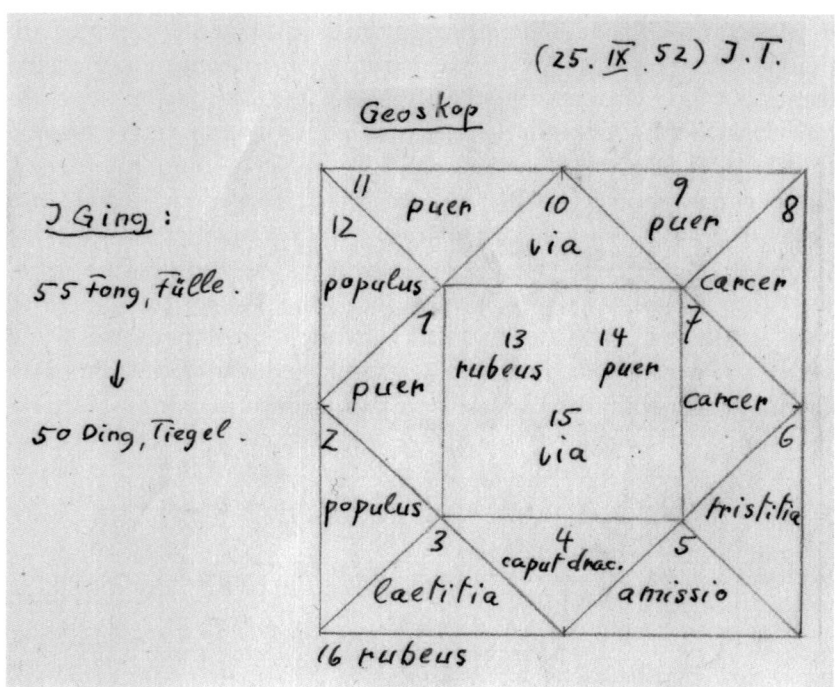

Fig. 6: Geoscope Ignaz Tauber, September 25, 1952.
I Ching: 55 *Fêng*, "Abundance (Fullness)" – changing to 50 *Ting*,
"The Cauldron".

"*Puer* in the first house shows him [Ignaz] as 'one who is becoming,' who is in a process of transformation, and who stores powerful forces in his unconscious not yet at his conscious disposition (*populus* in the second). He is growing in the unconscious. The third shows how it spills outwardly (*laetitia*) in daily relationships with his immediate environment, whereby the unconscious, however, pushes with vehemence through the open door. In the fourth house, *caput draconis*, lives the heritage of his parents; it wants out and to be redeemed. His backward ties want to be redeemed in forward motion!

Amissio, in the fifth house, has him suffer a loss because of his extraversion in the third and fourth; too much extravert movement in *laetitia* and *caput draconis* (his mother's temperament!). Here in the fifth, with his erotic speculations, he suffers a loss in his ability to regenerate, and thus experiences sadness in his work (*carcer*, sixth house). There he falls into a hole, and the entire unconscious falls on top of him and oppresses him with its weight; his body, too, weighs him down. At the moment he feels that marriage is a prison (*carcer* in the seventh), but has to endure it to learn about keeping boundaries. He is even trapped by the unconscious itself (*carcer* in the eighth), but here the prison is already spiritualized! Saturn squeezes out the juice through concentration, that is, he reveals the meaning. In the ninth, the youth appears again, but now on a spiritual level as *puer aeternus* (similar to Faust). This results in an outwardly movement (*via* in the tenth), the personality is unfolding. And similar to the boys' chorus in [Goethe's] *Faust* there now are 'many boys' in the eleventh – with his friends, illusions, and wishes. In the unconscious, the seed for new, expansive growth lies dormant (*populus* in the twelfth)!

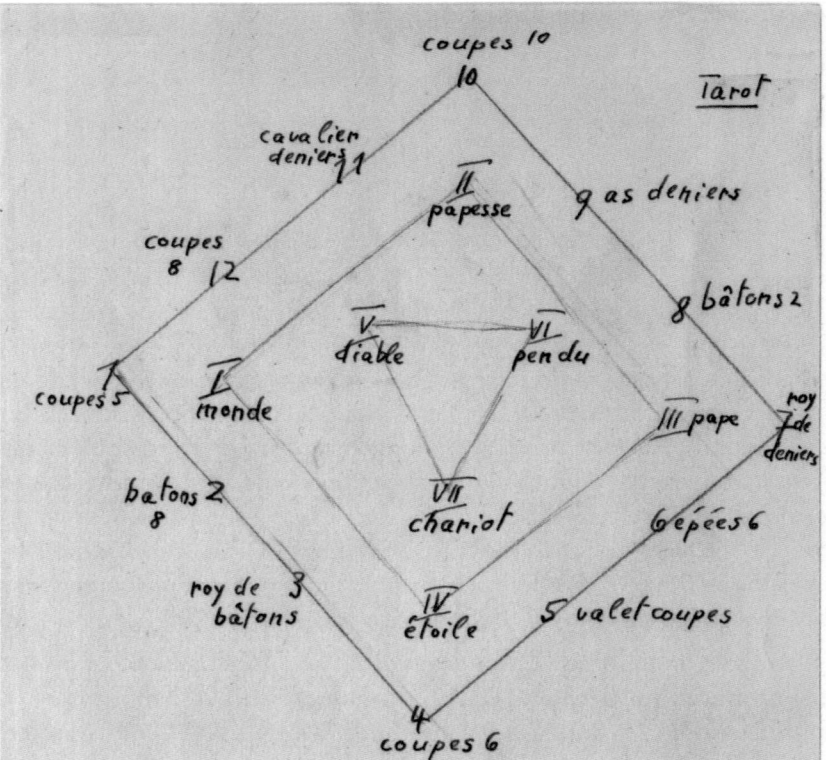

Fig. 7: Tarot Ignaz Tauber, September 25, 1952.

In the layout of the tarot, we first notice his rather feminine disposition as a natural human on earth (*coupes 5* on first place). The second place points to his masculinity that embraces all possibilities (*bâtons 8*). (The number 8 comprises all the planetary energies, 7+1; Mercury counts twice; in ancient Greece one of the gods always counted double.) In the third place, we notice his gallant demeanor towards his environment (*roi bâtons*); as king he does what he wants (parallel to *laetitia*, the overflowing joy in the geoscope). The fourth place, too, (*coupes 6*) corresponds to the fourth house of the geoscope: the outward overflowing (6 is the most potent number, fertile). In the fifth place we find a defeat again; as *valet* he is a servant here. In the sixth place (*épées 6*) insight brings sadness, which becomes fruitful (number 6) and lets him appear as a king of values (*roi deniers*). Independently, out of free will, he acknowledges the value of the prison and accepts it. *Bâtons 2*, in the eighth place, points to a relatively weak masculinity towards his unconscious; he is too modest. (Also, his unconscious is split between masculine and feminine.) The prison in the geoscope has a different effect here: the exuberance disappears. *Ace deniers* in the ninth place indicates the highest value – ace is oneness, the self. It's Sophia who manifests outwardly in the tenth place. In the eleventh place, the *cavalier* equals the boy of the geoscope: he belongs to a 'court' (many). And in the twelfth place there is the number 8 again, as wholeness, similar to the second, but a transformation has occurred, from masculine to feminine (second has *bâtons 8*; twelfth has *coupes 8*).

On place V, the *diable* would compare to the *rubeus* in the thirteenth of the geoscope: *puer* is being confronted by the devil, and if he doesn't take it very seriously, he'll be hung! (*pendu*, place VI) (compare to *Faust!*)

Place II, *papesse* is almost the self, the anima as the inner man (with light and darkness).

Place III, *pape*, refers to the self, *anthropos*, Jesus' memorial stone.

Étoile, on place IV, is also a symbol of the self; the self is calling and has an effect everywhere; it shows itself as light and signpost.

On place VII, *chariot* stands for the way of individuation, transformation."

Every word imprinted itself deeply. He wasn't tired at all; to the contrary, he seemed enlivened. So, I quietly slid a later geoscope of myself [fig. 8] on top of the others,

... and Jung simply continued:

"It starts with transformation in the new moon (*via, luna* in the first house), that is, illegitimately like a secret love affair (in closer vicinity to the sun one's own light would be lost!). The work with geomancy, the tarot, the records on synchronicity – all that seems to be a secret love affair for you, a *novilunium*.[23] There, sun and moon conjoin, but it is dangerous, because it's dark! You must be humble and careful, not too ambitious, by all means. The tarot, with *chariot* in place I also points to that. In the second house, you are an 'overflowing virgin' (*laetitia* in Virgo), actually unmarried, 'the mother drops out'[24]. This is avenged in the third house (*amissio*), because in reality you are no longer a young maiden.

In the fourth, with *fortuna minor* and Scorpio, the whole impact of your relationship to your parents kind of 'implodes' on you; the whole hereditary mass is arrested (here in contrast to Ignaz); in other words, it all remains inside, only the sting (of Scorpio) turns outward. This has to be compensated in the fifth house with this secret love affair, generating a transformation. Tarot with *coupes 6* on fifth place indicates 'fruitfulness,' which gives hope. In the sixth house, we see that your body (your most faithful servant) is experienced as a prison! It is under a lot of stress and withdraws, which, of course, shows up as *amissio* in the seventh, the house of marriage (relationship with Ignaz). The overflowing of the unconscious in the eighth (*laetitia*) is meant spiritually, not erotically. We find the same kind of 'ahead' in the ninth house (*caput draconis*). A *coniunctio*, union of masculine and feminine, the *hieros gamos* of Sol and Luna takes place in the tenth house, in the *novilunium* of May (Taurus, ruled by Venus). In the eleventh, you come into contact with likeminded people (the Psychology Club[25]), there is an exchange (Gemini, ruled by Mercury).

23 New moon.
24 Jung said it in English.
25 In this year, Sabi and Ignaz became member of the Psychology Club Zurich, founded in 1916, and ever since an important place for the Analytical Psychology.

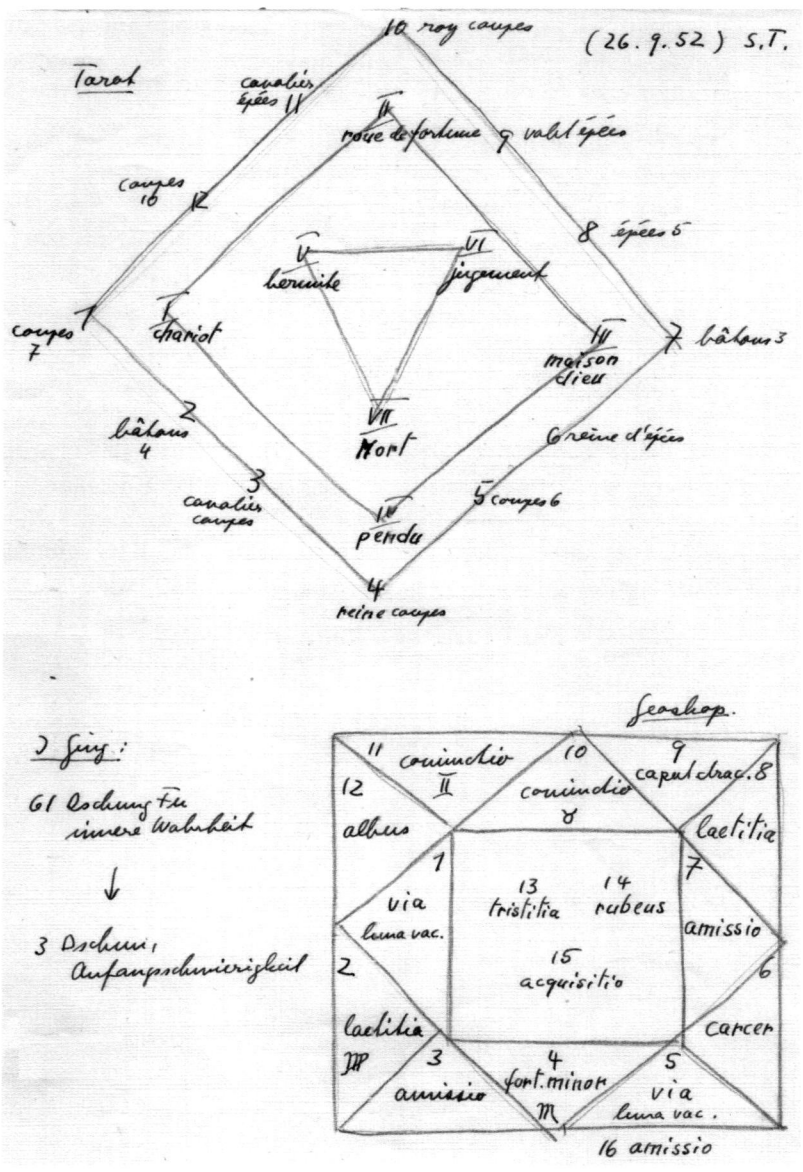

Fig. 8: Tarot and Geoscope Sabi Tauber, September 26, 1952.
I Ching: 61 *Chung Fu*, "Inner Truth" –
changing to 3 *Chun*, "Difficulty at the Beginning".

Finally, corresponding to the independent virgin in the second house stands *albus* in the twelfth, signifying an *anima candida*, the 'one in her own right,' the spiritual virgin."

Together we had undertaken a wonderful journey through the innermost world, where fairytales are true and where the truth is as just as in fairytales. Noon was long past. I quickly took leave, filled to the brim with life. Jung's eyes radiated happiness: This is the real world, isn't it; this is where eternity can breathe!

Immediately thereafter we went on a road trip with friends to the South of France. But this entire summer vacation seemed unimportant. Thank God, Jung had given me a task to take along: to give a concentrated description and an interpretation of all the geomantic figures, so as to completely absorb their essence. I was looking forward to those quiet hours in the tent at Les Beaux. Thereabout we also searched for authentic old tarot cards, unfortunately without success. As it turned out there had been a recent search by the police who confiscated and burnt whatever they could find. An old gypsy woman in Mossam laid the tarot cards for me and Ignaz, and she, too, lamented over the loss of her precious old cards. She told me that my 'minister,' 'father confessor,' was very ill – but that he would get better again. There was also something about a little child standing somewhere in the middle and around whom everything revolved. Further, she saw a project or some undertaking of mine that was in trouble and would become the source of many difficulties. It would cost a lot of time, but it would end happily. Back home I ought to be vigilant, for there was a woman ill disposed toward me! At the time of the reading, many things she said didn't make sense, and I couldn't explain them, but later I could.

Upon return, we heard about Jung's illness[26]. My sweet little girl demanded all my energy and attention, day and night. My psychological work was fraught with seemingly insurmountable obstacles – and my encounter with Mrs. X. was imminent.

During that time, I had the following dream:

> A bird appeared from within a stone and slowly became alive. I had to help it.

26 He repeatedly suffered from the flu and tachycardia (rapid heartbeat).

Fig. 9: Walking towards Jung's house.

Together with my youngest (Butzli[27]) I brought Jung a bunch of pink carnations for Christmas. We both had our arms full. On the long stony path leading from the garden gate to the entrance I told the little girl about the old wise man and his truthful life. After delivering the flowers we hopped from stone to stone all the way back to the gate, making a wish for him on every stone, and when nothing came to mind, we were not permitted to hop on. The mood was so happy and serene, as if Mozart in heaven was accompanying us with his music!

Küsnacht-Zurich
Seestrasse 228
7.XI.52

Dear Mr. and Mrs. Doctor!

Receive our most heartfelt thanks for the marvelous carnations, which in their fullness conjure up a complete spring into the living room and delight us anew every day. I have not yet had a chance to write to you, as my husband has unfortunately caught the flu, which has also affected his heart, although it has already recovered quite a bit. Now the flu is over and we hope that the recovery will continue. It is of course a big test of patience, but fortunately my husband is an exemplary patient. Your charming French bell maid is doing a very good service!

With best regards from both of us,
Yours Emma Jung.

---

27 Nickname for the youngest, Marianne.

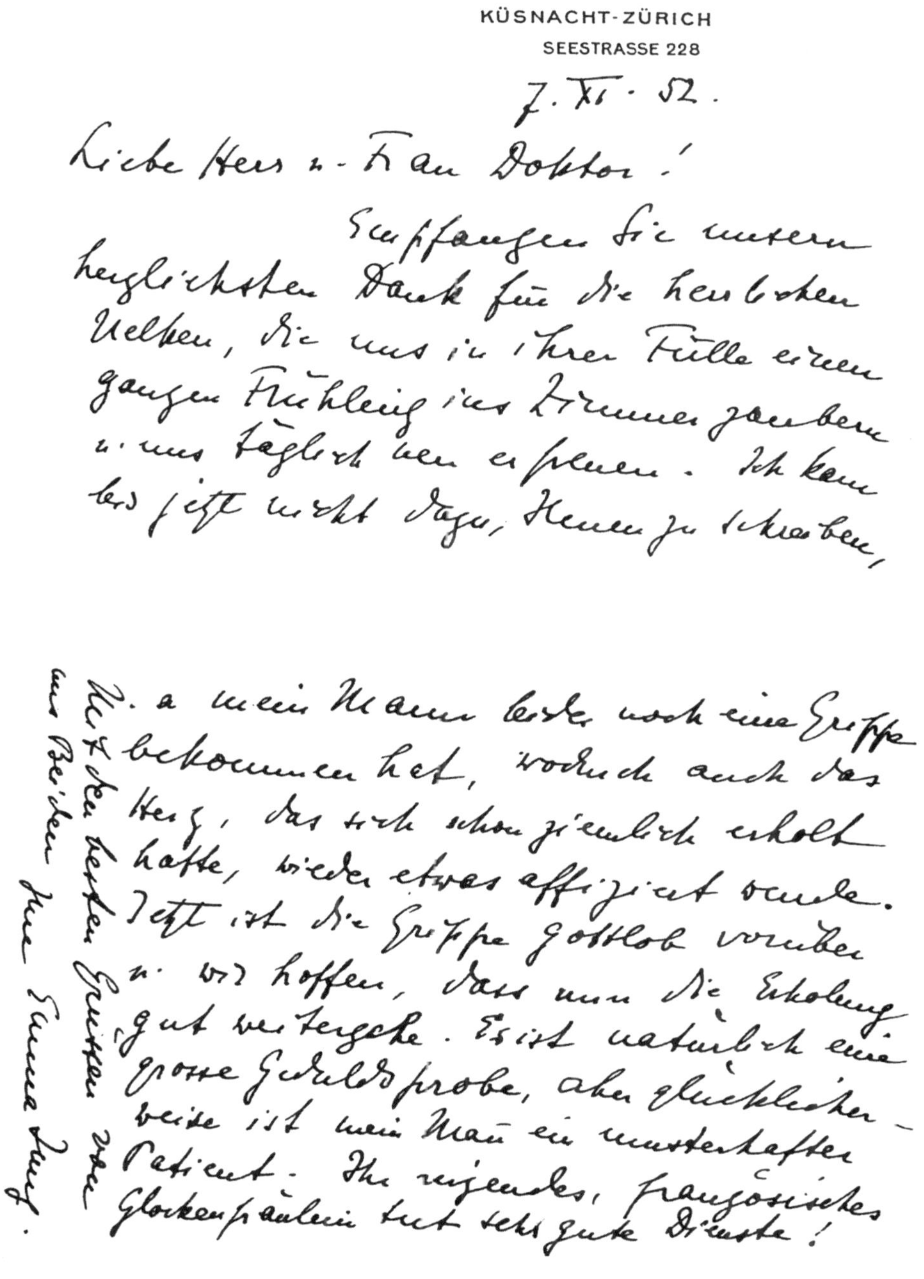
KÜSNACHT-ZÜRICH
SEESTRASSE 228

7. XI. 52.

Liebe Herr u. Frau Doktor!

Empfangen Sie unsern herzlichsten Dank für die herrlichen Nelken, die uns in ihrer Fülle einen ganzen Frühling ins Zimmer zaubern u. uns täglich neu erfreuen. Ich kam bis jetzt nicht dazu, Ihnen zu schreiben, da mein Mann leider noch eine Grippe bekommen hat, wodurch auch das Herz, das sich schon ziemlich erholt hatte, wieder etwas affiziert wurde. Jetzt ist die Grippe gottlob vorüber u. wir hoffen, dass nun die Erholung gut weitergehe. Es ist natürlich eine grosse Geduldsprobe, aber glücklicherweise ist mein Mann ein musterhafter Patient. Ihr reizendes, französisches Glockenfräulein tut sehr gute Dienste!

Mit den besten Grüssen von uns Beiden
Ihre Emma Jung.

Fig. 10: Letter of Emma Jung to I. and S. Tauber, November 7, 1952.

1953

New Year's Eve 1952/53 was horribly dark and heavy. I launched myself with desperation into my work, without a goal in sight.[28] At the beginning of the new year I was allowed to visit Jung. He was sick, indeed, and sad. I was ashamed to have had even the faintest expectations, and he immediately sensed my feeling and said,

"No, there is no libido left, no strength in my heart, and no creative impulse. And that's what you need; that's precisely what you came here for. It's totally natural and okay. But one doesn't really need an analysis when one has real, true relationships and is able to think psychologically. Just be real and true to yourself, and the people around you will be forced to be the same, which will create real and true relationships."

Could I perhaps lend him my strength of heart? He sadly shrugged his shoulders – maybe.

"Of personal matters I cannot speak right now, because that is immensely tiring. But talking about the work is neutral and less burdening." Then he mentioned for the first time a distinguished old lady who knew geomancy very well, saying that she will deal with the organization of the group work. "Honestly, she looks like a ghost and is part witch, but she is very knowledgeable and smart! Only, you may not be afraid of her!"

I plunged headlong into the cold water: I began with the recording of synchronicity phenomena at the hospital.[29] It often seemed impos-

28 See more details of this project in the Introduction.
29 Sabi rarely told her children about her visits to the Winterthur Cantonal Hospital. This one case, however, was deeply remembered: a young man was lying in a hospital bed with both legs amputated. He had slipped with his motorcycle on a railway crossing shortly after midnight and remained unconscious until the first train approached and the accident happened. The man had been on his way home from his mistress. He didn't want to tell his wife about this relationship; he didn't want to put her through this pain. But when he had awakened in the hospital and saw both women entering the room at the same time, not as rivals hating each other, but more like friends who were both happy that he was still alive, he had a felt sense of

sible to do justice to the various chores and tasks – and yet, I knew that they were all demanded by my inner self. I took care of my little daughter alone; during naptimes I rushed to the hospital where I tried to accomplish my task without making a great stir, and then back home again to my big, beloved family. And all this with 'lukewarm' maids. There were moments when I felt close to despair. Once in a while there came a little note from Jung, as encouragement and a reminder to see it through. Then I met for the first time 'the woman' prophesied by the gypsy. Though I'd been prepared, I fell headlong into her trap! It was a good lesson and I am eternally indebted toward her. Thank God, my dreams provided the opportunity to meet with Jung.

At some point, spring always arrives, so, too, in that year 1953. On 13 May I spent a wonderfully happy day in Küsnacht.

I met Jung standing in midst of the blooming spring garden and followed him, filled with expectations, to the little garden pavilion by the lake.[30] The magic of the place had an immediate effect on me. The reeds and waves were whispering,

> Time gone by –
> Am I ready
> For eternity?

Was I? I simply fell into it ...

"You are much too reasonable, that's why your heart is hurting. It's almost suffocating, because it is so imprisoned. You think 'nothing but real'[31] but you should also include *rubeus* and *puella* in your worldview! Those have to be integrated. Out of the so-called 'real world' you have to make a 'psychic world.' Life always has two aspects, and one always has to consider which of the two has precedence and 'counts' at that particular moment: 'my own action' and the 'act of God' (this is precisely how it is called in English law when, for example, lightning

meaning. The synchronicity liberatingly revealed a truth that he himself had not brought over his lips. A leaden heaviness was thereby lifted. (Report by Christian Tauber)

30 In dry weather, Jung occasionally received his visitors and analysands in this little garden pavilion.

31 Jung said it in English.

Fig. 11: Geoscopes laid out in the garden·pavilion.

strikes a house or there is flooding, because it is not one's fault and responsibility – corresponding to the *maison Dieu* in the tarot). In case of 'my own action' one is responsible; one is conscious, has a will, a reason, is rational and moral. In case of 'act of God,' one has to fulfill the will of God, one has to 'let it happen' (Zhuangzi) – I'm happening to myself, whereby often unreasonableness reigns and things happen irrationally. Both sides have to be lived. To weigh beforehand which side is to be given preference is difficult. For example, one simply cannot write a certain letter; there is no reason why not, but one simply cannot do it. Only later it dawns on one (aha, *this* is why it didn't work!). The reason only comes in hindsight, and the deed, or misdeed, is being justified afterwards – that is an 'act of God.' However, if the deed later cannot be justified, perhaps even condemned, then it was negligence or laziness (of one's own acting) and one is guilty. One's behavior has to withstand 'sincere consideration.' 'Act of God' always does.

Precisely because you are much too reasonable and realistic, the life of the soul (the psychic world) becomes so intense and vehement – all *rubeus* and *puella*, which elicits identification with them. Live more in the 'psychic world,' apparently unreasonably and irrationally, and you will integrate *rubeus* and *puella*. In this way they will loosen their intensity and at the same time become real. This closes the circle."

I asked him whether I was not simply too cowardly to live *rubeus* and *puella* in a concrete way. "No," he replied, "it's a fateful calling on which level you have to live it. *Puella* and *rubeus* are psychic factors that can't be dealt with on the level of 'popularity' because of your acute sense of reality – it wouldn't make sense anymore." And softly, but urgently, he added, "Should you ever do something 'unreasonable,' know that it would be an alleviation. Don't let it confuse your heart (that would be identification). Though it might be chalked up to you in outer life, for the inner life it is fine. Thinking like that protects against identification."

Then I asked him about the meaning of the following dream, which did not make sense to me at all:

Ignaz has to expand[32] in one of these two directions: either the vertical = 184, or the horizontal = 148. But he is supposed to do it in the vertical.

Jung commented that 1 symbolizes the (original) unconscious oneness, 4 the visible reality, the world, and 8 corresponds to man as a differentiated psychic vessel for the final oneness.

Now, 1–4–8 would mean to go from the unconscious oneness through the sensible world to the psychically highly differentiated final union. The divine One (1) is diffused in the world (4) and then recollected in a complete union (8).

If, inversely, the path for Ignaz is the outpouring in 1–8–4, this means that, after the unconscious oneness (1), he is directly seized by the divine spirit (8), and that he must realize this in the world afterwards (4). As an intuitive type, he first experiences the psychic world and only thereafter worldly reality (in the tarot correspondingly first *pape*, then *monde*). A woman first lives reality (4) and then comes to the final union (8); therefore her way is 1–4–8.

Lastly, I wished for his own geomancy mandala [fig. 12] to stand as a kind of 'banner' over this research project on synchronicity – it would always be a shining light above us.

I made a short, vague attempt at interpreting Jung's scutum and sent it to him. It remained without answer, so I assume that it might not have been totally wrong:

The tarot[33] shows on place I, the place of 'morning,' *impératrice*, a moving, urging, also supporting anima (goddess of fertility, Artemis). Place II, the place of 'noon,' has *justice*: reaction follows action, beginning of the second round in the dance of the 8, harmony and balance according to the inner law (justice has her eyes covered). Jung's lively connection between consciousness and the unconscious – one's own responsibility and the 'act of God' (Job). On place III, in the 'evening,' stands *force*, indicating the force of Yin with which Jung has insight into the Lion.[34] The wheel of fortune can be halted in order to behold

---

32 In German "sich ergießen", literally, to pour out.
33 Tarot: The square and triangle, in red, together with the second-outermost ring.
34 Jung's astrological sun sign is Leo in the seventh house.

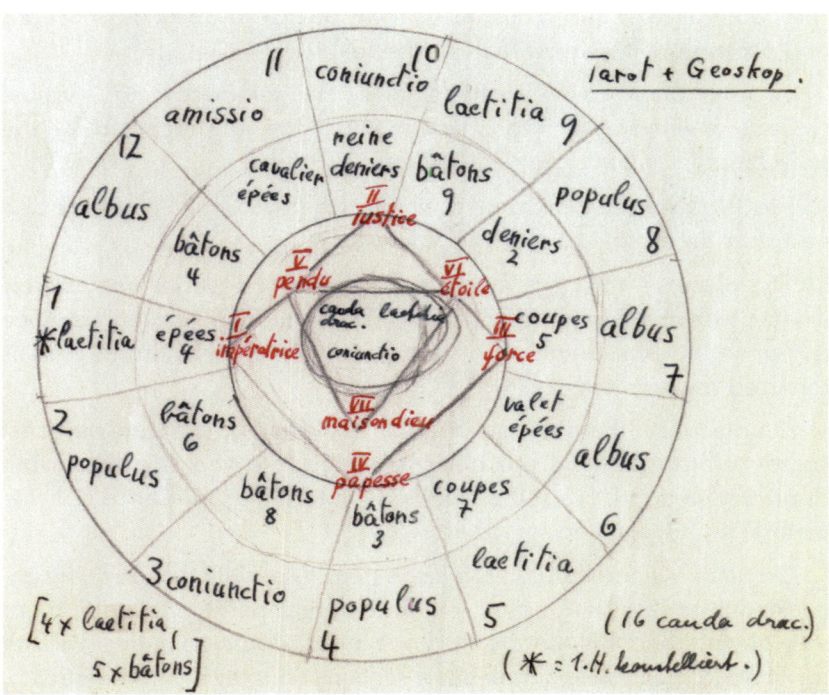

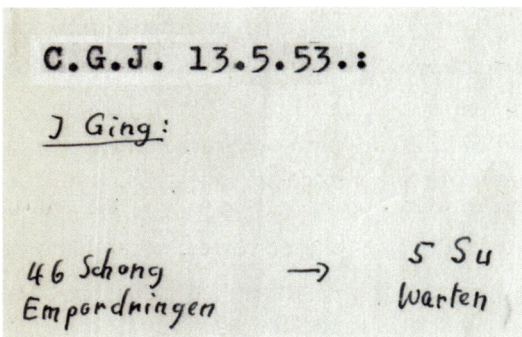

Fig. 12: Tarot and Geoscope C.G. Jung, May 13, 1953.
I Ching: 46 *Shêng*, "Pushing Upward" – 5 *Hsü*, "Waiting (Nourishment)."

the hub. Value of consciousness; in the ballgame, the ball is caught and passed on; invisible effect of the self.

Papesse on place IV, 'night,' signifies the self-becoming, invisible (veiled), a withdrawal into oneself; being lovingly received by the universe, the *anima candida*, Sophia.

I to IV rather spans life as a whole, whereas V to VII seems of a narrower timeframe to me.

The place V, 'the past,' has *pendu,* a violent reversal (may be his illness); loss of libido (gold coins are falling out of his pocket); sacrifice is demanded (the branches of both trees are cut back); the gaze is directed towards the sky (self).

On place VI, 'the present,' there is *étoile* (star), the transpersonal solution (both pitchers are being emptied into the stream); in the depression (night), the self is shining with fateful significance (1 + 7 = 8 stars) for himself and for others.

On place VII, the 'future,' is *maison dieu,* experience of god, the unconscious as fertilizing agent, enlightenment; perhaps development may never stand still. Logos shall not 'petrify' (tower), a lively ability for change must be maintained; a recharging with divine electricity. I believe that the archetype has a positive aspect in this position because of *papesse* and *coniunctio* (*iudex,* no 15) and *albus* (in the twelfth house of the geoscope). Also, *I Ching* # 46 Shêng, "Pushing Upward." Perhaps Jung's attitude toward *maison dieu* should include *papesse.*

1st house[35], *laetitia,* an 'aligned' personality, one with its goal, in appearance supported by the unconscious, undivided, whole and happy; together with épées 4, it means with real spirituality, the truth-loving sword (a constellated house, perhaps pointing to rebirth).

2nd house, *populus,* the collective (conscious and unconscious) became the task, which Jung tackles with fruitful masculinity (*bâtons 6*).

3rd house, *coniunctio,* the problem of the union of opposites is dealt with in the relationship with the closest environment, where

---

35 For both, tarot and geoscope. Geoscope: the outermost ring and the three signs right in the center.

the solution is achieved, thanks to the capacity for totality (*bâtons 8*) (Psychology Club).

4th house, *populus*, strong roots in both the masculine and the feminine element; a solid stand (*bâtons 3*).

5th house, *laetitia*, in life's experiments supported by the unconscious, 'appointed'; fateful encounters with the feminine (*coupes 7*; urging towards *8*).

6th house, *albus*, through his work Jung becomes the 'old wise man'; with his sword at his disposal (*valet épées*) – with discrimination he brings the self into the light.

7th house, *albus*, the self becomes reality in his relationships to other people; here we see a natural-human comprehension (*coupes 5*); warm humanness toward the other.

8th house, *populus* here requires detachment from the collective through individuation. The unconscious embraces duality (*deniers 2*), Devil and God.

9th house, *laetitia*, the unconscious leads him to a deep, powerful relationship to God (*bâtons 9*), (Job).

10th house, *coniunctio*, the fruit of all his endeavors is the *coniunctio oppositorum*, realized both in the profession and within, as the soul approaches values with Yin energy and thus controls them (*reine deniers*).

11th house, *amissio*, a loss of relations; isolation through withdrawing into himself, whereby his sword of discrimination becomes a messenger to the beyond (*cavalier épées*) for himself and others.

12th house, *albus*, though he might be isolated as the old wise man, he lays the seed for the birth of the self for all of suffering humanity. This seed is an accomplished mandala (*bâtons 4*), which will sprout because he is so completely in the truth!

13, 14, and 15 [geoscope]: There are two currents, one toward the inner, one toward the outer, which find themselves in a golden middle movement (here, too, is a requirement to grasp opposition). When in doubt, rather close out the world, and orient within because of *cauda draconis*, as 16. *Papesse*, too, emphasizes 'inwardness,' while *maison dieu* destroys 'outwardness.'

Similarly, the *I Ching*, in # 46 *Shêng*, "Pushing Upward," emphasizes patience, diligent growth around obstacles. Just as in:

> Beschäftigung, die nie ermattet,
> die langsam schafft, doch nie zerstört,
> die zu dem Bau der Ewigkeiten
> zwar Sandkorn nur für Sandkorn reicht,
> doch von der grossen Schuld der Zeiten,
> Minuten, Tage, Jahre streicht.[36]

It changes into # 5, *Shü*, Waiting (Nourishment): strength within, danger without. Strength in the face of danger doesn't rush; it can wait. Quietly gather strength.

The great lines are wonderful, for example: the transformation of soul in the image of the four women (I, II, III, IV): The beginning ("spring") with *impératrice, laetitia* and *épées* 4; then "summer" with justice, reine deniers and *coniunctio*; followed by a fruitfulness ("fall") in *coupes* 5, *albus, force, étoile* (*force* on earth; *étoile* in the sky), and finally the wise and loving guidance toward Sophia within ("winter").

[Here ends Sabi's attempt at interpreting Jung's *scutum*.]

At the end of that beautiful day in May, however, I found myself standing in front of my car, utterly perplexed: The keys were inside, and the doors solidly locked! Was I dazed, or had my unconscious 'fabricated' this beforehand? But no, there was no awakening as from a dream: I had to go back, ring the doorbell again, and shamefully confess my 'misfortune.' I called Ignaz and asked him to send me the spare keys by express mail. And then Mrs. Jung very kindly invited me for lunch. I was terribly embarrassed, to Jung's obvious amusement. But he had a way to cheer me up so that it became a very pleasant meal for the three of us, with open windows, sunshine and a smiling 'knowing' lake. The two were like my parents, changed and yet the

---

36 Last verse of Friedrich Schiller's poem, *Die Ideale* (To the Ideal): "Sweet toil, in toil itself delighting / that more it laboured, less could cease / Tho' but by grains thou aid'st the pile / the vast eternity uprears / At least thou strik'st from Time the while / Life's debt – the minutes, days and years." *The Poems and ballades of Schiller*, translated by Edward Bulwer Lord Lytton (Leipzig: Bernhard Tauchnitz, 1844).

Fig. 13: C.G. Jung in front of his tower in Bollingen, August 27, 1953.
(Picture taken by Sabi Tauber.)

same. I received and found myself engaged as mediator, transformed and yet, also, the same.

This is the year I turned forty. Perhaps the fates thought that it was time for intensive shadow work – and set Mrs. X. directly onto my narrow path. I was glad not to be able to evade her, coward that I am. In support, and as a reward, I was privileged to experience Miss Hannah's genuine courage and energy.[37] She gave me a felt sense of a wonderful righteousness. Catching my every thought of flight, yet never denouncing my weakness, she strengthened my own courage. "Seeking death is the longing for rebirth," she remarked wisely. Behind every word stood the proof of her own life. At that time she taught me the Chinese saying, which became the ransom that freed me from the very claws of my embodied shadow: "I appreciate the truth so much that I am economical with it."

And it was exactly for my fortieth birthday, August 27, 1953, that I received an invitation to Bollingen!

To start off, Jung encouraged me to continue my work with the synchronicity phenomena, in spite of the difficulties with Mrs. X. Concerning her power and hardness, he gave me the following explanation: "She would have to admit to far more of her own shadow, so as to be in direct contact with the earth. Because she doesn't have a 'stand' without such an earth-contact, she constructs a kind of coordinate system in her mind about the world and humanity, and forces everything into it subjectively and despotically. Synchronicity makes her insecure, and therefore she exercises power over us. But there is no insight with power, only with love.[38] *Qui amat cognoscit!*[39]

There are people who smash a motor that doesn't work, instead of checking with love what might be wrong."

Where I'm concerned, I should simply continue my work in the dark and stay open for everything. He told me how, for example, during

37 Barbara Hannah was Sabi's analyst.
38 See C.G. Jung, "The Type Problem in Poetry," in: *Psychological Types,* CW 6, par. 408: "... for where love is, power cannot prevail, and where power prevails, love cannot reign."
39 Who loves, knows.

his research on *dementia praecox*[40], he was under a constant fear of going insane. In the heat of summer he'd dreamed that suddenly an icy coldness set in. He thought that was the onset of insanity – but then, in 1914, war broke out. "But you can never forget that Nature is just as cruel and deadly as she is life-sustaining!" (Meaning, I cannot be too optimistic!)

As to my husband, Jung suggested that perhaps all of his anima was invested in me, and only if I don't hide out, only if I am completely real, open, and conscious, can he come to his own reality through mine. In that way, the unconscious no longer slides between him and his anima. Each of us has to find out individually where creative activity lies.

"Just like Mrs. X., so M.[41], too, would be startled by me being essential, which challenges the totality of the other. Oftentimes, female analysts would exercise power over their analysands at the end of their analysis, as soon as they act from their totality, in order to keep them 'down.' Conversely, male analysts simply evade the challenge and withdraw. The whole personality, and a clear and brave attitude is needed for a friendship to develop, a true relationship. Most people are afraid when one is one's essential self."

Then he asked me whether I had ever sensed such evasiveness in him. "No, never!" I answered with conviction, for that was precisely his greatest asset:[42] his total presence and his rock-solid reality. Actually, he continued, one should always be able to live essentially, but that was impossible. He therefore had learned to wear a mask and to 'make belief that he knew nothing,' so that his partner would be talking without inhibition. Insight into the other is a danger!

The lake was quiet and serene before us and within us. It was a boundless evening of *Tui*[43] – heaven wide open – like an invitation to my forty years. Jung might have sensed it too, for he started to tell me, "When I was deadly sick, everything fell off me; I had to forge a long and solitary path, and only those parts of my personality, that at

---

40 C. G. Jung, "The Psychology of Dementia Praecox," *Psychogenesis of Mental Disease*, CW 3.
41 Unknown.
42 Sabi wrote, "das Herrlichste" – literally, his most glorious.
43 *Tui*, "The Joyous, Lake," is one of the eight basic signs of the *I Ching*.

some point of my life I had painfully and laboriously integrated, came faithfully with me. Those have become eternal values."[44]

In the future I will bow deeply before every rainbow. It is a radiating symbol for me of 'overcoming,' and the only way from earth to heaven.

Then came a very crazy time; I felt like I was being flattened to the ground (only later did I comprehend that wheat is completely pressed down into the earth in order to grow). The poisoned arrows of Mrs. X., coming in my direction, were constant; they were well aimed. At home, Ignaz wrestled with an acute anima-problem. It was as if I suffered from a constant longing for Jung, and I plunged into the waves at high tide. Miss Hannah made an attempt at rescue. She had a way of showing me my flight from the earth and sounded an alarm based on a warning dream, saying that I wanted to be too self-sufficient, too independent. I should have let Ignaz feel my dependency on him, but my heart didn't want to play along anymore. Today, I am grateful to him! Fortunately, it was not too late.

Once again, into these dark times came a letter from Jung. I visited him in Küsnacht, with, and in spite of, my illness[45] for I knew that only he could see deep into my heart. It was a stormy day.[46] I put my hand into his and simply had to cry for a while. His wonderful benevolence radiated calmness and warmth over me. Through tears I asked him how could I possibly make water out of my inner fire, so that I could better tolerate lying still. He smiled gently, "Just like that – with tears." Then I shared my dreams:

> (1) Jung taught me exercises on the piano to train the independence of the right and the left hand.

Jung's comment: "To play the piano means using and living the feeling function. All feelings have two sides, positive and negative, conscious and unconscious. With these, one can be dependent or independent."

---

44 See *Memories, Dreams, Reflections* by C. G. Jung, chapter "Visions," p. 292 ff.
45 Endocarditis.
46 The infamous *Föhn*.

Fig. 14: Rainbow.

(2) At a lecture Jung is sitting directly behind me; the light is too glaring for him. He says that he would give me something (7 or 12 francs) if I'd be able to regulate (dim, soften) the light properly at the first attempt. I thought I could simply ask the waitress how the switchboard worked, but she showed it wrongly. I investigated the situation myself, and then my second attempt was successful. Some kind of curtain came down halfway and softened the light.

Jung commented that absolute clarity is a sign of poverty. With bright light the 'flair' is lost, the atmosphere, the nuances. Total clarity may not be desirable, otherwise life is lost. Day and night have to mix. Haziness is necessary too, but it can't be part of it if the light is too glaring. There has to be doubt. In a Chinese temple one corner is always left unfinished. Humans cannot be perfect, only God. A desire to be perfect is false arrogance, hubris. In the Barfüsser church in Basel, the highest nave was set up asymmetrically on purpose – out of humility! Clarity alone is too difficult to bear. What we know should be called into question from time to time, only then is it complete (not perfect!). "Nothing is totally true and that also isn't totally true!"[47] Absolute clarity is an absolute error.

---

47 Jung quotes Dutch philosopher Eduard Douwes alias Dekker, with pseudonym of Multatuli, see C. G. Jung, "A Study in the Process of Individuation," in: *Archetypes and the Collective Unconscious*, CW 9/I, par. 607; Letter to H. J. Barrett, 12.X.1956, in: C. G. Jung, *Letters*, 2 vols., ed. Gerhard Adler and Aniela Jaffé (Princeton: Princeton University Press, 1975), vol. 2.

1954

Then we looked at my newest tarot and geoscope:

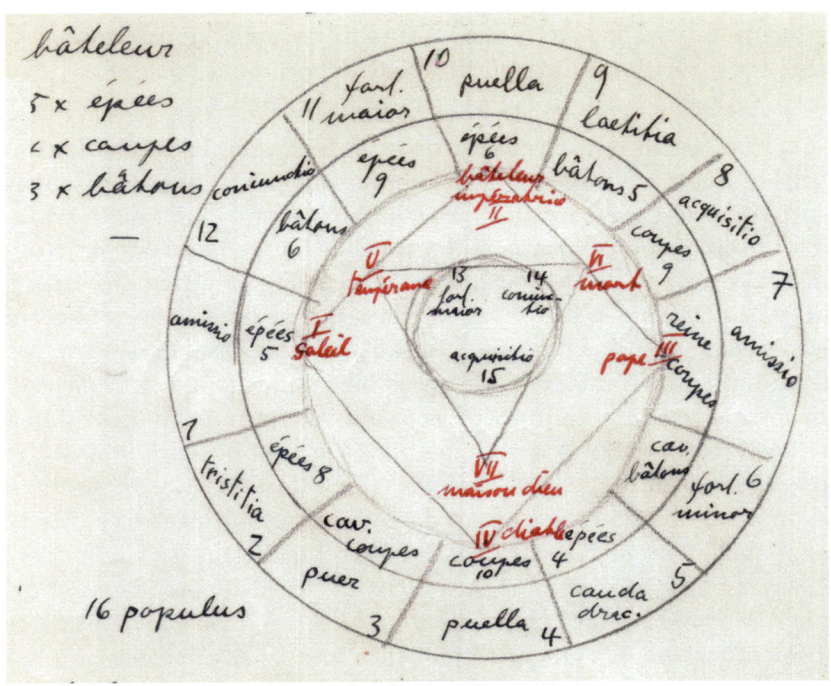

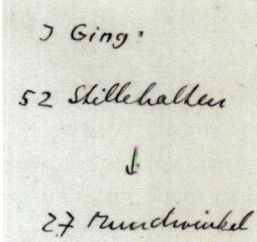

Fig. 15: Geoscope and tarot Sabi Tauber, February 22, 1954.
I Ching: 52 *Kên*, "Keeping Still, Mountain" –
changing to 27 *I*, "The Corners of the Mouth (Providing
Nourishment)".

Jung commented: "Many épées, that is a lot of spirituality, but also high values of *coupes* (*reine coupes*): large femininity – it's the problem of masculine and feminine within you."

Everywhere he saw something positive, as, for example, "no *deniers*[48] – well, those you don't really need!" Furthermore, "*fortuna maior + coniunctio*, 11, 12, 13, 14 – great destiny, big goal. 16 (*super-iudex*) tells you how 15 (iudex) wants to be understood. Here, it is success in relation to the unconscious (otherwise it could also point to appearance in the world, success in the collective).

In the fourth house, *puella* together with *coupes* means uncontrolled, natural femininity; in the tenth, *puella* together with épées is spiritualized femininity (through work!). *Laetitia* in the ninth house is an overcoming of *tristitia* in the second (source of libido). As a primary disposition you have a natural masculinity (épées in the second house). *Acquisitio* in the eighth house says, one acquires what before was believed to be lost (or counted as lost). Masculine signs are action oriented; one has to do something with them. *Puer / cavalier coupes* represents the masculine in a woman, the animus acquired in childhood, where *puella* is inferior. The fifth house is the secret preparation for life; *cauda draconis* is oriented backwards, so there is an inhibition here; you don't dare to come out (probably due to experiences in your youth). In the sixth house, the self is hidden; *cavalier bâtons* is a masculine animus as, for example, Faust at his desk. In the seventh house; *reine coupes / amissio* indicate a loss in relationships, a defect. With such a loss of relationship you are standing at the threshold of death! *Reine coupes* is really a royal vessel, high femininity, large capacity for comprehension, royal attitude (restraint). *Acquisitio* in the eighth house wants to say that, if it comes to a 'declaration' (that is, when it matters; when it is illuminated), you are feminine in your disposition, receiving, ready. You have a gain that way. In the ninth house, you overcome the obstacle and 'have an effect' (*bâtons*), (behind the masculine activity there is a positive sign).

48 No monies.

In the tarot, I–VII shows high intensity of life; accumulation of great things (*pape*, by the way, occurs frequently in all cases); V, VI, and VII point to your illness."

With regard to Ignaz, Jung said that he should not intuit; he should think.[49] Select a myth, for example, find all the instances where it is mentioned, and carefully record these texts; look where they occur and how they are related 'n each instance. What this myth meant for the Egyptian, not for himself! He has to explore the reality of the Egyptians, that is the truth, not what kind of meaning he finds in it. For example, what is the 'eye of Horus' and what was it for the Egyptians? With individual symbols he can proceed in the same way: put together images and texts carefully and make use of his thinking. Jung, for example, did not intuit what the number four might mean when he studied it, but he compiled the reality of the number four from all he could find in the world. The four is reality and truth; he had not to invent the correspondences.

Restored, and with a new found love for the darkness, I returned home.

> Thanks for your boundless kindness,
> for your heart, which I could feel today.
> Thus I will not freeze –
> May God have lost me not.

The darkness enveloped me gently once I had left everyday life behind and found myself alone on a recovery vacation. And there, time was extinguished as well.

> Slowly, all grief settles
> to form a solid ground
> which stands as heavy anchor
> in the abyss.

---

49 Concerning his research in Egyptian mythology. See also a letter to Ignaz Tauber, 22 May 1959, in: C. G. Jung, *Letters*, vol. 2, in which Jung criticizes him for his uncritical use of the amplification method. Jung emphasizes the necessity to know the whole available tradition of the milieu in question in dealing with a definitely historical text. On the basis of a dream, Jung warns him not to let himself be seduced by his intuition. He had lost solid ground because he was misled by his intuition.

There upon, gradually,
a pillar, stone by stone,
and, golden, there's a bow
leading up to heaven.

But the darkness also showed its uncannily wild and destructive side. As an encouragement to stand strong, Jung sent me a couple of books with the newest scientific insights, i.e. Pascual Jordan, *Verdrängung und Komplementarität* (Stromverlag, Hamburg-Bergedorf 1947)[50], and James Jeans, *Physics and Philosophy* (1943). They were fabulously clear and aroused my enthusiasm, for they all gave prime importance to the soul.

Strong hands
that stand like walls
before all harm
and never go away.
Help me live!
Help me believe
in the strength
of the soul.

***

Furthermore, there were Jung's letters to an English clergyman[51], which I got to read as well, admiring their wonderful strength. I made a translation for myself.

Water and heaven are my Thou!
Perhaps the door to people will close –
lonely I can see the winds,
blowing quietly across the earth:
Fertilizing spirit – timeless
it works for eternity.

50 No English edition available.
51 Victor White. See *The Jung-White Letters*, edited by Ann Conrad Lammers and Adrian Cunningham (London: Routledge, 2007).

This retreat gave me the gift of the essential *Yin*. To live it fully without coming under its spell is an art. Pray that my now inevitable afternoon nap may become a true *Yin* ritual!

Spring had returned, but the old wise man was tired and sad. He warned, "One should, as far as possible, withdraw all projections in life. They make life poor and steal libido. I don't want to be a 'myth' either, but a real man, a human being, not a god – otherwise each word of mine has either an annihilating or an eternalizing effect, and that is very burdensome for me. I simply lived my potentials, like any other, and did what I thought was right. One can, in fact, make projections to the point of self-destruction. Then one no longer has *gana*[52] at one's disposal; it seeps into the unconscious. Every relationship is aggravated and burdened through projections. It only starts to live when they are withdrawn. This is when real life can start! Otherwise one lives in an auto-erotic fashion, loving one's projection in the other. Things can exist in themselves; they have *mana*[53] in themselves; nature does and humans do. With the projection gone, the false glow falls away and one can see the true value. Nothing is ever only this way or that, but has multiple facets that are alive and reveal new ones all the time! Only when something becomes mythic, that is, full of the highest projection, is it 'only this or that' (that is, either godly or demonic!) We humans must live in reality, that is, have our own *mana* and real relationships!

Nobody knows what Christ was like as a real person; like William Tell[54] he is a myth. I only want to be real, without the burden and responsibility of a myth. The natural sciences work only with dry statistics; theology weighs everything morally. In that way, both lose their essential, real values. Psychology on the other hand includes everything and is therefore true, real life!"

I told him the following dream:

> I played the Bach fugues from memory on the grand piano, while he leaned against it on the other side.

---

52 C. G. Jung used the term for "psychic energy," derived from Spanish *gana* for "lust," desire for life.
53 Numinous power.
54 The Swiss hero figure in the fight for independence, eternalized in Friedrich Schiller's drama *Wilhelm Tell*.

Jung explained that he represented 'the other end' and thus gave me moral support. He accepted the situation: with him I could do more than without him. The expression of my feelings was still on feeble ground, he said; I have a need for it, but can't yet express myself sufficiently. It is most often in the inferior function where the greatest storms take place. With Jung at the other end, the feeling is adapted, while alone it is too uncivilized.

I told him about the grief I still felt, along with bliss, when contemplating a blossom in the spring. (While typing up my notes, now, in the spring of 1956, I'm happy to say that this is no longer the case. At long last I can experience the blessing of spring fully!)

Jung said, "this is melancholy because one cannot live one's feeling openly and fully. Then, of course, one is not as vulnerable as a flower in nature that might be plucked by anyone at any moment. Individuation grows on its own. It is the totally true and real way of a human being, his essential pattern, as in the example of the leaf-cutting ant.[55] One has to follow faithfully, go with the current, 'grow in the forest.' We must do what we hold to be right and what is possible. In that way we answer the question that our destiny puts to us. For example, I never would have wanted to become a gynecologist, so as to avoid having anything to do with women – and lo, how many women did I have to deal with in my practice!

Maybe you are losing libido at the moment, because deep inner realizations during your illness haven't found expression. Try with a spiritual[56] project on synchronicity. At the last convention in Brussels, the 'Rhine's experiments'[57] were discussed (parapsychology, telepathy), but they all talked past it! They don't understand my idea of synchronicity. It doesn't work causally, but meaningfully, and only

---

55 C.G. Jung, "On the Nature of the Psyche," in: *The Structure and Dynamics of the Psyche*, CW 8, par. 398: "The instinct of the leaf-cutting ant fulfills the image of ant, tree, leaf, cutting, transport, and the little ant-garden of fungi. If any one of these conditions is lacking, the instinct does not function, because it cannot exist without its total pattern, without its image."

56 Again, the German "geistig" as spiritual and creative.

57 Joseph Banks Rhine (1895–1980), an American scientist who published statistical tests about extra-sensory perceptions. From 1940 onwards, he corresponded regularly with C.G. Jung.

when emotion[58] is involved! One should read everything that has been recently published, follow up on the newest biological experiments, make excerpts, prove exactly where the thinking went wrong, and present my ideas about the living reality of the archetype. The principle of probability calculations is wrong. 'Mere coincidence' is more than we assume – it's not just 'chance,' it's all 'arranged'! Synchronicity is a reality!"

Jung told me that he'd like to leave out the astrological experiments in the next edition of his book on synchronicity, because, time and again, people get the idea that he wants to prove the correctness of astrology.[59] But that wasn't the point! His reservation is with the application of the theory of probability.

"The flying saucers[60], too, are a phenomenon of synchronicity: new life is coming from outside the earth, from a new standpoint. But it's like a 'spook in the stable'[61]: one doesn't talk about it, because it is dangerous!" Jung had been collecting material about this since 1946. It could be:

a) a mass-hallucination,

b) a subtle materialization through active imagination of a 'chap' on Sirius, for example (or anywhere else outside planet earth),

c) new apparitions of incarnation.

Focusing on me again, Jung continued, "You had to leave your family to witness that they could do without you. (I took a deep breath – what could he possibly know?) Now, don't slide back into your old life! By all means, find a spiritual task. Struggle for verbal expression, so that your libido can see the light of day and be at your disposal, otherwise it will keep flowing back into the unconscious."

In Jung's presence one becomes totally and essentially oneself. It is such a wonderfully free feeling. I wanted to keep it, always, so I

58 In German "Ergriffenheit," literally, being seized by an archetype.
59 Revised in the 1960 edition of C.G. Jung, The Structure and Dynamics of the Psyche, CW 8: see the editorial comments to "Synchronicity: An Acausal Connecting Principle," at the beginning of Chapter VII. Not revised in German Gesammelte Werke, vol. 8, 1967.
60 C.G. Jung, "Flying Saucers: A Modern Myth of Things Seen in the Skies," in: Civilization in Transition, CW 10, pars. 589 ff.
61 An ethnological expression.

asked him to give me my own special name (like in one of my earlier dreams, in which, at the Psychology Club, he had whispered a secret name into my ear). He only smiled. Perhaps he was helping me to my own name through my work on the synchronicity phenomenon?

For July 26, 1954[62]

What you, with your strength
created throughout life,
it shines broadly
into my darkness,
prohibits the dying,
orders a becoming,
awakens a holy plea.
Thank you, lighthouse, for the center!

With desperate zeal I put myself to work yet again. I was given access to Jung's library and 'allowed' to seek out the most recent literature. But it disgusted me like a swarm of insects sent out by the devil. It was such a confusing mess of concepts and languages that I could make neither head nor tail of it. I read and sorted, all the while gasping for air. I had a keen awareness of my inadequacy, but suspected that I couldn't simply abandon this assignment as long as it was so horribly uncomfortable for me. So, I made excerpts and tried to give some sort of 'answer' to the various scientists by demonstrating Jung's idea of synchronicity.

Jung's response to my paper seemed quite natural to me: "These people are simply too dumb, they don't know anything about the unconscious. This will take at least two generations. Why don't you stay with your own work? Moreover, this task would far surpass your intellectual capacity. One has to stay within the frame of what is possible."

But what did he mean by "your own work"? Perhaps I completely misunderstood him. At any rate, feeling quite liberated I put the paper on synchronicity to rest. I, for myself, understand the principle of synchronicity naturally. The moving archetype is like an arm coming up from the depth of the earth, the hand just below the surface and

62 For C. G. Jung's 79th birthday.

only the fingers sticking out, which we see in different places. The common root of the fingers – the hand and the arm – can only be guessed, as it is deep in the earth.[63]

visible: reacting phenotype

surface of the earth

invisible: living and moving arche-type

For me, parapsychological phenomena are a natural proof of God. My "own work," however, which Jung may have seen as a possibility within me, will remain a mystery. Did I evade in any way? Or was it a synchronistic misunderstanding? I simply kept on working by myself in the Jungian mode, even without a formal "goal and result." In fact, the absence of a goal is the premise for such work (as in an active imagination); it arises from the unconscious and has an effect in the collective.

> "The spiritual effort of the individual benefits the whole; conversely, individual neglect harms the whole."[64]

Then I dreamed:

> I sat at a table together with Jung, drinking wine.

Soon thereafter I sat in the vicinity of the strong tower at the shore of the clear lake, listening to Jung, and experiencing how a single day may become a "pearl."

During our conversation, Jung was saying that, "Mrs. X. may have a certain degree of pathology; she is a 'witch,' but that really doesn't have anything to do with you. It's your business if you fill her up with so much projection that she is damaging you! You are each other's dark side, the shadow, a piece of unlived life. She is scintillating,

---

63 See *Memories, Dreams, Reflections* by C.G. Jung, p. 4: "Life has always seemed to me like a plant that lives on its rhizome. Its true life is invisible, hidden in the rhizome."

64 Sabi Tauber put the two lines into quotation marks, but perhaps it is her own aphorism?

unreal, helplessly ungrounded. You represent for her a piece of young, real life, standing firmly on your ground, a happy wife and mother. This is why there is 'electricity' between the two of you. But if you try to avoid her and run away, many other 'witches' will come your way. Fate doesn't let you get away without working on your negative mother complex. You have to fill undeveloped land with real life! Your naïveté and insufficient experience cause you to make and 'fall into' projections. Imagine that you are walking a path, and on either side are 'pieces' (parts of your life) scattered about. You have to collect them all and take them with you!

The *detour* is the shortest way in the development of the soul! You, however, rush towards your goal with averted eyes and without picking up those elements of your life on the left and right. That's why you are insecure. The goal is completeness. One also has to be able to stand still and let things happen, not pursue the goal as stubbornly as a typical schoolteacher in Eastern Switzerland! Synchronicity exactly fits into your life. You have to experience it in your own life, 'for real.' With you, either everything is here (full of life), or there is nothing (no joy, no *gana*); these are extreme opposites to be dealt with, if one has no experience. With a goddam naïveté, like 'The Little Rose from the Säntis,'[65] You fall into the traps of Mrs. X.! You don't experience yourself enough. For this kind of work one needs better acquaintance with oneself, so one knows who one is and what one has to do. Your insecurity is 'unprejudiced life.' If you only see the goal, the devil lures behind every corner (for example, Mrs. X.). The shadow is so real; it lives itself out anyway. You only fall victim if you don't know your other side; otherwise you could say, 'Yep, have known this for a long time!' Something always happens when one inwardly says 'yes' to life. You look like a teenager, outright 'prohibitive,' full of expectations and longings. Say yes to yourself, then life will come to you! The light is only your will; God is in the shadow. Don't mix this up!

Someone said, 'The Lord wants it.' The other one pointed to him and said, 'No, *this* lord wants it!'

How can God test my obedience? Only if He wants something I don't want. But one cannot always just say 'yes;' each time one

---

65 A Swiss vernacular: like an untouched maiden from the Swiss mountain, Säntis. Opera "Das Rösli vom Säntis" by Franz Curti (1854–1898).

has to examine whether it is 'physically' possible to fulfill the will of God. Learn to accept the slightest hint of a feeling. It is often quite insignificant, but each time a piece of life wants to join you."

As an example, he told me of a female patient who was on her way to her session with Jung when she saw some beautiful early strawberries on display. Her impulse was to buy them and bring them as a gift, but then she changed her mind, thinking that perhaps it wasn't appropriate. When she arrived, she brought such a 'hellish animus' with her that he protested, asking what she had experienced just before the session. – Those strawberries were the little piece of rejected feeling, which is why her animus became so awful.

Jung confirmed: "Up to now you were a full-time mother and wife. A mother wants to give life. When your freedom returns, after the task is fulfilled, you must take *in* life! It wants to come back to you. For a man, it's the reverse: In the first part of life he conquers life, in the second he gives of it. Within you, there is too much land as yet uncultivated, then you don't know what's settling there – maybe Mrs. X. is planting her poisonous plants! Erroneously, she is still giving of life, and negatively at that, because she shouldn't do it anymore. If one wants to prove all that one can do, the effect is negative and poisonous (power-complex!). Seek life humbly! Beware, it wants to find soil in you!"

And then the door opened and Mrs. X. appeared in person – unannounced, as a complete surprise! She stared me down, speechless, then started to talk sweetly (in her strong Basel dialect) to Jung, addressing him as 'Carl.' Jung roared with laughter, "Now *that* is synchronicity!" Giving me a nudge, he added, "Now you can prove it!" She had brought some books along and wanted to explain something, but Jung cut her short, "Go now," whereupon, dumbfounded, she disappeared into the tower. I felt horrible and wanted to leave immediately, but he ordered me to sit down again.

So, I showed him my latest glass-painting (a church pane), depicting the sun, dripping into a bowl, and the blue cross.[66] "There we go,

66 Sabi had painted on glass several times. Here are meant the drops of blood from the wound of Christ, from which love flows. (According to oral report of Christian Tauber.)

exactly!" he exclaimed. "The sun is giving life (she[67] is dripping). You receive the substance of life from her. If it were a power-complex, you'd do it with bad means, but this way you only have to hold out the bowl. Just don't say no, otherwise the precious drops are lost – receive life, catch it! It *has* to be a church window, because you can see it only through a religious attitude. The colors show when looking from the inside out, not from the outside in. So, you are standing *in* the church (thus you don't have to be afraid to derail), and you are looking out, meaning you have visions. Church windows are visions!" With a laugh he pointed to the blue cross. "Look here, your cross of temperance![68] Perhaps cold rationality as well, an annihilating critique, wanting 'only the spiritual.'

> Und der Satan kommt verschmitzt,
> Wenn man einen Rausch besitzt.
> Und mehr und mehr nach diesen Schritten
> hat der Teufel ihn geritten.[69]

You have to know about your feelings and take them seriously, within the frame of what is possible, not with rigid principles."

A swan was swimming slowly toward us and called out. Jung got up to fetch bread from the tower, then handed it to me: I should feed the swan, and I did. Whenever a piece of driftwood came floating to the shore, I fished it out, for Jung's fireplace.

Jung is pleased that his books are better understood by the common people than by the unworldly intellectuals who have lost their instincts. When he gave lectures in America, he had asked for a small audience.[70] The organizers apologized for the crowd; it would only be for the first time because the regulations demanded public access.

---

67 "The sun" is of feminine gender in German.

68 Emblem of alcohol abstainers. The "Blue Cross" is a Christian organization in Switzerland for self-help in addiction diseases.

69 "For the devil comes mischievously / if one is drunk. / And more and more after these steps / the devil has been riding his back." In: Philipp Ulrich Schartenmaier (pseudonym of Friedrich Theodor Vischer), *Leben und Tod des Joseph Brehm, gewesten Helfers zu Reutlingen, am 18ten Juli 1829* (Tübingen: Georg Heinrich Reiß, 1829).

70 See also B. Hannah, *Jung. His Life and Work: A Bibliographical Memoir*, p. 164.

Fig. 16: Sabi feeding the swan with bread.

Later there would be less because the people wouldn't understand him anyway. But the crowd got bigger, so that in the end the police had to assist! (Apparently people could feel that this man was living what he spoke.)

Jung continued, saying that humility requires an unprejudiced attitude with a corresponding behavior. One should accept what next comes up with great humility and examine it carefully as to its value for life. If 'it' is appealing, one should say 'yes' to it, but with great trepidation, because one never knows whether it's right. Life is difficult, or it would be meaningless! One should keep secrets; they enrich us. This is why people invented mysteries when there weren't any. 'It' had to be kept secret. This gives security, independence, forms a personality. Many pastors don't understand the *Book of Job*, because they don't have a genuine relationship with God, only an assumed one. So, they have no idea of the terror of the religious man before God. The most important thing for man is his personal relationship to God (children education[71]). All of Job (whether from different sources or not) is built around this one experience: the relationship between man and God. People with a genuine religious sensibility understand this immediately. (Again, the simple folk!)

S. D. G.[72]

71 At the time, Sabi seems to be concerned how she can pass on religion to her children. See her question to Jung noted in the Colloquium May 29, 1957.
72 *Soli Deo Gloria*, "Glory to God alone".

1955

At the turn of the year 1954/55:

> For C. G. Jung:

>> Full of blessings
>> be your life
>> in the new year!
>> And true
>> may become, please,
>> that center
>> in spirit and meaning
>> where all our hearts dwell within.

> For Butzli (Marianne):

>> Make me truthful
>> in the new year,
>> so that I want the same
>> as you, dear God!

When I visited Jung for the first time in the new year, I was touched by how loving and caring he was. With increasing eagerness, he proceeded to explain why one shouldn't be a coward toward life.

"Especially the dark side of life has to be accepted wherever it presents itself; only by having lived and accepted this life completely is one redeemed forever. And there is only one situation where shirking something is allowed, namely when the burden of being a coward (the knowledge of it) is as great as the 'holy sin' one would commit otherwise." He said that he himself could not afford to be a coward, because he simply couldn't stand it. "I *had* to accept life. Exactly where one is a coward and shirks from the darkness, incest with one's children begins. What I don't do, my children have to do. Sexuality still has a totally different task besides begetting children."

I had read Elisabeth Haich's book, *Initiation*,[73] and so I asked Jung whether there wouldn't be a possibility of creating something like a "School of Initiation" within the framework of the Psychology Club. Jung pondered: "With an outstanding leader, it would most likely be possible, but not without. Perhaps there could have been something like a European ashram, similar to the East, where the disciples gather around a guru – but then I couldn't have written my books, and I simply had to write them."

In mid-February he sent the following letter:

> Dear Frau Doctor![74]
> Hex. 30 Li could give you all the information you need: <u>Care of the cow</u>: female principle of <u>acceptance</u>. (Δ = sign of the flames!) The fire serves <u>to raise consciousness</u> (it does not only give heat, but also light.) It flares up, goes out and comes back. It is the emotional element without which nothing is really seen and understood. It gives also you the light to find out which way is your way, if you can only rein in your animus. He usually advises you the wrong thing.
>
> With kind regards
> Yours
> C. G. Jung

This spring, Jung was healthy and exuberant. Right then it hit him like a thunderbolt: his wife had to undergo major abdominal surgery. He had lived so securely in this long-lasting partnership that it came as a real shock. Thank God, by summer they could both celebrate his 80th birthday with full confidence and quiet happiness. After the grand

---

73 First edition 1954. Elisabeth Haich (1897–1994) was Hungarian; she taught Hatha yoga in Zurich during the '50ies, '60ies, and beyond.
74 Liebe Frau Doctor!
    Hexagram 30 Li könnte Ihnen alle nöthige Auskunft geben: <u>Pflege der Kuh</u>: weibl. Prinzip des <u>Annehmens</u> (Δ = Zeichen der Flammen!) Das Feuer dient der <u>Bewusstmachung</u> (es giebt nicht nur Hitze, sondern auch Helle). Es flammt auf, erlischt und kommt wieder. Es ist das emotionale Element, ohne welches Nichts wirklich eingesehen und verstanden wird. Es giebt auch Ihnen die Helle, herauszufinden, welches Ihr Weg ist, wenn Sie nur Ihren Animus zügeln können. Er rät Ihnen meist das Verkehrte.
    Mit freundlichen Grüssen
    Ihr
    C. G. Jung.

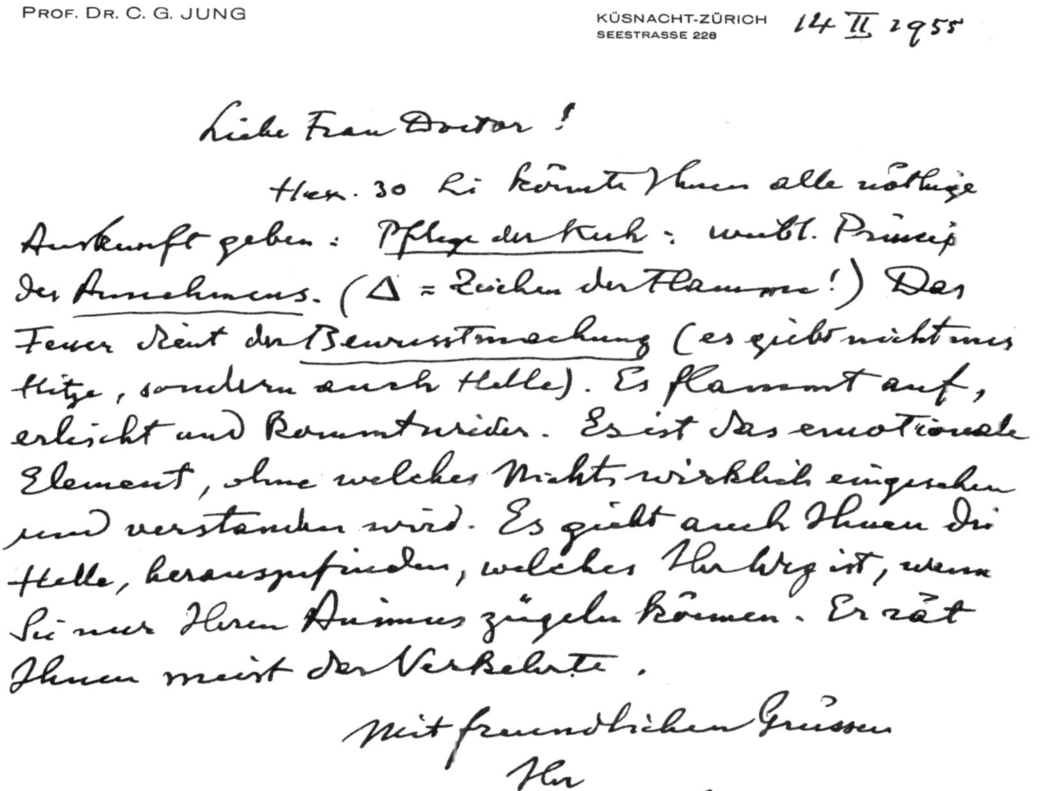

PROF. DR. C. G. JUNG

KÜSNACHT-ZÜRICH
SEESTRASSE 228

14 II 1955

Liebe Frau Doctor !

Herr. 30 Li könnte Ihnen alle nöthige Auskunft geben: Pflege der Kuh : weibl. Princip des Annehmens. (△ = Zeichen der Flamme!) Das Feuer dient der Bewusstmachung (es giebt nicht nur Hitze, sondern auch Helle). Es flammt auf, erlischt und brennt wieder. Es ist das emotionale Element, ohne welches Nichts wirklich eingehen und verstanden wird. Es gilt auch Ihnen die Helle herauszufinden, welches Ihr Weg ist, wenn Sie nur Ihren Animus zügeln können. Er rät Ihnen meist der Verkehrte.

Mit freundlichen Grüssen
Ihr
C. G. Jung.

Fig. 17: Letter of C. G. Jung to Sabi Tauber, February 14, 1955.

celebrations and bestowal of the umpteenth honorary doctorate, they danced a waltz together in their own garden to the music of the village band!

Every once in a while, I had had a dream about Mrs. Jung. She had been a living example to all of us women of how to love without being possessive, and how to suffer without turning bitter. She was wonderfully grand! Because of it, her partner gave her the greatest gift: the path to one's own God.

At the beginning of the following year she would no longer be with us.[75] He'll be carrying it with his wholeness, great and quietly – waiting.

Still, in that healthy, joyful spring I had the following dream:

> I am in Jung's garden. A young, strong elephant came by, saluted Jung reverently with its trunk – and then stood in our way on the stony path that Jung and I wanted to take. Suddenly I wasn't quite sure any more whether the elephant was good or bad. Its keeper gave a warning and then ran away into the darkness. Jung pulled his sword and yelled: "Padro!" (that was the name of the elephant). After that, I don't remember any more whether he stabbed the elephant to death, or whether it followed Jung willingly back into its cage, for I was shrouded in darkness.

Jung's first question was: "What do you feel when visualizing the elephant?"

I answered: "A lot of power."

And Jung said: "So that's the nature of the elephant. Overwhelming power, God-power. You are confronted with such a power. In the beginning, it was favorably disposed, but then you doubted whether it was good or bad. That you should not have done. You shouldn't have made such moral considerations – that's why the power turned negative and evil. To kill the obstacle (Jung with sword) is to analyze it intellectually. That is one possibility, but more important is to make oneself invisible (be shrouded in darkness). Because it is dangerous! One may not provoke this power! You should have stood there

75 Emma Jung died 27 November, 1955.

motionless and announced yourself. for example by talking loudly or calling its name. These are good 'bush-manners.' It means to somehow manifest oneself, to emphasize oneself, that is, to liberate oneself through one's own activity, to express the present moment, simply to react humanly. Then it probably would have left. You were not friendly enough toward this power. In such a case one has to completely rely on un-reasonableness to be sure to express: 'yes, I want to realize you!' That was the reason for the elephant to stand in our way: it wanted to be accepted, integrated. It is God-power that wants to incarnate. One has to learn to deal with such a superpower, for it wants to be part of you! Divinity is caught in its own power of creation, world-creating but blind (an animal, an elephant, for example). Thus, Job did not know God in the beginning; he did not fathom his power. You are at present under the pressure of the elephant!"

Then Jung gave me a couple of examples concerning 'bush-manners': Once he was traveling with an Englishman and an American in Africa.[76] Both called themselves 'gentlemen,' but only the American was: When he was in a bad mood, he stepped out of the tent, came back in and announced loudly, 'I'm in a bad mood.' This way everybody knew, himself included, and one could be on guard. The Englishman said nothing; he simply became unresponsive until the others were angry. He infected them. The same goes for infectious diseases: One also says, 'I have measles.'

A farmer rode his bicycle through the jungle, on a steep descent around a curve. Suddenly an elephant stood in his way. The farmer had way too much speed to be able to stop abruptly. In desperation, he sounded his horn (an instinctive move) – and the elephant took a leap sideways into the forest. The farmer had 'announced' himself, had expressed himself.

Jung's friend since childhood, Albert Oeri, was known to be very entertaining and witty in social occasions. For that very reason he was once invited to a fancy party (expected to be the entertainer). Noticing it, he simply could not say a thing anymore. Throughout dinner, the atmosphere was cold and stiff. Suddenly he said into the

76 This trip to Africa began on October 15, 1925, in Southampton, England. The American was George Beckwith, the Englishman Peter Baynes. See Blake W. Burleson, *Jung in Africa* (New York: Continuum, 2005).

dreadful silence, "I still don't have an idea!" (meaning, he was aware of his inner situation and expressed it). Everyone laughed and the ice was broken!

Jung continued: In this way one can liberate oneself from the pressure of an overwhelming power. At present, you are under such pressure. (The reason for the car accident in Bivio!) The elephant forces you into an unusual situation, so you can get to know and prove yourself. Only in life-endangering situation can one see what one is capable of. Just don't fail, by all means, and don't ruin God's "game of incarnation" with nonsense or sexual adventures! To prove oneself in the fire! In civilized, everyday life there is no opportunity for that. But everyday life and daily chores are like eating and drinking. We need that, otherwise we die, and God cannot incarnate himself. He can't do it on unhealthy grounds – not in folly and stupidity. Without the reality of everyday life, the plant of eternity cannot grow and thrive. It wants to grow in this world, here and now. God himself wants to grow!

Surely, through my encounter with Jung, something is growing within me. But I must not keep pulling and tugging at it, otherwise it cannot root firmly, and it will die.

Jung: This need to always do and accomplish something is Western extraversion and is wrong! Something can also be made in the dark, and it grows by itself. This is your practice now, because you are so active and impulsive, namely to do nothing, to endure, to let it grow in the dark. There is no need for "sins," that is a stupid idea. Live as if you had a hundred years to waste. That equals the realization of eternity.

So, I had to realize my feelings, to express them as best I could. Through my experiences with Jung I receive my individuality; I recognize myself in them and become myself. (Now I understand why he loves Goethe's poem, The God and the Bayadere so much!)

My everyday life got a new face. But it remains difficult to weave it into a worthy cloth for eternity. For if I drown in my daily chores, I become "senselessly unhappy" – there must be free time, not just for "happiness," but also for "meaningful suffering."

Fig. 18: Sitting by the well.

Out of light and bitter juice
made into a tree,
thus I root deep in the earth,
with every leaf and branch a "becoming."
I long for sun and wind –
come, move across my leaves
and call me your child.

Juppa, Avers-Tal, July 1955

In the mandala of the mountains
I sit deep down at the well,
praying all by myself:
God, do bring back light!
What is, say, "transference"?
a word so gray and cold –
hurt does not stop there –
only where the heart bursts open
and pours into the well,
completely and in its depth,
turning the water crimson –
such great distress –
and yet, not dead?
No, I must live, doubly strong!
And my wound, deep in the marrow?
Does it create this life?
Is it the source of heaven and hell?

***

In hot and cold
grow old!
and perhaps quietly
a bit wise – – –
so as to thank the far-away,
which brought the luminous stars
in the depth of night
to shine.

An Evening with C. G. Jung in Winterthur, October, 1955

> God, you sent us the wise one!
> Please, let him, with his hand,
> kindle for us eternal fire,
> and let us find him
> in the depth, where he feels
> that we, all seven of us,
> love him!

In the fall of 1955 it suddenly became reality: On a radiantly golden day in October, Jung came to our home for a visit! At 5 o'clock, I went to pick him up in our car, was of course half an hour too early and waited on the street. But when I finally pulled into the driveway, it turned out that he, too, had been waiting already for quite a while in front of his entrance. He had to do some errands on the way and guided me securely through the complicated maze of the streets in Zurich, all the while talking and joking. He expressed his unhappiness over the many misunderstandings around his theory of synchronicity and, in general, over the lack of followers.

Once we were on the quiet stretch to Winterthur, I told him that I was writing everything down about our meetings for my children to remember, and how I would always feel pain at first. Each time, the feelings of 'having missed out,' of 'having come too late,' would overcome me, but after working through the material, I'd feel gratefulness and a sense of freedom.

He responded by telling me about the demand of fate for detachment.[77] In youth, everything has to be lived very personally; projections have to be made by necessity. Only later, these can be recognized and withdrawn, and we become free and detached. He

---

77 Jung used the German word, "Unpersönlichkeit," presumably in the sense of not-personal, i.e. archetypal.

laughed, "Had you known me earlier, life would have become much more difficult for you, because the demand for detachment is there anyway, but when we are older, we can fulfill it more easily. Besides, everything has happened precisely as it had to, and that is always right!"

At home, the entry and the stairway were lit with candles, and our five children[78] greeted him like Santa, full of expectations. Butzli even said, "Welcome, C.G. Jung!" Once in the living room, he was asked to light the fire in the fireplace, where Jürg and Christian had prepared an artful sculpture with kindle wood. This act was supposed to symbolize how he had enlightened and spiritualized our place in the world, by putting the emphasis on the Otherworld. (It did not catch fire right away, and I was secretly glad about it!) We sang the canon Dona nobis pacem[79] for him, and immediately afterwards he began to tell us stories of his travels in Africa, enthralling us like a magician:

"We had pitched our tent by a brook close to the jungle. Every evening at the same time we heard a brief hissing sound very close by, a sort of coughing. Finally, I asked the porter who had come with us what this could be, and he said it was a lion. The next morning, I went looking for footprints and, indeed, found rather large pawprints on the bank. Now I started to feel uneasy and went to the chief, asking him whether that lion couldn't become dangerous for us. The chief replied quietly and in a matter-of-fact tone that this particular lion was 'theirs': they knew him well; he always came at that time to drink water. He surely wouldn't hurt anybody.

Leopards accompany the people on their pheasant hunts, skipping along, but only if the hunters use a shotgun – with courser rifles they are not to be seen or heard. On the pheasant hunt they accompany the people, from tree to tree along the path.

My companion always had something to deal with snakes somehow.[80] There are such white men who are especially vulnerable to snakes, and black people immediately take notice. They are the pueri

---

78 At the time, Roswith, 18; Jürg, 17; Christian, 13; Lotti, 9; and Marianne, 4.
79 "Give us peace."
80 This was George Beckwith, according to Blake W. Burleson, Jung in Africa, p. 34.

aeterni types,[81] those who are not grounded, who shy away from any sort of responsibility, wanting to be free and unbound, 'flying high.' They usually die early, and this is their way of being 'free as a bird.' One time we were *en route*, crossing a difficult terrain full of termite hills (about 2 meters high). Suddenly one of the porters shouted, *Atari!*, a warning call, meaning, 'stop, danger!' I immediately reacted and stood still, but my companion did not understand the call, because he didn't know the language, and kept on walking. Now a huge snake was about to attack him with lightning speed, and only in the last moment he was able to escape, thanks to his unusual agility. A bite would have killed him within a minute, for it was high noon, the sun burning hot, and water scarce in that region. He shot the snake. From then on he was terribly afraid of snakes and kept having unpleasant encounters with them. One night he was especially restless, imagining that there was something in the room or under his bed. At last, I angrily told him to be quiet and stay within his mosquito net, where he would be safe, even from snakes! The next morning, I suddenly heard a piercing scream: Just when my companion was about to put on his pants, a snake crawled out of them! Moreover, he was quite negligent in taking the necessary precautions. For example, I had to keep reminding him to put on his mosquito boots at night (because the dangerous insects sneak into the pajama pants and sting there). Still, one time he omitted to put them on and got very sick with malaria, so much so that we didn't believe he had much of a chance. He simply was 'marked.' Only much later, unfortunately, I got to know a dream he had had before our departure, namely that a man was bit by a snake and died. He did not tell me that dream because he believed that I was that man! So, he projected his own death onto someone else. Such people often endanger their fellow men. He wanted to talk me into another trip, but I preferred to return back home to my work. Later, he died in a car crash. His sister was driving; nothing happened to her at all, but he was immediately dead."

Meanwhile, careful not to interrupt Jung's storytelling, we had made preparations to roast the meat over the fire. But he suddenly stopped, saying matter-of-factly, "May I be part of the cooking?" We laughed and happily agreed, whereupon Jung gave us a most

81   Eternal youths (lit. eternal boys).

sophisticated cooking lesson. The meat had to be held into the open fire under constant rotation and seasoning. During his travels he had always looked out for the most exquisite ethnic recipes and learned to prepare them. In Bollingen he would always cook himself; at home the cook would ask him about menus and advice on how to prepare them. He knew hundreds of exquisitely rare and exotic recipes! "Cooking is earth," he said in response to our incredulous giggling. "Why should taste be less important than hearing? Cooking over the open fire is a difficult and dangerous matter. It is magic! The fire is hot and we get 'fiery' – a thousand different things have to be observed to make it a success. Of course, 'swearing' is part of it (as with sailing)! All cooks, male and female, are hot-headed people, a bit crazy, because they have to do with fire."

After he had emptied his glass of Burgundy, I asked Jung, with the wine bottle in hand, whether he liked some more. He declined resolutely, "No thanks, I only drink one glass" – then took the bottle out of my hand, "or one and a half" and poured himself some more.

Roswith played a Bach invention on the piano after the meal, which he enjoyed very much. By now, the room was very warm and became quiet again, as we gathered to listen to the continuation of Jung's engrossing story-telling:

"One day, I talked for thirteen hours straight with Freud![82] I was so pleased to be able to share all my secret trains of thought, and he listened with burning interest. At one point, however, we diverged. He suggested to make a dogma out of (his) science, to set firm boundaries against the 'dangerous occultism.' I, on the other hand, wanted to discover the mystery. I had just presented him with my perspective and he had rejected it as being crazy. I became silent for a moment, as self-doubts arose within me. Right then, there was a sudden, tremendous racket in the heavy bookcase Freud was leaning against, right above his head. We both were shocked, thinking that the case might crash. But not a thing had changed. In that moment an almost sacred certainty overcame me that my ideas were right. Something within me declared with a firm voice, 'This was the proof that I am right! And to prove that I am right saying this, another such

82 During the first meeting in February 1907 in Vienna. See *Memories, Dreams, Reflections* by C. G. Jung, chapter "Sigmund Freud", pp. 149 ff.

noise will follow!' And indeed, a second, equal racket followed immediately! The noise seemed to penetrate Freud to his very marrow and terror seized him. We politely separated. But afterwards I was stunned, 'How did you know? Why were you so sure? How could you make such a claim? Why was there actually a second racket?' But for the moment, it simply had been 'right' for me."

Surely, that moment had been of highest importance for all of humanity, which is why fate itself had to speak! From then on, the two men went their separate ways. Freud called Jung a 'prophet' and sought to fight him. Jung discovered the irrational and helped the unconscious to have a voice. Because he was so alone with his ideas and his way of thinking, he had to rely on the support of the unconscious. This he often experienced.

For example, Jung once dreamed, completely out of context that,

> An unknown lady was sitting in his office and telling him about her life. In the end he exclaimed, 'but this is a fantastic father complex!'

He continued, "... This exclamation woke me up, but the whole dream didn't make sense at all. The very next day a lady from Berlin sat in my waiting room, elegantly dressed, looking very sophisticated, in brief, *tirée à quatre épingles*[83]. She had come to me because of a phobia that simply couldn't be cured, though she'd been to several other doctors. The last one had asked her to leave, so as not to destroy his life, for he had fallen in love with her. My dream came to my mind, but there was nothing in particular about her father to be heard. Perhaps it had to do with her grandfather, I thought, and when I asked about him, she suddenly lowered her eyelids and became silent. This told me immediately that something about him 'had an effect.' As it turned out, this grandfather (as the Great Father) had been a Hasidim, a Jewish saint. But the family had kept it in the dark; one didn't talk about it. But something like this cannot be suppressed! A saint is alive in the blood of many generations to follow! This woman was lacking the respect for the sacred, the proper 'fear of God.' So, she was haunted by a phobia.

83 French, dressed to the hilt.

In the following night, I dreamed that,

> I was at a big party and that lady was there too. At some point,
> I was presented with one of those collapsible umbrellas (as they
> are available today; at that time, they weren't). I was supposed
> to unfold it, open it up, and then present it, on my knees, to the
> said lady!

Then I knew that I had to show her my own reverence for the sacred,
so she could learn it too. The opened umbrella signified both the reverence of, and the protection against, God. The phobia corresponded to the folded umbrella; opened up, it became the fear of God. I
told her the dream and how I interpreted it. The phobia disappeared,
and the eccentric lady changed into a true woman. Fortunately, she
survived the war!

Perhaps one should rather know about phobias, instead of insist-
ing on absolutely healing them. I remember a patient who was afraid
of open staircases. He had to avoid them everywhere. But once he
got into a shooting scene in the middle of a street. To get out of
harm's way, he aimed for a building to hide in, which, however, he
could only reach over an open staircase. While on the stairs, he was
hit by a bullet and died.

Another female patient had a life-long fear of Paris. I tried to cure
her of that phobia. When she was already much better, and quite a
bit older, she told me that she had decided to visit Paris together with
her friend. On the first day there she was hit by a taxi and died."

When we reminded Jung of the story told of Rev. Fink and his
wife, he corrected us: He [Jung] saw his wife as a 15-year-old girl
in the stairwell [at the Rauschenbach's home] for the first time and
immediately knew that this was his wife! He had even left the house
and told his friend that he had just seen his wife![84]

Now it was our children's turn to ask the old wise man a question. Roswith asked him how one could stay permanently in a 'higher
realm,' without falling down in between; or what was the shortest way
to the self, the one without detour. Jung laughed: "What looks like
the straight-way is often a detour, and the detour is really the straight

84 See B. Hannah, *Jung. His Life and Work: A Bibliographical Memoir*, p. 83.

way! The self knows this much better than we do. What seems unimportant or lowly to us may be very important and necessary to the self."

Jürg wanted to learn from an experience once and for all, so as not to have to make the same mistake twice. Jung answered, "You can never bathe twice in the same river, for the water has run downstream." Jürg grumbled, "But each time it is water." And Jung, "Yes, but not the same."

He continued, "Youth needs firm guidelines to grow up (as, for example, to always act like a gentleman, or to always be absolutely honest). In old age, the situation changes; increasingly, it depends on the 'how' instead of the 'what.' Jesus was the first to teach people that one's attitude is important – he went to school with the Essenes."

Between these conversations, Jung relaxed by waxing about cooking recipes from far-off countries. Christian wanted to hear more stories from the jungle, which blended nicely with the recipes, as Jung, during his travels, prepared most of the meals himself. And so he continued: "Once we had made a big fire pit in the middle of the jungle; ashes and some burning wood were still laying around in a large circle. The black people hopped between them with admirable grace and precaution, without ever getting burnt. I still had a bag of flour left that I absolutely needed to use up. I wanted to make 'Knöpfli'[85] and tried to give my black assistant an elaborate description of what it was. Suddenly he jumped up, clapped his hands and exclaimed enthusiastically, 'Knepfle, Knepfle!' I was completely surprised and baffled. He then told me that earlier in his life he had worked for a Swabian missionary where he got to know and love the dish."

Marianne had put her black doll into his arms and brought him from time to time a piece of apple or banana, which he always ate at once. Finally, we asked him whether he could paint the Latin vernacular, which he had given us in writing ten years ago, onto the sill of our fireplace. We were a bit worried that he might be far too tired,

---

85 Literally, "little buttons," a specialty of Southern Germany, Austria and Switzerland: Small amounts of dough are dropped with a knife into boiling salt water and cooked to perfection.

but he happily and joyfully accepted the task, painting the words very carefully and exact, including his name. Ten years ago he had written: *Omnia in se habet quo indiget.*[86] What he painted onto the sill was: *Omne portat cum se quo indiget.*[87] It surely has its own significance: We can 'have' something unconsciously, whereas 'to carry' is a conscious act; *cum se* is with oneself; *omnia* (plural) is all-encompassing, whereas *omne* (singular) is limited to one destiny.[88]

Marianne received a farewell kiss on her cheek, which she quickly wiped off. Jürg presented him with his carved leopard; Christian gave him his two-pronged stick. Jung left our home again in the soft glow of candlelight, after the children had bidden farewell with a canon, which he still enjoyed during the car ride back to Küsnacht:

> Wenn dieser Mann zu den Menschen marschieret,
> öffnen sich alle die Fenster und Türen,
> rum rum rudududum
> rum rum rudududum
> Ei, das ist ein wahres, ein wahres Gaudium![89]

Along the way, Jung happily commented on the Germans who were such good psychologists in theory, but failed in life, whereas the French who often acted with a healthy and natural instinct, contributed little to the science of psychology.

When we pulled into the driveway of his house at exactly 11 p.m., Jung declared with satisfaction that this was precisely the time he had had in mind for his return. Ignaz and I made our way back to Winterthur, both deeply content and tired. It was wonderfully quiet at home; the children had neatly cleaned up before going to bed and were already sound asleep.

86 It [the lapis] has in itself everything it needs.
87 It carries everything within that it needs.
88 "Omne quo indiget" is a repeated warning not to mix anything from outside with the content in the Hermetic vessel, because the alchemical *lapis* has "everything it needs." See C. G. Jung, *Mysterium coniunctionis*, CW 14, par. 749; and a letter to an unnamed couple, in: *Letters*, vol. I, April 10, 1946; see also C. G. Jung, *Aion: Researches into the Phenomenology of the Self*, CW 9/II, pars. 220, 256.
89 When this man marches to the people / all doors and windows open / rum rum rudududum … / Yay, this is a true, a true spectacle!

Jung later told us that the evening had been good for him; he had slept very well and woke up refreshed the following morning. As for us, there was a slight melancholic hue lingering in the days that followed, as we kept asking each other, "Remember?" Into our reminiscent mood a big box with the most delicious chocolate candies was delivered, with a note attached,

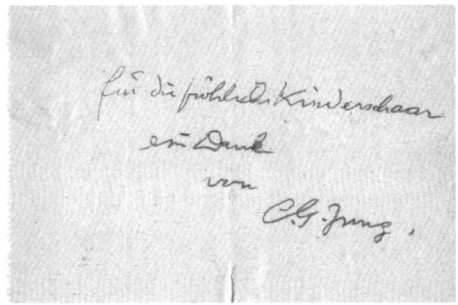

Fig. 19: "For the happy band of children, with gratitude ..."

October 24, 1955

Oh magician! We thank you!
You sat here!
Transformed the false world
into a true one,
the soul, as the wonderful,
into firm, clear reality;
it is ready
and flies out!
The magician won!

The most beautiful gift Jung had received for his 80th birthday was a delicately carved Sudanese crest of a mask: a gazelle mother with her young [fig. 20]. I so badly wanted to show it to our children. When I dared ask, he spontaneously invited the whole family for tea! It was three days before Christmas. We met him laboring heavily out on the porch, chiseling a tree and a Chinese aphorism into a stone slab. It was to be set beneath the freshly planted Ginkgo tree in the yard, and we all knew for whom it was.[90]

My dear children, never forget: From his grief, from the energy-loss of a depression, he created a 'power station!' Out of suffering – creation! This is why he has so much vital energy (available libido) at his disposition. *Vocatus atque non vocatus, Deus aderit*[91] is written over the entrance of the Jung family house.

90 The Ginkgo tree was a birthday present as well. The stone slab was for Toni Wolff. "The meaning can be read 'Toni Wolff *soror mystica*'", see *The Art of C. G. Jung*, ed. by the Foundation of the Works of C. G. Jung, Ulrich Hoerni, Thomas Fischer, Bettina Kaufmann translated from German by Paul Young and Christopher John Murray (New York: W. W. Norton & Company, 2018), p. 166, 172.
91 "Called or not called, God will be there."

Fig. 20: Sudanese crest of a mask (chiwara).
Originating from the region of Bamana (Mali),
at the time in French Sudan,
used for ritual dances.
(Foundation C. G. Jung Küsnacht)

1956

Perhaps I'm getting better at living through the storms within my heart, while all around me, the waves are subsiding. "To suffer because of others" certainly hurts, but it also leaves a vague feeling of impotence and insincerity. "To suffer oneself" is not easier, but it gives dignity and a chance to act. It is experienced as essential, right, central.

One day in March, with a heart in turmoil, I sat vis-à-vis Jung, his face lit by the evening sun. It seemed deeply akin to me, known since times immemorial. For a while, though, I was unable to summon up the courage to talk honestly about what was on my mind, until I heard Jung's encouragement, "Just say everything straight out, as essential as you can be!" My question nevertheless must have sounded rather shy and a bit nebulous, but his answer was unequivocal and courageous:

"What is right in the first, biological phase of life is not right in the second, other phase of life. There is a total reversal in values. If values and perspectives don't change, a neurosis will surely develop at forty, midlife. A complete transformation has to take place, lest there be death. The passage to the second phase starts at the darkest end. Men, for example, generally believe that it starts with sexuality (brothels are sustained by married men). But the development in the second phase must lead to the great eros that holds the human community together (which is transpersonal, not personal). Men get hypnotized only by the sexual character of this eros, but it's not sexual at all. If someone still tries to solve the problem on the sexual plane, he ends up in a depression because he missed the meaning. A man has to serve his anima (*la maîtresse*) like a knight, just as the animus should serve the woman and not dominate her! Then both are redeemed. In the case of identification, the servant (animus) has become master and vice versa. Animus and anima are true half-gods. If a man comes to feel his anima, he has to stop and say to himself: 'Still, be quiet, the goddess is present!' He has to go into submission and be committed to her. But if a man has only cursed and suppressed his anima, then of course she remains inferior, dull, and stupid. He has, then, to make her aware of her unconsciousness!

A woman who cannot include her soul in intercourse is mere anatomy. Women must have an enormous claim. Sexual intercourse in the second phase of life can oftentimes feel deeply humiliating for the wife in a marriage, if she functions as the legitimate prostitute of her husband. One must see it absolutely as it is. The real marriage begins where adultery seems to take place. At that point a true, real relationship may begin, actual love begins! If nothing is there, the marriage has no value. If one partner loves someone outside the marriage, it is his very own, personal business, perhaps following his innermost law. No special 'gestures' are needed. like touching, sexual intercourse etc.; they do not matter. The subjective inner truth is the absolute essence (independent of gestures); that is the innermost freedom. This problem reaches everybody who has a claim to spirituality – precisely because it means spiritual growth."

Then I asked, what actually is a depression?

Jung answered: "Whoever is standing too high is, in fact, depressed, that is, his expectations of himself are too high and he is living in the clouds instead of down to earth. He has to come down and see himself in the lowliest role. If it is a man, he has to let himself be employed as the servant of his anima. Face-to-face with a woman of value he must be aware of his own unworthiness, otherwise instinct does not live within the relationship. For example, at a party I may think of myself as the distinguished 'Herr Professor' and all the ladies behave perfectly (none of them will suddenly jump at my throat!) But if I am at the same time aware of my humanness, of my gorilla-nature, then instinct is alive too, is a reality that lives within, alongside. Body means reality. Sometimes the body is an abyss and one gets engulfed, while spirit flutters around by itself like a butterfly. A dangerous separation ensues that leads to death, for one lives outside of reality. Vitality in its fullest is experienced when one lives totally within the body and with the body! Every spiritual progress includes a better connection to the body. (Yoga!) An earthly union wants to form. Without connection to the body, spiritual progress is simply nonsense. Where a soulful connection exists, we should think:

'Beware, you are in higher presence!' A God or a Goddess is present. It doesn't matter who it is. It is a sacred mystery that belongs wholly to oneself. It is pure experience, and the freedom of the soul!"

It was precisely what I experienced right then and there, during this sacred hour of the evening. It was so strong that I felt like bursting. I simply had to cry. Jung said calmly, "As your husband I wouldn't understand your tears. I would get angry, just as I did with my wife, because, as husband, I couldn't satisfy that claim. These tears don't come from being sad, but from being alive, and from the presence of the god and the goddess. It is a claim of the soul, a soul-connection, which I can satisfy now because I'm not your husband, but a god. Your husband can't do this, because he satisfied your biological needs of the first part of your life. Soul-connections outside the marriage are absolutely legitimate in the second half of life."

I told him how there were moments now when I would feel life very intensely, as if before I had never really lived. "This is the joy of one re-born," he said softly into the serene peace of the evening.

***

In the middle of May, Jung brought his *mana* for the second time into our home, making himself available for an evening with us and our closest circle of friends.[92] Our house was filled with joy and expectation long ahead of the event. We all, adults and children alike, cleaned up our own rooms and then the whole house, as if in preparation for a very special 'holy day.' He felt it. His eyes were radiant, and the magic of his words filled our hearts with a sacred fire. He sat in Ernst Jung's 'grandfather chair'[93], which Lotti had fetched with a handcart. Our friend Peter brought his favorite wine. There were colorful flowers and candles everywhere. Those who had the courage to ask open and honest questions were greatly rewarded. We all listened with rapt attention.

92 Most of them practicing physicians and their wives.
93 Ernst Jung was a distant relative of C. G. Jung and the brother in law of Sabi Tauber.

An Evening with C. G. Jung in Winterthur, May 26, 1956

(At the time, we thought that any kind of "official" note-taking would disturb the ambiance. Thus, in the days that followed, Ignaz put the content of the seminar together w th painstaking care and a lot of dedication, and with the help of ou friends who had attended. As it turned out, Roswith, our eldest, st ll remembered most of it *verbatim* – she had secretly listened, together with her brothers Jürg and Christian, laying on the floor in the hallway – young, wide open souls.)

First question (Dr. Ernst Jung): How would you evaluate the psychological situation, on one hand of the European in the West with his overemphasis on intellectual psychic development, and on the other of the Eastern people, mainly the Chinese, who have seen their culture break down under the influence of the materialistic-technological mentality?

Jung's response: The world is split into two factions, separated by the iron curtain. The psychological explanation for this phenomenon is the fact that the individual human being is split too, and that the world consists of the sum of all the split individuals. Going back in history to investigate the origin of this split would go too far now. But we can proceed empirically: Let's say, some intellectual comes along who suddenly has fantasies about his wife or his mother. Or a mother has ideas about her children. Or a professor comes to me, frightened by his visions – for "only crazy people have visions." When he [Jung] shows him a book from the Middle Ages where he finds exactly these visions written down he is baffled. Indeed, in those times, such things were written down in books! If, for once, such an illuminated intellectual could see his unconscious, a whole archaic museum would present itself, of which the man doesn't have the foggiest idea. One has thought that a man is what he knows about himself, but there is one thing he hasn't reckoned with. One has forgotten that one is not the only master of one's house. Up to the Middle Ages one was aware of that. In this respect, the Reformation has sinned as well, pouring out the baby with the bath water, whereas the Catholic Church has maintained a relationship with the unconscious through its cult. Compared to the vastness of the unconscious, our consciousness fits into the size of a thimble. Admittedly, consciousness has made big progress, and we don't have to give it up, but we have to find the connection with the other, split-off side. Today's man has forgotten much of what was known in the Middle Ages, which is now dismissed as superstition.

The Romans, for example, still knew that there is a *genius loci*[94]. So, when they built a new town somewhere, they didn't yet know the god of that location. Therefore, they brought sacrifices to the local god and engraved onto a memorial stone: *genio ignoto loci*[95]. Today we travel to foreign places without taking into account that we are exposed to unconscious influences there, and that it would be quite reasonable to be a bit cautious.

Primitive peoples are aware of many places of sinister influence, and such "dwellings of the spirits" are taboo. While traveling in Africa, Jung was especially interested in those places and could explain their uncanny influence by the nature of the milieu. Once he asked to be taken into an ill-famed bamboo forest, situated at a 9,000-foot altitude in the Elgon region, "the place of the departed spirits." They had to bend down to walk along the narrow rhino paths, without making a sound on the bamboo leaves under their feet. All was deep dark green, above and below; it felt like being in deep water. He had two brave soldiers along with him, though they were breaking out in a cold sweat. One of them whispered into his ear: "10,000 spirits!" They had to be careful not to startle sleeping rhinos, as there was no way to escape their fury. So, they had to sing and whistle to chase them away. Once, a camera left behind on one of these paths was recovered the following day, completely trampled.

Primitive peoples cannot simply disregard the unconscious – that would be much too dangerous. When one is out of balance one must not undertake anything. One could, for example, come across a mamba, one of the most dangerous poisonous snakes that attack

94 The spirit of a place.
95 To the unknown spirit of the place.

on sight. One has to have the rifle "handy"[96] in order to be the faster one. Or one has to cross a river full of crocodiles on some slippery tree trunk: Whoever is not in balance might slip and fall to his death, or, for example, might lose his most important piece of luggage. This is why "the boys" shared and discussed their dreams every morning in front of the tent. If they were unfavorable, one had a day of rest. If they were good, one could go ahead with the trek.

This had been on a safari in coastal Somalia. Jung had tested the head boy's knowledge of the Koran and he himself had known more than the boy. After that, Jung had been respected as "the wise one" and had to decide whether the dreams were good or bad.

Who today would think of honoring the "unknown spirit of the place" with an engraved stone, "just in case"? Or slaughter a black rooster before buying stocks or bonds?

Richard Wilhelm has this interesting story about the rainmaker in China:[97] Once he came into a province that suffered from severe drought. The people had called for a rainmaker from the South. He came and sequestered himself for three days. On the fourth day it rained and snowed! Wilhelm asked him how he had done it, and the rainmaker answered that he hadn't done anything. He had noticed that the people here weren't in order, therefore he had to separate from them and bring himself into order. It took him three days to establish *Tao*, and then, of course, it rained. But he didn't *make* the rain – *that* he couldn't do!

This being in balance, translates for us Europeans as giving the unconscious a voice too. In this respect, the saying "let me sleep on it" has a legitimate, deep meaning: If you sleep on it, the unconscious is given an opportunity to have a say, either through dreams, or simply by letting one's mind be influenced by it. It is because Western man has "forgotten" all this that the world is split today, in the outer world by the Iron Curtain, in the individual by the well-known inner disunity. How can there be help?

---

96 Jung says it in English.
97 "The Rainmaker" – a well-known and often quoted story among Jungians. See B. Hannah, *Jung. His Life and Work: A Bibliographical Memoir*, p. 128.

There are examples of a wrong Western kind of thinking: Röpke[98] proposed the oppressive idea of the *Herrenmensch* (member of the master race), a kind of club for the elite, that is, another Nazi remnant. Impossible, for who makes the selection? Before such a "committee," Jung would have failed. Based on his critique of the universality of the causality principle (written while still a student), any committee would have classified *him* as "subhuman." The idea is not only unworkable, it is wrong. Equally wrong as the recent experiment "Zurich whereto?"[99] Everything is wrong that wants to impose something new on people as a collective, as a mass. This is the well-known misconception: "the masses will do it." Karl Barth[100] is said to have had thousands of disciples, whereas only a small group has gathered around Jung. One may respond: Hitler had many more people than Barth; Jesus even less than Jung!

Here is yet another example of wrong Western thinking: One assumes that education in the natural sciences gives us an accurate picture of reality. But the "norm" of the natural sciences is not an existing reality at all; it is an abstraction, only a statistical means. Let us consider a bed of gravel, for example. We just found that the average weight of one stone is 145 grams. Then we ask a student to bring us a gravel stone with exactly that weight. He might be looking for hours! Not only are statistics not reality; they also awaken wrong ideas about the reality. The way we think is referred to as "realistic," but in fact, it is not real at all! Reality is never an average, never a "norm"; it is variety. "Normal" isn't the so-called "norm," but the diversity.

A physician, therefore, should never treat patients with categories of pathology, but always keep the individual sick person in mind. If you simply have "a hysteria" in your office it says about as much about this patient as, for example, she belongs to the white race.

Just as absurd is the statement, "treatment according to Jung." I don't have a method; every person is new and unique. I used to

98 Kurt Röpke (1896–1966), Nazi General in World War II.
99 Mass evangelization, 1956, in Zurich under the leadership of pastor Emil Brunner. The campaign was titled "Zürich wohin?" under the slogan "Spirit of Revival." See Frank Jehle, *Emil Brunner: Theologe im 20. Jahrhundert* (Zürich: Theologischer Verlag, 2006).
100 Karl Barth, a Swiss theologian (1886–1968).

interpret about 2,000 dreams a year. But just as a Catholic priest confesses his sins before holding mass, I said to myself before each interpretation, "well, good heavens, I don't understand this dream at all; I can't say a thing about it; I don't have the foggiest idea," to prevent any kind of theoretical prejudice.

In the natural sciences we live in a totally artificial world, abstracted from reality, and that's why the scientist has a hard time finding his way around in it. The statistical truth is the way of stereotyping society, something we take over from America, which is not at all different from communism. All recipes that say, "one should, one must ..." are wrong. Nothing is improved with them. Real change can only come about when someone starts to do "the right thing" every day; then it will be heard from miles away! Then the millions who don't do this are diminished by one, then by two etc. So, this is the task: that each one works on himself to heal the split within.

Now something about the Chinese: Nobody would have thought that such a highly evolved culture with such an orthodox people could break down so quickly! But, just what do they still know about their high culture? I asked a Chinese professor what he thought about the *I Ching*. He was embarrassed and evasive, as if I had asked an astronomer about astrology, or a surgeon whether he also practices chiropractic. Some time into the conversation I learned that once, the professor and a friend of his had each consulted the *I Ching* oracle. "Were both oracles meaningful?" – "Yes." – "What consequences did you draw from this?" – "None." This is also the reason why India with its many illiterates is endangered by communism, in spite of its old culture, because people don't understand their culture any more. Nehru has tried to maneuver, but it is a dangerous game!

Second question (Mrs. Dr. Mimi Fopp-Fink, Flims): In your *German Seminar*, 1930, you made a remark that touched me deeply: "With the church's fight against gnosis, many deep truths have vanished or have been turned into nonsense. So, for example, the word of Christ, 'When two or three are gathered in my name I am among them,' is completely distorted. It should rather say, 'When two are together they are not without God. But if someone is alone – verily I tell you – I am with him; he shall lift the stone and find me there; he may split wood and I'll be there.'"[101] My question is whether God is also with one who is alone, or only present within the community.

Jung: Indeed, this passage has been distorted in the interest of the community, to strengthen the Church. In a collection of such "Sayings of Christ" (Logia Iesou), contained in the Oxyrhynchus-Papyri[102] from the first century, we find, for example, a conversation of Christ with his disciples. One of the questions is, "How can one get from earth to heaven?" Jesus says, "It is the fish and the birds that bring you heaven, therefore strive first for self-knowledge, for you are the city, and the city is the kingdom!" This answer is about the instinct of the unconscious animals, how the fish find their way and the birds build their nests, and likewise man, when he is well connected to the instincts and to his inner images. ("Metropolis" – mother city – center – the town – the kingdom.) The kingdom of heaven is not to be reached with ladders, corresponding to the belief of various religions; it is within man. That is the self of man, the Unknown, Christus in nobis[103], the kingdom of God. Therefore strive first to know yourselves! Here Christ touches on the secret of individuation, self-realization.

In the Indian religion, the primal being is Atman Purusha, the primeval man, who sacrificed himself in order to build the world. My ego is the personal Atman, and he is identical with the transpersonal Atman. "He covers the world everywhere two handbreadths high and is within my heart two thumbs high." It means that the ubiquitous God is contained within me in the smallest form. I am a split-off particle. The "I" is an illusion, a trouble maker that gets us entangled in the ten thousand things. There are people who believe that Christ was familiar with Buddhism. In the second century before Christ, Buddhist

101 Translated from Bericht über das Deutsche Seminar von Dr. C.G. Jung, 6.–11. Oktober 1930 in Küsnacht-Zürich, zusammengestellt von Olga von Koenig-Fachsenfeld. Mit Beigabe von 51 Photographien, Stuttgart (Privatdruck), 2. unv. Aufl. 1931, S. 81 f., Anm. 3. See also C.G. Jung, "Seminar 5 March 1930", in: Dream Analysis. Notes of the Seminars Given in 1928–1930, ed. by William McGuire (London: Routledge, 1984).
102 A group of manuscripts discovered during the late nineteenth and early twentieth centuries by archaeologists at an ancient rubbish dump near Oxyrhynchus (modern el-Bahnasa), Egypt. The manuscripts date from the 1st to the 6th century AD.
103 Christ in us.

monasteries sprung up in Persia. After the conquest of Alexander the Great, there were relations with India.

Another interesting source is the *Liber Enoch*, the apocryphal *Book of Enoch*, from around 150–100 BCE, which, at the time, was very popular. There, the "son of man" figures as the steward of justice, the advocate of man before God. Christ has identified himself with the steward of justice. When he calls himself "the son of man" he took it directly from the *Liber Enoch*: The son of man, chosen by God, who ensures that humans are justified before God. For the old Jewish theologians, Yahweh was a paradox. On the "Day of Reconciliation," the high priest would go into the sacristy of the temple where he would see the splendor of *Adonai*.[104] And the glory spoke, "My son, give me your benediction!" and the priest would bless him, adding, "And mayest thou always remember thy good qualities more than thy bad ones!"

Yahweh was in danger of falling into oblivion with the emerging Greek spirit. Many Jews only spoke Greek. Jesus was the reformer who saved the Jewish religion by saying that "God is good." This is why he saw Satan falling from heaven. He saved the Jewish religion by affirming that God is good.

The *Apocalypse* brings back the "Fear of God." The old, terrible God reappears. When Yahweh gets angry, he himself hides his faithful under his throne, lest he strikes them dead.

Abraham didn't want to come down from the altar before saying this to God: Had he killed his son, then Yahweh would have broken his word, because, as it is said, "You promised me my seed in Israel." Yahweh said, "In the future you will always blow the *Schofar*[105] on the Day of Reconciliation." This was so that Yahweh would remember that he *almost* broke his word.

In the 89th Psalm we find the antinomian[106] idea of God, which disappeared in Christianity. That God is the *summum bonum* conforms to the Jewish Reformation.

104 Another Hebrew name for Lord.
105 Bock horn.
106 Free of moral laws.

It took Jung years to track down the apocryphal texts that had been left out of the Bible. The *Liber Enoch* records the expectation of the great Essene community that the "Son of Man" would come to help humanity gain its rights before God. We may compare this to the "parable of the shrewd manager" (Luke 16:1-9), who, having administered faithfully, reports to his master. God is pleased with this, because this man acted alertly and with agility. Ignorance is the greatest sin: "Man, if indeed thou knowest what thou doest, thou art blessed; but if thou knowest not, thou art cursed, and a transgressor of the law."[107]

Christianity did not simply fall from heaven. Its history reaches as far back as Egypt. Think of the three times fourteen ancestors of Christ,[108] assimilated from the coronation of the Pharaoh, where fourteen ancestors were placed ahead of the procession.[109] Because of these relations Christianity immediately got under the skin of the Egyptians. Recently, a German-American scholar devoted his dissertation to uncover many more of these interesting parallels. But his findings were not accepted by the universities.

As Jesus said: "He who is near me, is near the fire, and he who is far from me, is far from the kingdom."[110] Fire *is* burning!

Third question (Dr. Hans Baumann-Barandun): I have trouble bringing together knowledge and faith.

Jung answered, that neither can he believe in what he doesn't know. Either one knows something and then there is nothing to believe, or one doesn't know, and then it would be even harder to believe – it would be immoral! Now, he doesn't speak here of the faith that may be given to one as "charisma," as grace. Jung's father

---

107 Uncanonical saying, see C. G. Jung, "Psychology and Religion," in: *Psychology and Religion: West and East*, CW 11, par. 133.

108 Matthew 1:17.

109 See Marie-Louise von Franz, *Creation Myths* (Boston, et al.: Shambhala, 1995), p. 304 f., 312; C. G. Jung, *Mysterium Coniunctionis*, CW 14, pars. 2, 8 f.; Marie-Louise von Franz, *Aurora Consurgens. A document attributed to Thomas Aquinas on the Problem of Opposites in Alchemy* (Toronto: Inner City Books, 1964), par. 424.

110 *Gospel of Thomas*, logion 82, translated by Thomas O. Lambdin, in: James M. Robinson ed., *The Nag Hammadi Library* (Harper Collins, San Francisco, revised edition 1990).

was a minister, and in his youth he always had disagreements with him. It went against his morals to believe certain things. Otherwise, one might also believe, for example, that a certain Mr. Meier is a scoundrel.

Faith and knowledge are not opposites, because these concepts lie on different levels. Objects of knowledge are facts. The stories in the Bible obviously are not meant as descriptions of facts – as such they would be either impossible or nonsense, like, for example, the Trinity, or the Immaculate Conception. The same holds true for the pronouncements of alchemy. They were always viewed from the perspective of chemistry, and thus considered chemical nonsense. Both the Bible and alchemy talk a symbolic language. Once we understand that, everything becomes clear. Consider the Immaculate Conception, for example: a divine female figure unites with the Holy Spirit; a virgin, untouched by any man, is pregnant. But Mary is not the first, the Egyptian Isis and many others were her predecessors. Here, Catholicism is much smarter than Protestantism, by declaring these goddess images to be forerunners of the Almighty Truth. A virgin can indeed be pregnant by a spirit. There exists in all languages an expression for spiritual pregnancy. And from this emerges the savior of mankind, the Son of God.

The Jews say that Mary was a hairdresser, and that Joseph got her pregnant out of wedlock, so she had to give birth hidden away in a manger. Mary represents the feminine that is innate in every man. But in intellectual men the feeling function is often undeveloped, just as for beautiful women beauty is often valued higher, at the cost of thinking. This is why a well-to-do man can fall in love with the cashier at a bar: it concerns his own inferior function. So, the French writer Gérard de Nerval, in his *Aurélia*[111] describes his love for an actress, doubting time and again whether she could really be his one great love, the saint, the goddess: "Après tout, c'est une femme ordinaire de notre siècle"[112] – and by God, she is it! And already he was insane. Poets have the ability to bring out their inner image – Goethe's

111 On June 9, 1945, Jung gave a lecture to the Psychology Club Zurich on Gérard de Nerval, and his autobiographical *Aurélia*, "the history of his anima and at the same time of his psychosis." Jung's abstract is reprinted in *The Symbolic Life*, CW 18, par. 1748.
112 Jung says it in French: "After all, she is an ordinary woman of our century."

Gretchen (*Faust*) and Mignon (*Wilhelm Meister's Apprenticeship*) are the only German examples; other than that, we only find them in the French and English literature, as, for example, She in Rider Haggard's *She*[113] and Atlantide in Pierre Benoit's *Atlantide*[114]. This kind of love is numinous. Hands off, a goddess is present!

The Holy Trinity and the question of the third and fourth comes up in many religions, also in Plato's *Timaeus* and in the scene of the Cabiri in Goethe's *Faust II*[115]. It is connected with the structure of the human psyche.[116] The fourth function is the inferior, which is why it often leads to dubious experiences. They are not necessarily divine (one might even get in conflict with the police!). Precisely because they are not only divine [in the Christian sense], the term "numinous" (the old Latin *sacer*) is better. We are dealing with the most ordinary, every-day things, which, in their ordinariness, we simply don't recognize as sacred. The fourth in the Holy Trinity is either the devil or Mary – the *mediatrix* or *creatrix mundi*[117]. Whereas men have banned the devil from heaven, for reasons of responsibility toward their *Weltanschauung*, women have a better way of dealing with him because they don't have ideological prejudices. Remember the little story in Anatole France's *L'île des pingouins*[118]? There, an old, almost blind priest blessed a group of penguins, taking them for humans, which provoked a difficult conference among the church fathers in heaven. They discussed whether the penguins had received a soul through the sacrament, or whether the sacrament wasn't effective in this case because only humans have a soul. Finally, God the Father referred them to Saint Catherine of Alexandria as their judge, because she was the most saintly of women. She decreed that, of course, the animals received a soul through the sacrament, for the sacrament can never err. But they are animals, after all, so, turning to God the Father, she said, "*C'est pour cela, donnez-leurs une âme, mais une petite!*"[119] Women's logic. This is why Mary, as the representative of the devil,

---

113 Rider Haggard, *She – A History of Adventure* (London, 1887).
114 Pierre Benoit, *L'Atlantide*, first publication 1919.
115 Part II, Act II, lines 8160 ff.
116 See C. G. Jung, *Psychology and Alchemy*, CW 12, pars. 203 ff.
117 The female mediator or creator of the world.
118 *Penguin Island*, a satirical novel, first published in 1908.
119 "Therefore give them a soul, but only a small one."

the protectress of all sinners, was taken up into Heaven, which was a pretty smart move.

Another physical impossibility seems to be the "feeding of the five thousand." However, in the *Vulgata* of Hieronymus[120], we find written in the Lord's Prayer, *"Dona nobis panem supersubstantialem,"* meaning, "Give us our super-substantial bread"[121]. Spiritual nourishment is capable of endless multiplication.

Pueblo Indians call themselves "the sons of the sun." Jung had been impressed by their great dignity and, next to them, felt like a ridiculous puppet[122]. Later, through a correspondence with the chief, he learned where this great dignity had originated from: Jung had asked the chief why he had written that the Americans would fare badly, were they to send their missionaries to the Pueblos. He answered, "The sons of the sun help their father sun with their ritual every morning to climb the heavens. If that should stop, then the Americans would lose the sun too!" – What if we had such a commission, too!

Catholicism has preserved a cult, which allows for a relationship with the powers of the unconscious, whereas Protestants threw out the baby with the bath water. One does Yoga – meaning that the West seeks access to its own culture via a detour through the East, while the East is doing the same thing through the West. A Chinese professor of philosophy confessed that he only gained access to the *Tao* by reading the booklet *The Secret of the Golden Flower*[123].

120 One of the four church fathers of late antiquity, who translated the Hebrew Bible into vulgar Latin.
121 The substance of this bread is beyond all substance. The term "super-substantial" still exists in some orthodox Bibles.
122 See *Memories, Dreams, Reflections by C. G. Jung,* chapter "The Pueblo Indians," pp. 246 ff.
123 In 1931, Jung's and Sinologist Richard Wilhelm's joint work appeared in English as *The Secret of the Golden Flower: A Chinese Book of Life,* translated by Cary F. Baynes (London and New York), containing as an appendix Jung's memorial address for R. Wilhelm, who had died in 1930. Today, see C. G. Jung's commentary on "The Secret of the Golden Flower," CW 13, pars. 1–84. (For "In Memory of Richard Wilhelm," see CW 15, par. 74 ff.)

Many people have two drawers: one for the weekdays, where they store their knowledge; the other only for Sunday, where they store their faith. Jung tried it too, but – the experiment failed miserably.[124]

An American professor of theology complained in a letter of so many esoteric expressions in the *Book of Job*. Asked for an example, he mentioned the *hieros gamos*, the wedding of the lamb. These, however, are really customary specialty terms and have nothing to do with esotericism. But that is how the humanistic education is being cleaned up, so that a theology professor is no longer familiar with Greek and Latin expressions.

[End of recordings for this evening.]

> Thank God, this night
> the moon held vigil
> over hearts,
> which in holiness,
> touched by the mystery,
> experienced heaven and earth
> and trembled.

Shortly thereafter, I received the following note:

Küsnacht, May 27, 1956

Dear Frau Doctor!

I would like to express once again my gratitude for the pleasant evening in your hospitable home. Only seldom do I have such a sincere and open-minded audience that resonates so deeply with what I have to say. This I probably owe to you and your dear husband's careful preparations and attention.

With best greetings,
Your devoted C. G. Jung

---

124 As faithfully noted, Jung here used a very vulgar Swiss German formulation for emphasis!

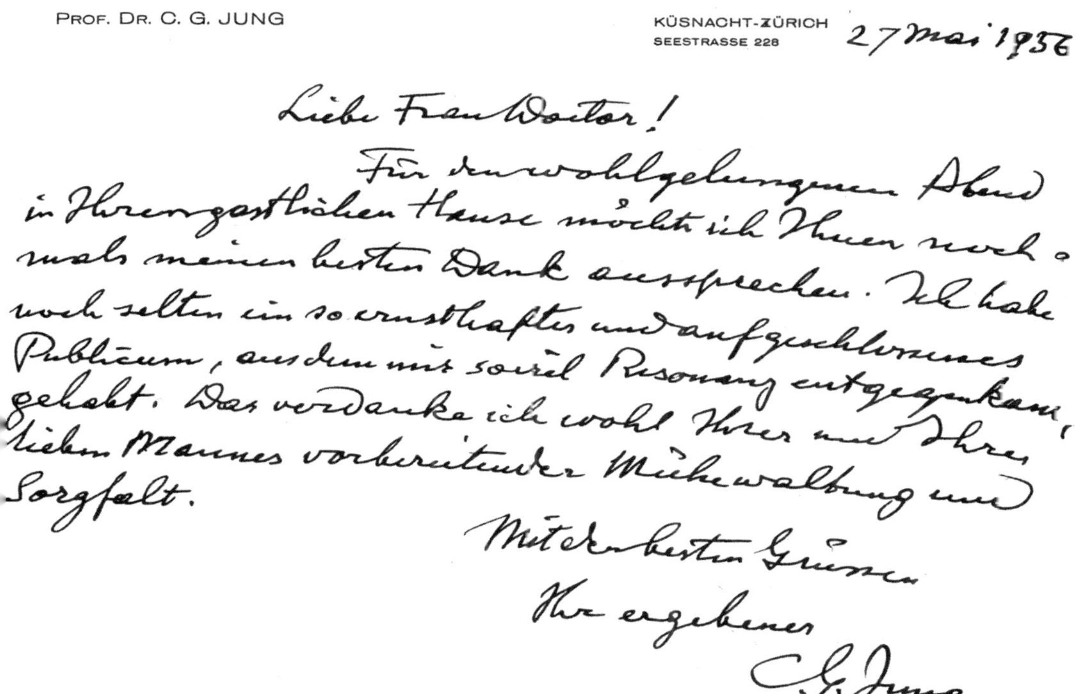

PROF. DR. C. G. JUNG

KÜSNACHT-ZÜRICH
SEESTRASSE 228

27 Mai 1956

Liebe Frau Doktor!

Für den wohlgelungenen Abend in Ihrem gastlichen Hause möchte ich Ihnen nochmals meinen besten Dank aussprechen. Ich habe noch selten ein so ernsthaftes und aufgeschlossenes Publicum, aus dem mir soviel Resonanz entgegenkam, gehabt. Das verdanke ich wohl Ihrer und Ihres lieben Mannes vorbereitender Mühewaltung und Sorgfalt.

Mit den besten Grüssen

Ihr ergebener

C. G. Jung.

Fig. 21: Letter of C. G. Jung to Sabi Tauber, May 27, 1956.

1956 – Journal Continued

Half a year has passed. Am I wiser now? Perhaps a little bit – how else would I deserve the gift of an invitation to visit Jung in Bollingen? And so, on this last day in October, I'm driving through golden autumn splendor with a solemn mood of celebration. The car is part of me; I am the golden trees; the people gathering fruit in the fields, that I am too: A big, sacred harvest! And yet, perhaps a world war has erupted.[125] Thank God for the inner world!

As I'm approaching the lake, the sun breaks through the clouds with an intense light – dear radiant sun, warm him well! He is sitting in his dark den, sipping tea and inviting me to join. He wants to know the latest news. Perhaps, he ponders, the extreme tension might gradually discharge in smaller eruptions in the East, hopefully preventing another world war.

Then Jung gives me the tour of the tower, showing me the re-modeling he did, the carved stones I haven't seen yet, while talking about his plan of painting the ceiling. He is incredibly active – and a real artist! At last I follow the old man in his heavy wooden clogs up the small trodden stairs to the tower room. It is warm here and cozy, but the air weighs heavily. One has the feeling of important things happening here all the time. He stretches out comfortably in his old, shaky armchair (which, I fear, threatens to break down at any moment), lights the pipe, and looks at me – and under this gaze one is transported at once into the core of the universe, the place where fate is forging the future.

Jung starts speaking:

In the second half of life people change. The eros of a woman becomes masculine, active, almost brutal at times. The man becomes feminine in his eros, passive, and thus suddenly understands the

---

125 The Suez Crisis in October 1956, as well as the invasion of Hungary by the Soviet army in early November 1956, posed a threat to world peace.

feminine psyche; he is longing, expecting, and waiting, like a young woman. The woman starts to talk "objectively" and to see the things like a man. He, on the other hand, wants to be sexually "introduced" (*ars amandi*[126]), but the woman refuses because she doesn't want to be his mother. It just doesn't work anymore; the cogwheels don't fit together any longer. It is a very difficult time and one must not become embittered. The only salvation is insight and an understanding of this transformation.

The man becomes effeminate, almost to a degenerate degree. The woman experiences a spiritual heightening and is in danger of degenerating into masculinity. She wants to talk "matter-of-factly," get to the essence, call things by their true name. She is seeking a clear religious attitude, "honesty,"[127] and only what has meaning is important, everything else is nonsense. The man, on the other hand, loves the twilight; he is seeking to lull in eros, and everything takes on a mystical glow (*"O zarte Sehnsucht, süßes Hoffen."*[128]) It seems to be a cruel joke of nature. The change happens gradually after midlife, which is why the physical aspect of the relationship is no longer essential, like it was in youth. For the woman, it becomes often meaningless, a waste of time, not essential, not convincing. Outside the marriage, with another man, it might work for a while, but then the same problem would surface. Biologically, it is a joke nature has with us, but psychologically the process of maturation is implied.

There is a Persian myth to demonstrate it: After death, man has to go across the bridge *Chinvat*, which for one person seems wide, for another narrow. One gets across, another falls into the river; one meets a beautiful maiden on the other side, another an old hag. It means that the transition is dangerous! For the "righteous" the transition is not dangerous and he meets a maiden; for the "unrighteous" it is dangerous and he meets an old hag.

Such is the inner meaning for a man who is evolving his feminine side: he realizes his unconscious, nuances of feeling from which he forms a woman (a feeling-infused darkness). In his youth, the man is clear and determined; he has firm intentions, an enduring will. He first

126 Reference to Ovid's elegy *The Art of Loving*.
127 Jung says it in English.
128 O! tender longing! sweetest hope! (Friedrich Schiller, *The Bell*).

develops his logos. The young woman has vague wishes and goals; she lacks differentiation. She is passive, she adapts to her man. Her interests are drawn to this and that; she develops her feeling first, and logos comes second. Man develops his logos first, then it all reverses. For the woman, increasingly more weight is given to the animus – he forces her to name things, to recognition, the search for meaning, development of logos, lucidity of feeling, spiritual development in general. The man, through his anima, is driven away from logos into the feminine sphere, has longings for feeling states. Just look at all those who sit in bars, flirting with the waitresses. They are looking for *Gemütlichkeit* – a cozy atmosphere. This is why alcohol is such a danger, because it induces the longed-for state of non-clarity. It is perhaps a rather comical outer expression of the man, but, inwardly, it's the doing of his anima, the carrier of his future. Then he meets the maiden and not the old hag!

Anima and animus become the carriers of life; man and woman stand still. Hence there are dire consequences if a man hasn't worked on his anima. He will fall from the [Chinvat-] bridge. For the woman the animus has the positive, alive energy that gives life its meaning. The man feels in his anima a transfigured power that creates "ambiance"; she has a motherly aspect wherein he feels contained.

Comprehension! Insight!

If the woman insists on describing everything with words, being overly discriminating, the atmosphere is spoiled. For him, it has to stay blurred, in the twilight, warm, full of hope and longing.

Jung continues by telling me that he experiences the most meaningful period of his life right here and now, in Bollingen. Here he leaves the world of thought and intellect behind, and existence becomes timeless. He forgets who he is, living in relationship with Mother Nature, touching on endlessly profound, enigmatic things without wanting to understand them, only touching. Being in touch with the trees, the stars, and the water. Everything has a secret charm, touching on the great depths in man. But no talking! He, who earlier in his life aimed so much for clarity and consciousness, now takes great pleasure in not understanding, not clarifying something. He lets it fly in and out unhindered, while drifting somewhere else.

"That's usually how women are," he said. Earlier he'd had terrible resistance against such fickleness. Once he sent his wife to town, to go buy little bags for the grapes (so the wasps could no longer get to them), and waited impatiently for her return. She came back with 200 dust cloths – she had ended up in a fabric store where there weren't any grape bags, so she thought … He became terribly angry![129]

"This whole transition, though, is a path we only take reluctantly. This path is, biologically, nonsense; one finds it ridiculous. But woman's way to clarity and man's way to twilight, both, are paths into the *Bardo*[130]; they are mystical paths. In the *I Ching*, the woman is presented to the 'Mountain of the West'[131] only when she is in clear possession of her logos; conversely, the man only when he has already left all clarity behind and can say, 'I don't know.' (At this point Sabi remembers lectures where she should have gained clarity!)

I've already forgotten what I've written. Something has taken me away from it, far away. I'm living in a semi-bemused twilight and love the not-understanding. I am no longer aware of my responsibility. In a way it is a moral defeat, this twilight, and the aversion to clarify it. I'd like to let everything rest, and this, however, is real progress – inwardly. There are then women who get on your nerves with their urge for clarity! But this is not necessarily possession! One absolutely must have first attained a state of clarity. A man who has always been in a state of confusion will be possessed by his anima and devoured by the Great Mother! Women, too, are in danger of being possessed by the animus – then they are ridden by an opinionated devil! Their urge for clarity may get on a man's nerves. A strong animus is always a danger; he is god-like! I have had a very strong anima, otherwise I would never have come to psychology. This is why I had to work in the first place. Neither would you have come to psychology without your strong animus."

---

129 See also B. Hannah, *C. G. Jung. His Life and Work: A Bibliographical Memoir*, p. 64. ("I remember that he used this example once in a seminar to illustrate unadulterated animus thinking.")
130 A concept from Tibetan Buddhism, designating an "intermediate existence" between two incarnations. Here, Jung might have used it as a term for the afterlife. See also C. G. Jung, "Psychological Commentary on the Tibetan Book of the Dead," CW 11, pars. 831 ff.
131 *I Ching*, Hexagram 17, *Sui*, "Following."

I brought a dream from September 13, 1956 (in brief):

> By passing through horse stables I gained access to a mansion. I had to greet the owner personally. He was like a god, came very close to me, and wanted to enchant and tempt me with all the pleasures of this world. But I was not allowed to look at him; I had to fix my gaze on a point at the horizon. It was almost impossible; the temptation was maddening. But I was able to do it. He gave a sigh of relief, thanking me for my steadfastness, saying that I had redeemed him, but I wasn't allowed to go with him to his castle. I had to continue my life here on earth.

Jung commented, "By all means, you have to fix your gaze on this point, that is, you have to keep your goal in mind with all your might, otherwise you will lose your consciousness – and God wants our consciousness; he needs it for his redemption. If you keep your eyes fixed on the far-off point, the castle always remains close by. That's how it's supposed to be. The beauty of this world is a true divine power, and one comes under its spell by looking at it directly! You may not enter the castle, lest you lose consciousness, and then God would feel betrayed, for, by Himself, he is an anonymous power without a reflecting consciousness. One has to keep the goal in mind, then the power follows. In a man's psyche, the sorceress in the castle spins a web around him; he is being abducted like Merlin and has to go on in the twilight, swaying blindly, moved by currents, suspended, swimming. Then the magic being stays close, just like you have the castle close by. But if he would enter directly, he'd be swallowed up by the terrible Mother, and then the Mother is betrayed! The man must have already won clarity when he enters the twilight, otherwise he is lost!"

Jung, then, pointed out how the two of us, Ignaz and I, are especially blessed in being able to understand each other, because of our opposite typology: Ignaz, by nature rather feminine, has now a desire for clarity, so his task is to find clarity while simultaneously being in the twilight. He is grateful for "gifts of clarity" from my side. I, Sabi, on the other hand, by nature rather masculine, now love "ambiance" and all things incomprehensible, while at the same time must struggle for clarity and meaning. I am grateful for Ignaz' warmth and his irrationality! Anima and animus are only valuable on the inner path, the path to God!

Jung had lit the petroleum lamp. Two hours had passed; it was the dark of night. And the Holy had come between us. He accompanied me to the gate. I was walking in the eternal realm. After the gate had closed behind me, I went to the lake shore and had to emerge both hands deep into the water.

A dark, solid tower by the lake –
hidden, unmoved,
holds a room deep within
filled with humanness and warm light
wherein the old wise one
lives – and, softly,
a veil hovers around him,
and whoever perceives it
loves
the sacred!
And his hands are both on fire –
woe –
but he cools them deep in the lake.

S.D.G.

1957

Mother Earth had held us in her grip for another long winter. Now she is trembling in her dark, innermost core. Outside there is no sign yet that thunder has touched her, but soon the life force will burst forth, a new source, flowing and quickening all beings. Spring is coming, in March 1957!

I am still heavy with darkness, though, and cannot find the source. Is it buried forever? Is there joy of life, even for the tired and for those who can see? (Such is my mood as I am once again facing Jung.)

"For heaven's sake – you yourself are sitting on your source, blocking its flow!" he thundered. "You have become a stylite[132], so thin and ethereal! Are you sick? Why don't you eat?" I am desperately fighting my tears. He continues more quietly:

> "Doch im Erstarren such' ich nicht mein Heil
> Erschauern ist der Menschheit bester Teil.[133]

Your animus has wrapped you up in one big vapor of ideas, rendering you blind for what is close, true, and alive! Don't be so complicated! Tolerate your warm, genuine feeling, even if it hurts the damnedest! You want to avoid the pain, so you incarcerate your feeling in a deep cellar and close the door. Well, and then what happens? The animus takes its place with his empty haze of ideas, and you sit in the dryness. Life is wiped out. Thank God you're not that prissy, so I can talk with you *in fractura*[134]. You have to be like a child and take yourself completely seriously. You have to make gifts to your empty heart, follow your 'appetites,' really do 'stupid things,' only the animus thinks one will be laughed at. You may never again suppress your feeling, lest life become a wasteland. Take it seriously; 'it' is always right!

---

132 "Pillar-saint" (*Säulenheiliger*) – an ascetic spending his life on a pillar, preaching, fasting and praying.
133 Faust speaking, "Yet not in torpor would I comfort find; / Awe is the finest portion of mankind"; Goethe, *Faust II*, Act I, Dark Gallery, verses 6271 f.
134 Straight forward, directly and bluntly.

Le cœur connaît des raisons, que la raison ne connaît pas.[135] Who doesn't live this truth doesn't live, he dries out. Never think how the people around you might react – it only matters what it means to you. The simpler one is, the greater is life, for then it is on the level of nature. Whenever you feel that your life force is vanishing, simply ask your unconscious, 'What do you want?' Seek your own water, your own source, otherwise you automatically drain that of others. One has to concretely seek life! I, for example, let my hand sometimes go along my bookshelves, and all of a sudden there is a kind of inner twitch. That's the book I take out – and look here, there's meaning! That's what my unconscious wanted to tell me. Or, I might simply look all around me, questioningly, and discover a face in a rock. I paint it and talk to it – and life is with me! I've also had moments smoking my pipe imploringly, until it occurred to me that I could write X a letter. That was it! Or I had the desire to visit Y, so, for once, I could tell him *that*.

Libido is inclination! Pay attention to where it is inclined within you; be mindful of your 'desires.' To look for a source means to dig in the dirt until it becomes increasingly wet. Then one first has to let the dirt settle until one can collect the clean spring water. That is reality: to dig into life!"

My eyes grew wide open in wonderment. I mused, "You really are an artist!"

He laughed freely, "Life *is* an art – unfortunately we have to learn this lesson anew, because we are distorted by culture to such a degree that we have forgotten how to follow the flow of water, like an underground waterway, that is, to follow the potentials in a totally irrational manner. Pour water onto a plain, and it will immediately find even the slightest gradient and start to flow. We have to do it the same way. That's what we have to learn again, to be as simple as the water. But we are at war with ourselves. Criticism suffocates our heart, which, after all, has been created by God, so we must love it and listen to it at all times!

135 "The heart has reasons that reason doesn't know." A famous saying of the French philosopher Blaise Pascal, 17th Century.

A gnostic, a Carpocratian, once pointed out that one should find a different reading for the particular paragraph in the Bible where Christ says, something like, 'Before you place a gift onto the altar of God, go and make peace with your brother, otherwise you will have to appear before the judge and be dragged into prison.'[136] Taken subjectively, related to yourself: 'Make peace with the brother *within you*, before you stand before God.'

Sometimes it is helpful to simply write down all that comes to one's mind, whatever wants 'out.' It frees the imagination. Once, a very cultivated lady came to see me. She was a professional in a high position, with a lot of responsibility. But the joy of life had left her. Duties and manners had suffocated her heart. I suggested that she might do just that: write down in a journal whatever came to her mind, even if it was bad or impolite. The next time she came in, she threw the journal onto the table with a provocative gesture, 'Well, there you go!' And what did I find in it? Nothing but slurs! Even some that were new to me – I could even learn from her! But from then on, her imagination was liberated and the source of life was freed. With her sense of duty and politeness she had sat like a cork on the bottle. Now the cork had popped and she was liberated!"

Listening to Jung I became acutely aware of how much I still suppressed, and how that was blocking my way to life. To my own astonishment I told him about my longing for him, a feeling I most of the time locked up deeply, so that I didn't know it myself any more – for fear of dependency. I would like to be entirely free, only belonging to God and never attach to another human being again. It is too painful. The direct way is better. I said, "It is the sacred within you that I love so much, so I only want to belong to it and not be attached to you!" My own words frightened me. But he only shook his head:

> "Willst du den Perlentau der Gottheit fangen,
> Musst du nur unverrückt an seiner Menschheit hangen.[137]

---

136 See Matthew 5:25f. (King James); and C. G. Jung, "Psychology and Religion," CW 11, par. 133. [See also notes of Ignaz Tauber, June 8, 1957.]
137 "If you want to catch the pearly dew of God / Just hang unshakably on to his mankind." A saying by the German mystic Angelus Silesius (1624–1677).

Born hermits are very rare. The world would have disintegrated into single cells, were it not for a connect'ng eros holding it together. This societal cohesion is only achieved by a free libido that is not bound up by family. You need contact with other people; your free libido wants to achieve something. Accept life where it approaches you! You have a warm, sincere feeling, but if you don't use it, the animus takes its place and messes it up. Why don't you write me letters – try it (it's not so easy, by the way, to write a truly meaningful letter!). That is legitimate, and I will profit from it too. And then the animus is in his right place. Only where he *replaces* feeling is he wrong."

And he told me again the example of the strawberries.[138]

I told him, that now and then I have the desire to talk to other people,[139] but lack the courage and thus often decline to engage, because I don't have a degree and therefore have no "right."

Jung replied, "When there is joy and desire, it is right. You must accept it, *for your sake*! Why shouldn't we talk to each other, as far as humanness goes? Simply react naturally. You might want to call it 'psychological counseling,' just not 'analysis.' But you can still charge a fee because it takes time, and time costs money these days. Even a little bit of consciousness has the effect of a magnet on others; it is sensed all around. On one of my crossings to America, I kept running into a lady dressed in black. It seemed to me that she had something to do with the East, but of course I had no idea. On the last day, she suddenly stood beside me at the railing and – I don't know how it came about – told me her whole life story in the shortest time. She had spent half of her life in the East and was on her way to her husband in Japan after burying her son in Berlin. Afterwards she was embarrassed about her candor; I was a stranger after all. But I could comfort her, explaining that, at bottom, I wasn't 'really' a stranger. By the way, this happens to your husband Ignaz as well. But he should be careful with his somewhat unbridled intuition that everywhere aims directly for the center, as with the trunk of an elephant. Only, he lets himself be pulled way too much into things. He participates too strongly with his heart, and that burdens him far too much. He should

138 See above p. 77.
139 She means as a psychological or astrological counselor.

consciously distance himself and not accept too many psychological cases!"

Jung wants to spend the whole month of April at Bollingen to experience springtime. In May he might come for another visit in Winterthur. I asked him whether there was really no wish we could fulfill, or gift we could give him. "Just become simple, very simple, like water – that is my wish … and never forget, keep doing something for your own heart – à *fond perdu!*[140]"

It poured in buckets, as I slowly drove out of the gate, and from Küsnacht back to Winterthur. In between is Zurich, and while stuck in traffic I suddenly remembered the beautiful spring dress in a shop window that had tempted me a few times already. This time I stopped – "for my heart, à *fond perdu*," it sang within me – and I entered the store and ordered the dress. Strange, I found it to be absolutely right. Then I drove along a country road towards the forest and cried, until I myself became the continuous, mild rain.

"In May I might come again to Winterthur." That's what Jung had said. Which May, I wondered, could he have meant – the one in the "Otherworld" or the one here? It all depends whether our eyes will open. Suddenly there is a telephone call from Mrs. Jaffé, late in the day: "Prof. Jung will be at your house on the 29th in the evening." How could I have doubted! As always, he had talked about the real, natural May!

Ignaz and I picked him up in Bollingen, much too early of course. But Jung, too, was ready, lovingly outfitted by Miss Bailey with hat, cane, and coat. He teased her on the way out, to be sure to let him back into the house late at night! We drove back to Winterthur in snail-tempo, holding our breath while listening to his outrageous ideas about flying saucers. It was more thrilling than an adventure novel. There already was a finished manuscript ready in the tower.[141] How will the world receive it?

At home, meanwhile, the children had welcomed our guests, so that Jung entered a living room that was crowded, warm, and almost

140 French, literally "unrecoverable," meaning "without expectation of reward," "off the books."
141 C.G. Jung, "Flying Saucers: A Myth of Things Seen in the Skies," CW 10.

bursting with anticipation. Roswith welcomed him at the piano with a piece by Brahms, whereupon Ignaz addressed him.

(Participants: Families Tauber and Ernst Jung, Peter und Helen Stierlin, Maria und Hans Baumann, Läuchli, Rupli, Mimi und Jacob Fopp-Fink, Arnold Renold, Alice Rüsch, S. Keiser, L. Zimmermann)

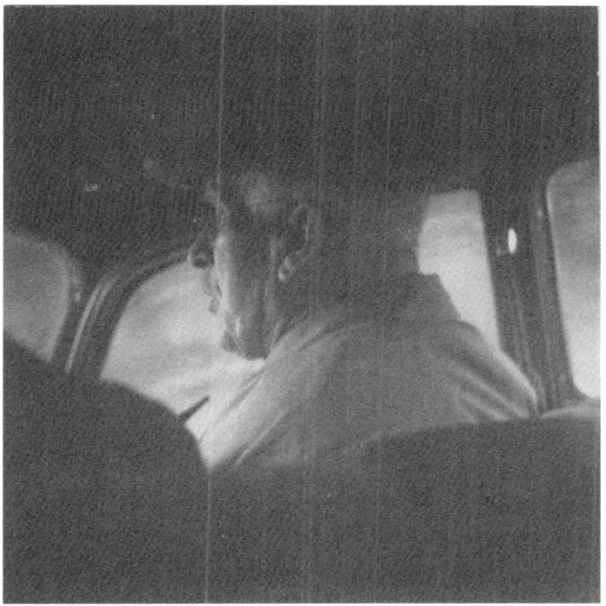

Fig. 22: C. G. Jung being fetched at Bollingen, Mai 29, 1957.

Colloquium May 29, 1957

Visit and question hours by C.G. Jung in the circle of friends of Sabi and Ignaz Tauber, Winterthur, on May 29, 1957.[142]

On the Shadow

Ignaz Tauber: We thank you, Professor Jung, that you have come to us today, and we would like to begin by posing a question about the shadow:

Did Christ himself advise suppression of the shadow, that is, of his dark side, and was it historically conditioned? Or, is that a later interpretation of the church? And, second, is it today, with a Christian education, possible at all to have a true relationship to one's shadow, to one's dark side, without getting in conflict with Christianity?

C.G. Jung: [It is not so easy to answer your question,] because it belongs to one of the last questions one comes upon. This question especially I've been asked not too infrequently.[143] It truly is a serious problem, because in general, is it not true that Christ is regarded, even in liberal theology – and there especially – as a *human being*. As a consequence, we must assume that he had what we call a shadow, that is, a side that is less perfect, less glamorous, which therefore doesn't correspond to the ideals of perfection. This, as you well know, is what the orthodox view avoids – precisely the arch-orthodox belief of Catholicism – where Christ is absolved from the *macula peccati*,

---

142 A portion of the discussion was recorded live by Christian Tauber. The text (in German) and 3 CDs were published as C.G. Jung, *Über Gefühle und den Schatten. Winterthurer Fragestunden*, (Zurich and Düsseldorf: Walter-Verlag, 1999). Here, they are reproduced in a practically unchanged version. For example, the footnotes and the parts of sentences reconstructed by the editor at the time are taken over. The notes in Sabi Tauber's typescript are essentially identical.

143 See, e.g. C.G. Jung, "The Spirit Mercurius," CW 13, pars. 239 ff.; or, for a comparison, "Jung and Religious Belief," CW 18, pars. 1584–1690.

that is, from defilement through sin. He is *sine macula peccati origina-lis*, he is born and conceived outside of original sin. His mother, too, is outside the realm of original sin, that is, through the dogma declaring the *conceptio immaculata* – introduced a hundred years ago by Pio Nono[144]. From this perspective Christ is therefore without blemish. On the other hand, through the reports of the church father Irenaeus of Lyon, at the beginning of the third century, we have knowledge of the Gnostic theology, which assumed that Christ was indeed born with a shadow, but that he cut it off, and from then on lived without a shadow. Now, it hasn't been revealed what the Gnostics assumed happened with this shadow. But from the gospels one may conclude that it is the devil himself, for, according to those reports, Christ distanced himself from the devil: "ὕπαγε, σατανᾶ! – away from me, Satan!" (Matthew 4:10) And with this he split from his dark side once and for all. Which, in fact, should be so, if the church's doctrine of the *summum bonum* were to be valid. That means, it is valid within the church. Namely, not only in Catholicism but also in Protestantism it is said that God the Father is the *summum bonum* and doesn't have any darkness. But where hell is now supposed to be, and the devil, that remains unexplained. That is outside the domain of the Father – that is simply overlooked; it is not mentioned how the devil fits into the almighty power of God. Jakob Böhme[145] wrestled with this problem. But then he was also a Gnostic, and the Gnostics are always insulted for struggling with questions that the theologians have brushed aside as uncomfortable. In truth, they were theologians, for example Valentinus or Basilides; the great Gnostics were great theologians. Valentinus, for example, was even *papabile*[146]; he aspired to the bishop's seat in Rome. He didn't make it, though, but he must have been a superb theologian – one who, in contrast to the others, was able to think. The others only imagined things; they didn't think, whereas he was accountable to himself for his beliefs. Among the new finds of Egypt, in this Gnostic library,[147] we have an original script from the Valentinian school, the so-called *Evangelium veritatis*, the Gospel of

144 Pope Pius IX, 1854.
145 Christian mystic (1575–1624).
146 Worthy of, or eligible to be, pope.
147 See C.G. Jung, "Address at the Presentation of the Jung Codex," CW 18, pars. 1514–1517 and 1826–1834.

Truth, where, contra to other fathers of the church, he tried in a reflective way to extract the quintessence of Christianity. He probably was a highly educated Roman who asked himself the question, "What does Christianity really say? What does it really mean? What is this story about the incarnated God?" He basically tried to elaborate on the essence of Christian thought. These people thus came upon the problem: "πόθεν τὸ κακόn?" ("Where does evil come from?")[148] This question comes from Basilides, the great Gnostic, who concerned himself especially with the question of evil, and hence with the problem of the shadow.

So, for these Gnostics it was clear that Christ was, in fact, born with a shadow, but that he cut this shadow off from himself, and this shadow became the devil. We must assume, therefore, that there is an original assumption, that is, a *sous-entendu*, mind you, an *unconscious* predisposition – that has to do with the nature of Yahweh, the Yahweh of the Old Testament – that Christ originally was also a *coincidentia oppositorum*, a coming together of opposites, a unification or union of opposites.[149] This union then split into two, through an act of ethical decision as it were. The other half would be the "dark brother." This fits with the history of symbolism, in that Christ and the devil have a whole series of symbols in common. For example, the devil is "the lion," and Christ is "the lion," *Leo de tribu Juda*[150] or, "He [the devil] is prowling around like a roaring lion, looking for one to devour" (1 Peter 5:8). Or the eagle and the *stella matutina*, that is, the morning star, Lucifer. Both are *lucifer*[151]. This points to an original oneness that was split through an act of will. As it were, the original oneness is still in his father, namely the Jewish Yahweh. Yahweh is a *coincidentia oppositorum;* he has both sides, a light, positive side and a dark side. On the one hand, isn't it so, one should love this God; on the other, one should fear Him. But you have the same thing in the New Testament, where this very Saint John, author of the gospel and perhaps also the *theologus* to whom the *apocalypsis Joanu*, the Revelation of John, is ascribed[152] – and this is truly the apostle of

148 See C.G. Jung, "A Psychological Approach to the Trinity," CW 11, par. 249.
149 See C.G. Jung, "The Personification of the Opposites," CW 14, par. 200.
150 The lion of the tribe Judah. Genesis 49:9: "Judah is a lion's whelp."
151 Latin, "bringer of light."
152 See C.G. Jung, "Answer to Job," CW 11, pars. 698–741.

love *par excellence* – comes to the conclusion that the *evangelium aeternum,* which is revealed in the *Apocalypse,* should read, "Fear God! Rediscover the fear and the terror emanating from Yahweh!"[153]

We'd also have a later example: look at our national saint, Niklaus von Flüe. He had a vision of God that was so terrible that people could no longer look into his face – he had such an expression of terror on his face that they shied away from him. He himself was so terribly impressed that he had to meditate a long time before he was able to transform this God into the Holy Trinity once more. He did it with the help of a little booklet from a mystic of southern Germany. He could neither read nor write, but with the diagrams contained in this booklet he was able to reinterpret his vision into the lovely Trinity, a painting that is still hanging in the church of Sachseln. The painting is from the end of the 15th century. He needed a whole process.[154]

This is similar to Ignatius of Loyola who also had a vision of Christ, but in the form of a luminous snake. It seemed so lovely and beautiful that he thought it had to be something good, the Christ. But then he had doubts and thought that it could have been the devil after all. So, then it was the devil![155] – There you see how close those things lie together.

This decision of Christ, this separation from the shadow, is a historical process, which belongs to that time. At that time a general refinement of moral critique took place. One started to realize that the "thou must" or "thou must not" was all-too primitive, and that there are also sins of intent, which are a lot worse than what one might be able to achieve with those laws of common decency. Meaning that the reason is not being touched upon, because the reason lies in the moral, ethical attitude, and not in such rules of decency. At that time, the whole world of the Greek gods, including the Roman and Egyptian, perished due to the scandal of their conduct. One found that they were immoral and indecent gods who displayed every kind of human weakness; as a result, they were ridiculed. This process lasted over a few hundred years. It was a moral critique leveled at the gods,

153 In *Memories, Dreams, Reflections by C. G. Jung,* "School Years," pp. 36–42, Jung reports on his own, early experience with the dark side of God.
154 See C. G. Jung, "Brother Klaus," CW 11, pars. 474–487.
155 See C. G. Jung "The Holy Men of India," CW 11, par. 957.

and because of this they ultimately perished. This means that the *phenomena*, which originally led to the naming of the gods, had remained. For example, we are only seemingly free from Wotan. Wotan – the phenomenon of Wotan – is present, and in a highly interesting way, at that. In the biography of Niklaus von Flüe, for example, there are wonderful accounts of "Wotanic" experiences[156], such as with the chronicler from Lucerne[157], when he writes that Wotan is roaming on the alp of Pilatus.[158] It doesn't say "Wotan," but the "Wuotis army." He himself went up there once and stayed overnight with the alpine herdsman and dairyman. During the night he heard lovely music and many people circling around the hut in both directions, a whole procession. In the morning he asked the herdsman what that had been. He replied, "Well, yes, that was the 'Wuotis army.' These were the blissfully deceased." This is the positive aspect of the raging army[159], the "blissfully deceased." Whoever sees them belongs to them, and whoever encounters the Wuotis army is robbed and assimilated by them, and abducted through the air, and so on. That is a Wotanic phenomenon that took place even at the time of Cysat. I could give you a whole bunch of other such cases in which you'd see clearly how what was originally called "Wotan" still exists. Especially with people of Alemannic or German origin the phenomenon is extraordinarily succinct. It is of absolutely no avail to say, it's all nonsense, it's superstition, or some such thing – the psychological phenomenon still exists. We are not done with this yet. It is present either way.

Exactly the same is true for those assertions of the Christian mythology: it is another name given for similar phenomena. And this is why the problem of cutting away the shadow is a historical problem. It is a psychological problem: At that moment, when the morality refines itself – when the moral problem is removed, so to speak, from the level of police ordinance and transferred to the human heart – from that moment on it is a psychological problem, which it wasn't

156 See C. G. Jung's essay "Wotan," CW 10, pars. 371–399.
157 Renward Cysat (1545–1614), *Collectanea Chronica und denkwürdiger Sachen pro Chronica Lucernensis et Helvetiae*; ed. by Joseph Schmid (Lucerne: Diebold Schilling Verlag, 1961–1977).
158 See also, *Memories, Dreams, Reflections by C. G. Jung*, p. 230.
159 The German noun, "Wut" (rage), and the adjective, "wütend" (raging, furious, mad) are etymologically related.

at all originally. At that time, it was a problem of statutes. This is why there was the negative confession of sins in Pharaonic Egypt – the soul's confession. When the soul comes before the last judgment, where the heart is being weighed, a negative confession is made: "I did *not* steal the belongings of the orphans," or, "I did *not* cheat the widow," and so on. But *what* this person actually did wasn't said. One only said that one did not infringe on the police ordinances of the universe, like, "There was, in our region, no known criminal record on this person." In a passport, a passport application, or a character reference, it doesn't say that one is a decent human being; it only says that, "It is not known that this person (for instance) cut somebody's throat." This is the negative confession of sins of our bureaucracy, since they refer to others and not to themselves.

Approximately at the time of Christ, the negative confession of sins of old Egypt evolved into a new consciousness: "I did do it." One discovered that it was a question of attitude and not just a simple offense against police ordinance, but that it was a concern of the human soul. The story in the New Testament of Satan's severance confirms the presence of this gossip, or of this philosophical idea, as well as other symbolic matters in the New Testament, for instance the relationship to Yahweh and so on; we don't have to dwell on it any longer. It simply illustrates, so to speak, a problem of time.

Today, we are under the influence of the medieval development of Christianity. We are used to thinking in this particular Christian way, namely in the style of the *summum bonum* and "God is only the good;" "God is not paradox;" "all evil is shadowy and doesn't even have real substance;" "it is merely the absence of good."[160] Therefore, one doesn't think anything at all, for if one were to think, one would know that if there is no evil, if evil *is* not, neither is there good. What's the point? There is no white if there is no black and no black if there is no white. But nobody gives it a thought. It is most astounding what is believed; as soon as one starts to think a little bit, one makes the most incredible discoveries.

I once had the imprudence to state that, in Catholicism, Christ and Mary are not human beings but gods. Then a Jesuit came to see me;

160 See C. G. Jung's position on the teaching of the *privatio boni*, e.g. in CW 11, pars. 456–459.

he was a professor of theology at the university of Munich, a very intelligent man. He said, "I've read your *Answer to Job*." I said, "Oh yes? Wow, that surprises me!" – "Yes," he went on, "I did read it. Of course, there is much one could say about it." – "Indeed," I said. "But *one* thing I have to ask you: How can you assert that Christ and Mary were not human?" I answered, "But that is a very simple matter, this is totally clear. You have to admit that we are all born in original sin. We are human. Christ and Mary were not born in original sin. Obviously, they are not animals, so therefore they must be gods – what else is there? – angels, or some such thing. But they are not human." To that he couldn't say anything, because he had never thought about it before. He had never thought about it at all.

Or, for example, another theologian, this one a Protestant. Now, the Protestant theologians claim that I devalue, so to speak, the religious ideas by "psychologizing" them, by saying that it is psychology. For these people this is devaluing, because for them the soul has no value. For me it does have a value. For those people the soul doesn't represent a value. Therefore, it is devalued. They claim that when I say, "God" it's nothing but a "psychologism." I say, "God is what I imagine." If someone can prove that He is something else, I'd be very grateful, for it cannot exactly be proven. But when I say, "God is a conceived image of my making," that doesn't mean that God doesn't exist! I only say, "That which I can comprehend is a conception." That is something I know about Him. Beyond that, I know nothing. I only know that this is my conception. Everything I know about God is my conception. Everything I know about the world is my idea about it. Beyond that I cannot assert anything. Yes, one can *believe* all sorts of things, but *I* can't believe, I can only know something.[161] For if I don't know it, well, then I honestly don't know it. And when I believe it, then I don't know it. But why should I believe something that I don't know? It could just as well be false. So, I better not believe it. And if I know something then I don't need to believe it, for then I know it.

---

161 See also *C. G. Jung speaking. Interviews and encounters*, ed. by William McGuire and R. F. C. Hull, (Bollingen Series XCVII, Princeton: University Press, 1977), p. 428. John Freeman's interview with C. G. Jung on the BBC television program "Face to Face," March 1959.

Well then, that theologian – I met him by chance during a vacation – asked me whether I occasionally discuss matters with theologians. I said, "Yes, yes, quite a bit, with Protestants as well as Catholics." – "Oh, but that is very interesting, what do you talk about?" Then I said, "Just now I'm working on such a case. I put the question to several theologians, namely how modern Protestantism relates to the question about the concept of God in the Old and the New Testament: How does Protestantism deal with it?" Two theologians didn't answer at all. These are people at theological faculties. Those didn't answer at all. One of them told me, "Yes, that is a difficult question; I first have to think about it." Eventually, he concluded that for the last thirty years nothing has been written in the theological literature about the concept of God, only about Christology. And then he said, "Yes, but this is really very strange. This question, in fact, is very easy to answer." Then I said, "Would you be so kind as to answer this question for me?" – "Yes, with pleasure! The concept of God in the Old Testament is simply a somewhat archaic matter, whereas in the New Testament this concept is more differentiated." Whereupon I said, "Look here, my dear colleague, now *you* are committing the psychologism that you reproach me of. Now, God is obviously nothing but a concept – please." But later, when he gets into the pulpit, he constantly waxes on about "Dear God." So, He has to be there, since he is talking about Him. Conversely, if *I* talk about it, it's a psychologism. Whereupon, of course, his jaw dropped! He had never thought about it either. For the first time, the thought occurred to him that he himself had committed a psychologism. This is why it's so difficult to speak about these things, because people cannot think about them. They are archetypically anchored; these things are *plus fort que vous*[162]. As background they are so self-evident that one doesn't even notice that they are there. Archetypes are the utmost self-evident thing, which is why one isn't aware of them. Because one doesn't notice what is self-evident at all.

In our time the problem has simply come alive. And, in fact, clearly through what happened historically. There are only a few centuries in which such disgusting atrocities occurred as in ours. It's simply horrible. And that tore open the problem of evil. We simply can't pretend

162 French, "stronger than you."

any longer that it is a μὴ ὄν, a non-being[163]. It is an optimistic view that evil is only a shadow. Evil is a reality. Or then, Good isn't either! But one cannot assert that only good exists and evil doesn't. It *does*! Every father confessor knows that as soon as someone has confessed his sins, and regretted them, he is relieved and goes around the next corner to sin again. Nobody can live without sin. We can sin with every breath we take. People who think that they are very respectable and only do the good ... Yes, when you look into those backgrounds where the surface presents especially clean – beware! There are sins of attitude, and, God knows, in this regard I am not optimistic. Now, it is a fact that there is no human being who doesn't sin, or who could ever hope to come out of sin. He'd have to be dead. But not before. When he can't sin any more, it stops. This is simply a fact. Nobody can convince me that it is different.

When you look at the saints ... well, dear God, who has to carry the burden? Who, for example, cared for the wife of Niklaus von Flüe when he left so-and-so many children and his wife, to retreat into his hermitage? Yes, there he was a saint! And his wife and children could herd the cows or some such thing. But he was out of the game. Just like Tolstoy who, in his old age, also quickly wanted to become a saint and gave his wife all the money. He still lived off it anyway. These are child's games.

Once I met a real saint. Unfortunately, I can't give you more specific biographical details. But, for three days I talked with him, and every day I sank a few fathoms deeper into my sinfulness and imperfection. At the end of the third day, there wasn't much left of me. The next morning his wife came to consult with me. Well, then I got to see another picture of this glory! I flew the fourteen fathoms out of the earth up again and was perfectly restored. I had my nose full. I realized, "Well, this now is the so-called saintliness."[164]

Of course, there are also very decent saints; this I readily admit. But these live through endless stretches of darkness and absence of God. Read, for example, *The Dark Night of the Soul*, by John of

163 See e.g. C.G. Jung, *Mysterium Coniunctionis*, CW 14, par. 86; or *Aion*, CW 9/ II, esp. chapter V: "Christ, a symbol of the self," pars. 68–126.
164 See C.G. Jung, "The Relations between the Ego and the Unconscious," CW 7, par. 306.

the Cross.[165] Or consider, for example, the highly original Therese of Avila. From some of the anecdotes one can see very well what she really thought. Once she was on an outing. A wheel broke and the carriage fell to its side. She had to crawl out from under and then said, her gaze turned toward the sky, "Now I understand why you only have such few friends!"

Of course, nowadays, we are confronted again with this historical question that has slumbered for two thousand years: "What is it with the dark side?" – Yes, if we were less conscious it would be easy, then it would pass by as an aside. Then one is not that good, not that clean; one is not that morally aware, and one simply doesn't see it and it somehow slips away. Yes, one was in a bad mood and quickly stabbed someone to death – it can happen to anyone. In this way, one just goes about life looking straight ahead without discernment. One winks at it; one simply doesn't look too closely, and so it goes. But if someone wants to struggle with it in principle, then the great difficulty arises! Then the question comes up: what does theology say? What a physician has to say is apparently irrelevant anyway. A doctor is known to be a highly dubious authority. He may give totally amoral advice and, in certain circumstances, even let a thing slip by. In this regard, physicians are known to have no conscience. But the theologian, he needs to step up. What does he have to say? How should one deal with all these questions? Because we can't ignore anymore that man is "good." "*Tout est parfait sortant des mains de l'Auteur des choses; tout dégénère dans les mains de l'homme,*"[166] it says at the beginning of Rousseau's *Émile*. The fact that we know that evil is real – as real as good – *that* poses a highly difficult problem for theology. It is a revision of the prevailing theological point of view. I can't help either; I'm sorry, but so it is. I'd love to spare you this, but it is an extremely difficult problem, namely, how to deal with the shadow side?

It is a problem that has various aspects. We pretend, or we like to imagine, that we know how to deal with the shadow, or as if the

165 See C. G. Jung: "The Psychology of Transference", CW 16, par. 479.
166 French, "everything is perfect when it comes out of the hands of the Creator; everything degenerates in the hands of man." In the original text, "Tout est bien sortant des mains de l'Auteur des choses; tout dégénère entre les mains de l'homme."

problem consisted in how *we* deal with the shadow. But we don't imagine how the shadow deals *with us!* During an English discussion with theologians, an old, witty priest said, he wondered why one posed the problem thus: "He entertains evil thoughts – I always found that they entertain *me!*" He got it! We don't have a choice. The shadow, after all, is an archetype, and it is such that it takes you, it seizes you. Nobody is such an idiot as to commit a glaring sin intentionally; for the disadvantages are so great that one avoids it on one's own accord. Either one collides with the law – and that's an uncomfortable thing – or one collides with one's wife or with one's husband, or with a colleague at work, or with the public in general. And that's very uncomfortable. Such a thing is prohibitive; one doesn't do it. What one can avoid there, one does anyway. But the devil is that these things seize one. One doesn't have a choice; one doesn't even have time. The sin is already committed before one realizes that one is committing a sin. One simply falls for it, and on top of the damage one has the ridicule. One is simply in a damn situation. Of course, the moralist says, "Well, but that you should have avoided it." – "Yes, of course, I should have avoided it, if only I could have! But the devil is, it happened before I realized it. *C'était plus fort que moi.*[167]" This is the situation, and it gives the whole business a completely different perspective. One cannot, in such cases, decide before – decide ethically – "do I want it this way or that." These are the rarest cases.

In reality, most of the time something uncomfortable simply happens, which afterwards one regrets, as if one could have avoided it. It's just like when someone falls into a crevasse. He can only say, "Why am I going into the mountains?" But going into the mountains is part of normal life, after all, and one can fall anywhere. Not that he wanted it, or that an ethical decision made it necessary to fall down here *in order* to commit a sin. That, in fact, was the way the Gnostics thought. They thought they *had* to commit sins – by invoking the archangel who had to protect them while they committed their sins – because otherwise they couldn't be redeemed from their sins, true to the principle, "You cannot be redeemed from a sin that you did *not*

---

167 French: "It was stronger than me."

commit."[168] Therefore, *tableau*! We must commit sins so that we can be redeemed. Because those we didn't commit will be unredeemed in all eternity. From what should we be redeemed if we didn't commit sins? In this way they [certain Gnostics] ended up in antinomy and libertinism and abominable orgies, where they sinned vigorously.

Luther knew this. He knew, for example, what the melancholia and depression of his friend Melanchthon was based on. This is why he told him, "Melanchthon, you don't sin enough. *Pecca, fortiter pecca!* Sin, sin mightily!" That was Luther. He knew that his [Melanchthon's] depressions were related to him being an intellectual and scholar – there is, notably, a typical intellectual habitus in his pictures – always floating a bit above himself, so, naturally, he got a depression. De-pression means to push down. This is how he was pushed down from these heights. And where does one land when one is pushed down? Down into the dirt, into a wholesome dirt. Thus, Luther said to him, "Accept it! *Humilis sis!* Be modest!" We belong to the Earth and the Earth consists of matter, or of dirt, like clay. Dirt is only matter, but in the right place, and one gets "into dark matter," which one *also* is, and not intentionally, but one is led into it. Why else would it say [in the Lord's Prayer], "lead us not into temptation?"[169]

Our daughter said, when her grandmother tried to teach her the Lord's Prayer – she was seven years old – "I won't pray that." I asked her, "Why not?" – "God doesn't lead us into temptation, that is evil." And she persisted. I didn't tell her this. But, when you consider, the almighty, the all-knowing, the greatness of the Godhead, about to lead those little aphids on earth into temptation: what an idea! This is precisely as if a father or mother, who have absolute authority over their children, would lead them into temptation to do something wrong, just to be able to punish them afterwards. A horrible idea! But it *is* there, and that is to say, this God has a dark side, and he *means* it! This is why Christ says, "lead us not into temptation," because, in this regard, there is divine intention. Meister Eckhart says in his sermon about Sin and Repentance, "God has burdened those He loves most with sins beforehand. And the apostles – were they not altogether

---

168 See C. G. Jung: "Woman in Europe," CW 10, par. 271; *Mysterium Coniunctionis*, CW 14, par. 277.
169 Here the tape was changed. A few words are missing.

deadly sinners?"[170] He, too, knew that it corresponds to the will of God that man also has to go through the darkness, and that there is no redemption without a price being paid for it. This is a hard lesson. I didn't make it up. It just is that way. I didn't insert this part, "lead us not into temptation" into the Lord's Prayer. Neither did I whisper it into Meister Eckhart's ears. I'm only a physician who has seen the moral problem of his patients. I had to tell so many of them, "Yes, that is difficult; this is a damn situation into which you've maneuvered yourself. You fell into a hole, but how could you come out of a hole if you never were in it? How could you in any way ascend to anything if you hadn't been down before? How did you live at all when you were walking on the clouds?"

To Americans I'm fond of saying, "Mary had a little lamb. It was as white as snow. But once she took it down to Pittsburgh…" – and now look at the damn thing![171] I don't know whether you understand this American slang?

Ignaz Tauber: Not everybody does.

C. G. Jung: That's a famous nursery rhyme: "Mary had a little lamb, his fleece was as white as snow." But once she took it down to Pittsburgh. Pittsburgh, you must know, is black from soot. And now look at the damn thing, this is how it happens that, precisely, moral people who are ethically gifted, end up in situations in which they have to get out of a hole. But they can't get out of it if they never were in it.

I can't really discuss this issue as a moral problem, rather as a psychological problem: Whoever has never been down, cannot climb up. Whoever has never been down, was never on this earth. And what, after all, is the meaning of our existence? Should we all be tigers, cute tigers, that only eat apples? A vegetarian tiger – that's simply an absurdity, a sick thing. And so is a human being who doesn't live on earth and doesn't pay tribute to the earth. This, one doesn't do of one's own free will. Nobody pays taxes of their own free will; to the contrary, it is always a bloody must, which – one could say, thank God – we can't avoid. But the one to whom it happens doesn't say a thing.

170 Meister Eckhart (German Mystic, 1260–1328), *German Sermons and Treatises*.
171 Jung recites in English.

We're simply exposed, and we have to acknowledge that we are at risk. *Pericolosamente vivere* – life *is* a risk! And if it isn't, then nothing has happened. Then you can say with Voltaire on his deathbed, when he was asked by the Abbé, his father confessor, "*Regrettez-vous tous vos péchés, Monsieur de Voltaire?*" – "*Mais oui, mon père, et surtout ceux que je n'ai pas commis.*"[172] That is true, that is colossally true! That is the problem.

I hope to have answered your anxious question in this regard. It is a question about human defeats. And that is a form of war. I didn't create this world the way it is, not at all. You'd have to put the protests to heaven against how the world is organized. But what would it be like if we were all good? Then what? Nothing at all would happen! There wouldn't be a need for religions, churches, nothing. There wouldn't be differences anymore. There wouldn't be a gradient anymore. There wouldn't exist a goal anymore, because the goal would have been attained long ago. We'd be born with harps in our hands, singing songs of praise our whole life long, and nothing else. We would be bored to death. There's also no energy without gradient; gradient means opposites! One who doesn't have inner oppositions is not alive; that is a dead neurotic who only groans, but doesn't live.

It is somewhat similar to being exposed to illnesses. It could happen that one's leg rots off, why not? That's very sad, but to which authority can we turn to complain? It's a fact, a misfortune. If a man abandons his wife, or a woman secretly cheats on her husband – yes, that's a misfortune, but something to be reckoned with. Consider for once how primitives live; that's highly interesting. They handle it with a lot of tact. It is essential, not so much *what* one does, but *how* one does it.

Even something dubious can be done in a way that is moral. Let's say, for example, "I'd like to cheat you out of five hundred francs. I'd later give you six hundred. You'd only have to refrain from connecting the two cases." [Laughing.] Yes, this is how it happens in reality, doesn't it? There are no recipes. In this respect, we've fallen out of police rule. There is no "you must not" or "you must," because none of these rules fit the individual situation. The individual situation is

172 French: "Do you regret all your sins, Mr. Voltaire?" – "But yes, my father, and, most of all, the ones I did *not* commit!"

always different! And there is only the individual decision, and that's where it shows if someone acts morally, or whether he doesn't act morally. In all these complicated matters, he has to come to terms with them himself, and not with the judge. There is no universal or collective ethic that can live up to casuistry. In each case, one has to investigate who does what. This "what" of the so-called ethical deed is by no means in all cases clearly determined. Even when there is a name for a certain situation, it can be in a particular case *toto coelo*[173] different from another case that has the same name. It is often a tragic decision; often it is a secret in an individual life. But we do need a secret. Evidently, people who don't have a secret (because they are too dumb to find out something that could be secret) have to invent secrets. They have to found secret societies, for example. They have to invent some kind of initiations that are "secret." Take any such secret society; when you examine the mysteries of that secret society, you find that there is nothing in it that would have to be kept secret. There is nothing at all secret – it has been divulged somewhere long ago, and it isn't even worthwhile to keep it secret. Take, for example, one of the Rosicrucian societies of today – they have such fabulous secrets! But if you examine them – oh, pity![174] – you have to laugh. They are no secrets at all. There's nothing. It's not worthwhile. They only say, "These now are highly secret things that one has to hide." Why? – So that, for God's sake, they have a secret, namely to keep their individuality.[175]

This is why nature herself is forcing many people into situations they simply cannot talk about, because it would be too embarrassing, and then they do a lot better. Why? They have a secret. They are someone in themselves. They are not sullied with all the other people, not stained with other psychologies; they carry their own psychology. They know themselves, have experienced themselves – and that is what is actually meant! I don't know whether this is understandable. Should I not be completely understandable, then it isn't necessarily

---

173 Latin, "by the whole extent of the heavens" – meaning: *diametrically* different.
174 In Swiss German, *oh herrje!*, literally, *oh Lord Jesus*, like the American "jeez," invoking Jesus without fully acknowledging it.
175 See C.G. Jung, *Mysterium Coniunctionis*, CW 14, par. 312; and *Memories, Dreams, Reflections* by C.G. Jung, pp. 20 f. and 41.

because I'm unable to express myself clearly or forcefully enough, but because the *problem* is so difficult. It is a new problem. We have to make a change in attitude here: If something happens to another person that we find loathsome, we have to think that he is pitiable for what has happened to him, and not that he is a "bad guy," or that he must have brought it upon himself, and so on. That's nonsense. Instead: Nature has seized him and done something with him! The majority of people are poor devils, who simply are victims of a merciless nature or of a merciless God. Why does one say, "He is the Just One?" Or the Most Lovable? These are all just apotropaisms, attempts at "appeasement"[176]; one wants to humor Him; it's a euphemism. One gives a good name to something highly dangerous. The "black sea" for example, feared for its storms, is called *Pontos Euxeinos*, the hospitable one, the hospitable sea, when in fact it is terribly inhospitable. *That* is the truth.[177] If, therefore, one evokes any kind of doubt – and this doubt is precisely evoked in our time – then one is a harmful person; then one has to somehow be silenced, because one doesn't say such a thing; it would be too terrible if one would lose the ideal of the *summum bonum*.

But our reality – let's think, for example, about the iron curtain, let's think about the hydrogen bomb, let's think about the unthinkable that threatens with the overpopulation of the earth! Well, Good Lord, then we don't feel so optimistic any more. This we can't formulate any longer in the language of traditional Christian optimism. Which, by the way, is found in a small place, as all essential benefits only come into effect when one is dead. That's when those paradisiac conditions unfold which, here on earth, typically are lacking. So, now I stop; now I've given an example.

Ignaz Tauber: Thank you very much. In that case, I think we now take a little break.

176 Said in English.
177 See C. G. Jung, "A Review of the Complex Theory," CW 8, pars. 206 f.

On Psychological Insights

Ignaz Tauber: Hans Baumann wants to speak.

Hans Baumann: I wrote Prof. Jung a letter with a problem that has already preoccupied me for a ong time. It was quite difficult to precisely formulate my question in that letter. I've been thinking about it again, and it ends up being the following: In regard to our scientific insights we naturally only have our human sense organs at our disposal, and insofar as all our insights are human insights. But the object we recognize is outside of the human condition. On the other hand, wherever we occupy ourselves with psychological problems, it is an introspection. We are, therefore, in considering the question, simultaneously subject *and* object. And for me personally, that makes all psychological insights, in a certain way, doubtful in regard to the numinous.

C. G. Jung: Yes, this is in effect a somewhat complicated epistemological problem. There are certain things we must first clarify.

Let's take the natural sciences, for example. In the natural sciences you have a so-called real object that is in no way tied to your psyche. It is independent. I mean, you can die and the object is still there. With the psychic it is apparently a wholly subjective business, in that it only functions as long as you psychically function. Apparently. But if one examines this more closely, we are actually dealing, in the case of the natural sciences, with insights that hinge on an external object that is difficult to recognize. Which means, they are conditioned by the object. How difficult these observations are, demonstrates, for example, modern nuclear physics. It is extraordinarily difficult to get a picture of what's happening in nature. Here we come to a point (as you have correctly emphasized in your letter) where the experiment, or the observation, disturbs the process and distorts it beyond recognition, so that you either can observe it only in part, by sacrificing other things – because if you want to see one thing you have to sacrifice the other – or that the reliability of the observation is completely put in question by the uncertainty principle[178]. It is therefore not an easy

178 By Werner Heisenberg.

thing to see the "object as is." We are always "on the way towards it." It follows that all insight is in some way anthropomorphous.

Let's take, for example, Niels Bohr's model of the atom, the planetary model. That is an anthropomorphous model. If we sort of compare the electrons with planets revolving around a core, it is not really accurate. Because an electron is rather an electrically charged cloud that cannot be compared to a tiny planet. These are exactly such "anthropomorphisms," which also occur in natural sciences.

Now, in psychology it is also a matter of dealing with the perception of certain processes that are difficult to discern, which actually lay beyond, or are the basis of, our psychological observations. This you see for example with our dreams. It is not even certain that they are the way you remember them, but are probably quite different, yet unrecognizable. Only upon awakening do they clothe themselves in images. As processes in the unconscious they are virtually unrecognizable, equally as much as the processes in the atom. This is why the conceptualization in modern psychology of the unconscious has remarkable parallels with the terminology of nuclear physics, simply because they both come up against the unknowable. Now, our idea of psychology is that which I know about these inner processes. That is psychology.

Recently, a university professor told his students that we didn't really need psychology, because that was what one knew about oneself anyway. This is exactly as if a professor at the medical faculty would say, "Anatomy you don't need, that's what you have, what you are! And physiology you don't need either. After all, you can digest without knowing anything about physiology. You don't need a textbook in order to digest. This you are; this you do, you do it every day!" This shows that there is a general prejudice that assumes the psyche is what we know about ourselves. But in truth the psyche is precisely that which we don't know about ourselves! What we know about ourselves is our consciousness and its contents. This consciousness, however, is considerably disturbed by objective processes, which in themselves are unconscious and unknown to us; it finds itself in opposition to them. But we can experience them indirectly through their effects on consciousness, borrowing from it certain images for illustration [of those objective processes].

[In an analogous fashion] we create a model of the atom from certain characteristics that the atom presents, and which remind us of certain conscious contents. A *model*, is it not? And in the same way we create, with what consciousness allows us, models for the processes of the unconscious. But these processes are the essential ones. If they did not exist, our consciousness couldn't function at all. I couldn't pronounce the next sentence if I didn't have the cooperation of the unconscious. For these are fundamental processes. These are processes that have to do with the instincts and that have instinctual forms, which one calls archetypes. The archetypes in themselves can't be formulated; we don't know them; they are not visible. Rather, they are present as active factors, somewhat like the crystal lattice in a mother lye. There is a lattice system, an invisible lattice system, in a completely amorphous mother lye, which, at a certain point of saturation, i.e. when the point of saturation is attained, becomes effective, namely in that ions are compelled to take certain axial positions through this hypothetical, non-existing structure. These, then, cause the molecules to settle along these axes, and especially in the axial intersections. And from that a crystal forms.[179] Exactly thus it happens in the unconscious psyche. We have an axial system, that is, an archetypal system, which is the foundation of all conscious forms, let's say, all principal forms. Because our consciousness is, in turn, also conditioned by the outside, by the non-psychic world, by the material world, the "world of bodies in motion," which is the definition of reality. On the other side, however, there is a non-existing, potential axial system that represents the objective psyche. You can very well compare this to a crystal. You could say, "This is the psyche of a crystal." The crystal has an axial psyche. It's the same with us. We also have a mathematical foundation of the human being, the psychic human. You can observe this in mandalas – there we have a definitive or mathematical structure, an axial system, that brings about infallibly, and in the uncanniest way – certain things that seem quite miraculous to us. But it is a mathematical structure, as for example the so-called "3 + 1" structure of traditional mandalas. Let's take one of the best known: the symbol of the trinity plus one (the

179 See C. G. Jung, "The Psychological Aspects of the Mother Archetype," CW 9/I, par. 155.

devil). That's a quaternity. That's an axial system, and it's simply an externalization, a projection of the psychic axial system. It follows that we have in the psyche the so-called subjective conscious processes – these are admittedly subjective – *and* the objectively present psychic foundations, which are, strangely enough, not personal but general. These are the same with the Indian, the Chinese, or the African, or whatever, always the same, in spite of our consciousness being *toto coelo* different. This, then, is the collective unconscious, which is impersonal – as impersonal as, for example, the human liver. The human liver is approximately the same in a Chinese, or an Indian, or an African, or an Eskimo. Just as the heart and all the fundamental vital functions are about the same. They are not personal. It's not your personal prerogative to have a heart, or your personal achievement to have a stomach. It's not a personal, but rather an objective matter. The fact that you have a psyche is an objective matter. You don't owe this to your own efforts. Neither is it a willful decision of your parents. Rather, when you are born, you are born with a psyche – in fact, with this psyche, which is everywhere, which even the apes still have, and the dogs, and so on, an animal psyche, a natural anthropoid psyche, to begin with. It's an anthropoid psyche. And that is objective, an objective crystalline system. For example, cooking salt simply has a cubic nature. Water has a hexagonal structure. It simply has it, so this it is [categorized]. If it doesn't have it, it's not water. You cannot suddenly discover water that crystallizes in another system, or cooking salt. It's impossible, it's part of it. And so, to every living being belongs a psyche that is objective, which we didn't seek, which is present before we even know it.

Hence there are, for example, children's dreams that are dreamt at a time when there is not even a continuous consciousness present, where consciousness consists of islands that only later come together as continents. Children can have dreams that anticipate their whole life. It is already planned; it is the fundamental design. In such a design, in such a dream, a psychosis may show up, for example, later the child develops schizophrenia. Or some great catastrophes may appear [in a dream] – and yes, they occur. Or ideas that later will determine the life of this child already [appear] in its earliest dreams.

And, these are dreamt at a time when consciousness is not even continuous. That is the objective psyche.[180]

Perhaps you've also had the experience of a talented astrologer quietly telling you your whole life story from your horoscope – and it is accurate! That wouldn't be possible if not everything were fundamentally laid out and aligned in a synchronistic manner with the positions of the stars. That is incredibly simple. If one has seen it a few times one is convinced. So, I ask my patients quite unabashedly and shamelessly, "Do you have your astrological chart with you?" Then they blush and say, "Yes, just by chance." Sometimes they opine that I might be just another biased idiot who would consider such a thing an incredible stupidity. No, it turns on quite a few lights. It is truly astonishing. And sometimes very uncomfortable. Once I had an assistant who later committed suicide. Years before. [...][181] There is such an astrological system. At the time, I calculated the charts myself because I wanted to find out how they worked. I saw that he had a symbol. There is a symbol for every degree of the zodiac, from the ascendant, from the moment of birth. A horse grazing, unaware that it is stalked by a tiger. The commentary, already printed and available long ago, read, "One who will prematurely disappear through suicide. Before his time." And so it was. I had a tremendous shock when I discovered this. At the time I couldn't yet tell why this would have to happen. But then it came to pass. Such things make a deep impression, even when once in a while it isn't true. But it provides a perspective; it is interesting.

So, it happened to me, for example, in 1911, when I got acquainted with these things, because I studied the history of symbols at the time. Then I realized the overwhelming importance of astrology in antiquity. It had an enormous influence. I first wanted to know something about it before making a judgment. Then, a little booklet from 1595 or 1596 came into my hands, from an old colleague. He'd been professor of medicine in Würzburg, a certain Mr. Goclenius, at the

---

180 C. G. Jung, *Children's Dreams: Notes of the Seminar Given* 1936–1940, edited by Lorenz Jung and Maria Meyer-Grass, translated by Ernst Falzeder with the collaboration of Tony Woolfson (Princeton: Princeton University Press, 2008), passim.
181 Here the tape was changed again.

end of the 16ᵗʰ century.[182] He'd written a nice compendium, a kind of
vade mecum for physicians at that time, concerning diagnosis based
on chiroscopy, that is, the study of hand lines. Then there was something else … what was it? Ah yes, then mainly a treatise of astrology
from a medical perspective. Very interesting! Therein one finds the
first individual horoscopes and rather smart questions, for example
about the psychological relationship between murderer and victim,
how this is expressed astrologically. The interesting thing is that they
are related; the two have similar constellations in their charts. At any
rate, there I read how he'd written categorically, *"Mars in medio coeli
semper significat casum ab alto"* – Mars in the zenith always signifies
a fall from high above. And about two weeks later the chart of the
German emperor came into my hands. He had Mars *in medio coeli*,
meaning, he was a belligerent lord, not an emperor of peace as he
was called. Whoever has Mars above is, according to old tradition,
of a belligerent nature. And then [came the question], "How can the
German emperor – by God – fall?" One couldn't even imagine such a
thing at the time! But lo and behold, three years later it came to pass.
Then I told myself, "Well, heavens, there must be something to this
business!" Then I started to preoccupy myself seriously with it, and I
found that it was the old psychology. It was the old psychology, based
on the objective-psychic. The case with the objective psychic, you
see, is such: I have a certain character and a certain individuality, and
that consists of imponderables. It's something like when you give a
wine connoisseur a special wine that you know where it comes from,
and this wine connoisseur can tell you, it's such-and-such year, such-
and-such location, and so has to be such-and-such vineyard. This is
possible. And so, too, is man imprinted at the moment of his birth
with the location, the country, his environment, the whole *kairos*, the
moment in time. And this is expressed in the horoscope. This is why
you can already discern certain predispositions in the horoscope (the
birth chart), which sometimes later in life might play a very big role.

---

182 Jung owned a copy of this textbook of medicine from Rodolphus Goclenius:
　　*Uranoscopiae, chiroscopiae, metoposcopiae et ophthalmoscopiae contem-
　　platio* (Frankfurt, 1608). He mentions it in CW 18, par. 1818, and in C. G. Jung,
　　Dream Analysis. Notes of the Seminars Given in 1928–1930, ed. William
　　McGuire (Princeton: Princeton University Press, 1984), p. 458.

Astrology, in fact, is coming into full bloom in our time, not in the Middle Ages. There it was in its infancy. In our time, astrology is at its peak. But when you open the encyclopedia, it says there, "as late as 1722, Lord so and so had a horoscope made for each of his children." That old fool! Such superstition! And, of course, the idiots who wrote this didn't know a thing about it – that real astrological literature only exists in our time! Only today have we a science of astrology. Never before have so many horoscopes been cast. I know a professor of philosophy in England who taught an introductory course in astrology – at an English university. Voilà, that's the situation! In Switzerland we are a bit backwoods; this I would like to have said, mind you: a bit backwoods.

Well, I am not here to make an apology for astrology. But that such a thing is possible and has legitimacy is only so because there exists an objective psyche. The psyche is not a random thing, nor an accident, but a definite, functional disposition that is more or less identical for all human beings, just like the physiological and anatomical dispositions. Just like everyone has a sternocleidomastoideus[183], so he also has a certain archetype. And just as the body is composed of various organs, so the psyche consists of various archetypes, of inborn forms. These are not inborn ideas, but forms of psychic happenings. They are forms of instinct. Instinct is not simply a dynamism that does something; rather, instinct is specific and therefore has a specific form.[184]

183 The primary actions of this muscle are rotation of the head and flexion of the neck.
184 The tape recording stops at this point. To conclude from notes of some listeners, Jung came in the following to speak on the *effect* of the archetypes.

Notes of the Continuation of the Colloquium

[No tape recordings exist of the continuation of this evening. Sabi and Ignaz Tauber and their guests have subsequently reconstructed the following notes of the questions and answers. We reproduce them here as they were collected by Sabi.]

He'd talked to us from 4.30 until 7 pm, with only a short break in the middle.

During the break, I asked him a question that weighed heavily on the mind and heart of a shy, honest young mother: How can one teach religion to one's children if one doesn't have any oneself? Jung responded drily and matter-of-factly, that, in such a case, one just doesn't do it. One simply doesn't do anything. But, I continued, what if one knows that they need it and one would like that they have it? Jung: Well, then one has to work on oneself until one attains a personal *religio* – one can only pass on what one has oneself.

Now we all moved closer together, to make room for Roswith and her cousin Verena. They performed a self-choreographed dance in black-and-white that was to demonstrate how our young generation imagined the relationship of light and dark. Christian underscored the performance on the piano with Cyril Scott's "Negro-dance." Jung much enjoyed it and said that he had learned something, namely how flexible a human being can be, and how important it was that one can fall and get up again! Sitting close together and every which way, a few among us also had the courage to put forth a question of our own to Jung.

The following notes are from Mrs. Mimi Fopp, pertaining to Jung's comments on a question that was asked: Instinct is highly conservative, and it is specific. Our psyche relies on instinct. What happens when opposition is present? Well, then there is an archetype that tells us what to do. What will happen with today's powerful oppositions in the world? A unifying process! Something will happen that is expressed through a savior figure who will unify the opposites, forge a bridge. The psyche is objective, like hands and feet. It lives on throughout the world when a person dies. The archetype is everywhere, like the sun.

Therefore, we are able to understand people from other countries, from India, China.

We no longer know what Christianity really means; we have fallen out of it. The numinous archetype is an experience which we don't make; it befalls us. Saul-Paul, for instance, is thrown from the horse, becomes blind, but he doesn't do it, he doesn't say, "I am an unconscious Christian." Such an experience is not our doing. The numinous experience only happens when we pay the tribute. If the concept of God is not empirical, it does not affect us, it is an empty word. I need to know where I am touched by the will of God. It is said, "The Lord will spit the lukewarm out of his mouth."[185] The lukewarm don't suffer hot or cold!

Thinking is so difficult; this is why most people judge. Where God is closest, danger is greatest. The Christian faith is no longer part of life; it is only words. If the god concept is not empirical, it doesn't touch us. I need to know *where* I am touched by the will of God!

(The following notes are from Mr. Renold.)

Question from Dr. Jakob Fopp: What has astrology to say about the situation of the world today?

Jung [noted in keywords]: Astrologers view it in connection with the discovery of the planet Pluto[186]. He is the Lord of the Underworld, something dark, remote, the devil, far from humanity, the earth, the sun; lacking light; a cold element. Manifesting in a figure like Hitler or Stalin. This astrological fact coincides with the situation of the world. In earlier periods one didn't think of such matters – the splitting of the atom; the splitting of the world through the iron curtain, or the message: "I'll be coming home over the North Pole," (as a relative wrote him on a postcard). The earth is getting smaller and smaller, and completely new conditions will arise. There is a great psychological restlessness; minds are divided. We have psychic epidemics, like National Socialism, or a utopia like communism, which are totally

185 A reference to the Bible: "So then because you are lukewarm, and neither cold nor hot, I will vomit you out of My mouth." (Revelation 3:16, New King James)
186 Pluto was discovered in 1930; till 2006 it was listed as the 9th planet, since then only as one of the "dwarf planets."

closed to criticism. The Christian faith is out of touch with life, or else is pathological.

Another question: Why was China so open to communism?

Jung: Because the social standards are so miserable. The Chinese are now becoming more honest and cleaner. In this respect, communism was partly beneficial there, but it also did horrible damage. The Chinese no longer understand the old Chinese culture. Jung knows of a Chinese professor teaching Taoism only after having read about it in *The Secret of the Golden Flower* – Jung had drawn his attention to it – and only then he understood its meaning.

After all, we are in no better shape with Christianity: We no longer understand the symbols either. Or India, with its two and a half million gods – a religion tremendously rich in symbols, which, however, is no longer understood by the intellectual elite. With the mind of a journalist you don't get close to these things. To drop the old is theology's sin of omission. These days, an American professor at a theological seminary no longer teaches students in a church-dogmatic fashion, but psychologically. In Europe we are not yet as "advanced." Explaining symbols can only come out of personal experience, not as an intellectual mind game – this is why pastors fail. As a whole, it is alarming how the theologians circumvent hot issues. Theologians deal with each other carefully. Catholics have to be terribly careful not to say anything wrong. But the same goes for Protestants. There have been pastors attending my seminars, but it is dangerous for them. They could come into dangerous conflicts. Nobody tells the theologians what kind of a dilemma theology is in today. Psychology brings conflicts of conscience and questions that cannot be answered. Theology never got clear about what the unconscious is. The will of God has to be experienced empirically, not just theoretically; otherwise it's just empty talk. Theology is dead, wooden. The public is extremely hungry for elucidation in a psychological-religious way. He had seen this in his patients. Then pastors would have an easy time filling their churches.

Question from Dr. Läuchli: Where are the boundaries between psyche and matter and how far have points of contact been identified?

Jung: When the psyche wants the body to stand up and then it does stand up, this shows that the psyche has power over the body. No psycho-physical causality would be possible, if psyche and the body had no points of contact. The psychic is a characteristic of matter, and matter is a characteristic of the psychic. I don't want to pass metaphysical judgment, but for me, even inorganic matter has a psychic component. Crystals, just like plants, have life: they grow, they develop. I couldn't talk about matter without also speaking of the psyche. There will come a time when psyche can be proven materially. It has to do with the size of the atom. The transition is made when we no longer distinguish between inner-psychic and objective fact. We are still fascinated by the idea that the brain conditions the psyche, yet the psyche is far more expansive. The psyche of the other is my psyche too.

A question about number as an example for archetypes: Was the number discovered or was it invented?

Jung: It is something abstract. It was *invented* as a means to count, but it was *discovered* as an archetype. The number is present in the quantity of things, and furthermore as a being in the collective unconscious. A mythological statement for number is, for example: "One" is the One and the All; it is also simply one, which presupposes a duality. It is a symbol of God, the One, and the All-one. "Two" is separation and desire. "Three" corresponds the mediation of the two. A whole philosophy of the gods is expressed here! Number *per se* is an archetype and non-perceptual. Illustrative is the number as quantity, a property of mathematical things, a property of mathematics. Number as archetype is the father and mother of all philosophy – the most beautiful fantasy of middle Europe!

"Three" as God-father, divine mother, and son is a *hypostasia* (concretization, representation of things); one wants to know that something *is*. True understanding is only possible when one can retrace the unknown to known principles. The psyche can be expressed as an idea. Vice-versa, if we can prove a material fact as congruent with psychic laws, then we have understood something. A psychic law is, for example, the current of libido as an energetic law. Or the model of the atom according to Einstein's theory of relativity or Planck's quantum theory.

Quoting Antoine de St. Exupéry: "It is not the stones that make the cathedral, it is the cathedral that bestows significance onto the stones."[187]

Jürg was preoccupied with his school paper about suicide, so he asked Jung about it.

Jung answered: A person who carries around suicidal thoughts I'd only try to convert and hold back up to a certain point. He is, in fact, a murderer! In my mind, a murderer deserves the death penalty – so he does it to himself. Whoever is capable of destroying a life is not worthy to live, that seems clear to me.

Roswith still had the improvised performance on her mind and wanted to know what Jung thought about it.

He said, it is good for young people to improvise once in a while, whether on the piano or on paper, because one gets to hear other voices; one gets in touch with another world and can take it in, and so one gains a wider horizon and a more open sense for the future. Moreover, it is a creative act that exposes itself to critique, which is very valuable for human beings.

Jung went on to tell us of ultra-modern paintings he had seen, depicting "holes." Artists express the future. Those artists work in the fourth dimension! There, the body is a hole. For our conscious, materialistic three-dimensional world the psychic world represents the fourth dimension. Seen from the psychic world, however, the three-dimensional world of the body presents as a hole! In the fourth dimension, objects are objectless.

As an amplification, Ignaz mentioned the East-Indian concept of Nirvana, the illusionary world of Maya, Plato's cave parable, and from Goethe's *Faust*: "*Am farbigen Abglanz haben wir das Leben.*"[188]

We had the warm feeling that Jung was comfortable sitting among us. But there is an end to everything. This end became a beginning for those present, as they were all deeply touched. Jung received

187 See *Flight to Arras.* (French title: *Pilote de guerre*, 1942.)
188 Faust speaking: "On this your mind for clearer insight fasten: That life is ours by colorful refraction." J.W. von Goethe, *Faust II*, Act 1, Charming Landscape, verses 4726 f.

Fig. 23: High up in the tower.

an especially kind farewell from "the Junglis,"[189] who now were no longer distant relations but "dear relatives." Ignaz was the driver on the way back, with me, Roswith, and Jürg in the back seat, ears and hearts wide open.

Thus, we arrived in no time at the forbidden railroad crossing. Jung invited us into the quiet tower. He gave us a petroleum lamp and motioned that we were free to roam. Carefully the four of us went up the stairs, past a thousand precious objects. At the very end hung a Tibetan ghost trap, and in mid-space floated a crocodile, wood-carved dancers, and masks. In the room at the top we discovered a bundle of loose sheets of paper, covered with the neatest and most careful handwriting: the manuscript on the *Flying Saucers*. Solemnly, we pulled out three apples from our pockets and put them next to it. We filled the room with thoughts of gratitude and a thousand good wishes, then quietly retreated down the steep staircase. Jung smiled while offering us a drink. Outside, in the courtyard, we sang a couple of canons, which he and Miss Bailey seemed to enjoy greatly. The two accompanied us for a bit, until we reached the meadow next to the tall trees. There, all six of us joined hands in a circle and sang the canon, *"O klage nicht, wenn Morgennebel dich umwehn, denn schöner wird die Sonne, die Sonne niedergehn."*[190]

Our heartfelt wishes were rising up to the bright stars in the dark sky, with a hue of melancholy.

Ignaz, however, had an appointment with Jung in his pocket that would afford him one of those peak experiences from which we see our whole life backwards and forward; one that we often can only "remember" later.

189 Ernst Jung and his wife Ruth, older sister of Sabi.
190 "Ah, do not complain if morning fog surrounds you, for then the sun, the sun, will set more beautifully yet."

Fig. 24: Farewell.

Ignaz Tauber with C. G. Jung – June 8, 1957

[Notes of Ignaz Tauber on his visit with C. G. Jung in Küsnacht, Saturday before Pentecost, noon. In anticipation of "dark times," he took notes as carefully and truthfully as possible.]

In my childhood I had occasional moments of insight – a hunch, a feeling of participating in another world that was very close and yet very remote. It was like a glimpse into eternity and infinity. It was ecstasy and deepest pain simultaneously, because of the loss of such "knowing." After my talk with Jung I was seized by a shiver of happiness as if in an atmosphere of Pentecost, with a felt sense of having found this other world again – a world permeating and containing ours, but not contained in it – and that, under the guidance of Jung, I would be able to find my way around in it, and to perceive this as the essential task of my life and its deepest meaning.

C. G. Jung's elucidations: Insight into the problem of the shadow is very difficult because of the *Zeitgeist*, which is always a spirit of heaviness. One is completely caught in it, and it is extremely difficult to free oneself from it. As soon as one takes the gods as principles perception changes, and one immediately understands that this is the principle of incarnation. When God becomes man, he enters the dark sphere of humanity. But Christ rejected the devil, dismissed the dark side of God. Therefore, incarnation has not even taken place yet! Only now, in our time, the complete incarnation of the *Anthropos* is happening within each individual human being. At that point the relationship to an exterior God disappears, because one has God within.

There are testimonies from astrological symbolism for every eon. We are now approaching the astrological Age of Aquarius. The symbol shows two wavy lines: the upper and the lower waters. Above is the sphere of the sky, atmosphere; below the heavy, humid air, close to earth. That reminds one of the Book of Genesis: There was a separation of the upper and lower waters, when the devil appeared in the world. God didn't say that he was pleased. It was Monday – moon-day!

Helmuth Jacobsohn[191] writes that it is very easy to demonstrate the transition from the astrological eon of Taurus into Aries. At the end of each eon there is a basic change in the perception of God, a new aspect is revealed. Today, we are faced with the task of the union of opposites. Now the incarnation has to be *truly* accomplished, and not in a disinfected body, but in the real and natural human being. There is a colossal change in the concept of God:

1. to acknowledge the dark side of God, and

2. to know that oneself embodies God.

How can this be digested? Certainly, no longer with the Christian ethic! It is no longer, "Go away, Satan!" One has to recognize one's own face in it! This needs tolerance and psychological insight. Otherwise we are defenselessly exposed, because there ensues enormous distrust in oneself and others through the awareness that there is also a commensurate shadow. This awareness is paralyzing at first, until one has generated the necessary tolerance. It is only real if one is tolerant with oneself in the first place – otherwise it is only a *bon mot* for others, empty talk: "Well, you should ..." The others notice immediately that he doesn't do it himself! This is the great difficulty. Theologians, too, got wind that it is about a transformation of the god image, which is absolutely necessary. It is in accordance with God's will, for he really wants to incarnate! (My idea: This is why the Christians hope for paradise after death, because there they participate in God's being. God's incarnation on earth is the exact opposite.) God was intent, but Christ rejected the dark side. It had to be like that. It is still necessary today, lest people fall into the dark side. It is terrible!

(I had told Jung that I now understand why I couldn't integrate the shadow: because I didn't yet have the moral strength, and anyway only recently came to recognize the core of the problem.)

It is a fearful thing to fall into the hands of the living God! (Hebrews 10:31) One needs morality. If Christ had realized that the devil was

191 Two writings that Helmuth Jacobsohn had sent to C. G. Jung (*The Dogmatic Position of the King in the Theology of Ancient Egypt*, and *The Dialogue of a World-Weary Man with his Bâ*) aroused Jung's enthusiasm. From then on Jacobsohn gave lectures at the C. G. Jung Institute in Zurich. Jacobsohn was able to visit Jung regularly 1951–1961.

also his specific despot, then I could apply the principle of Christian charity toward the devil as well. The Gnostics already knew this. The Bible reads:[192] If someone says to his brother: Raca![193], he is doomed to hell fire! If someone wants to offer a sacrifice and realizes that he has something against his brother, he should first go and reconcile with him, and only then bring his gift to the altar. The Gnostics interpreted this as: first go and reconcile *with yourself* and then bring your sacrifice.[194] One is one's own closest brother. This is one of the most difficult things. It presupposes insight and psychology.

In Egyptian mythology, *Horuer* (the older Horus) had one body and two heads – one was Seth's. They both hold the ladder for Osiris on which he climbs up to the heavenly plateau. It means that the opposites are necessary if one wants to arrive at the heavenly plateau. He is the union of the two. It is nature's logic, of which one can only become conscious over time, when one is at one with oneself.

Depression is a purposeful reaction. With one's conscious mind, one always arrives in the upper sphere and finds it very positive. In truth, however, one is separated from reality; one is in a subjective balloon. One has to follow nature's logic. After all, we have these natural processes within ourselves.

As long as I'm afraid of them, I'm in danger of being led astray. If, however, I'm not afraid, then the danger is much smaller than we think – quite to the contrary, then it goes the right way. But we don't have the necessary trust. Remember the legend of the Rabbi, who wanders through the countryside, passing on teachings to his disciples, such as: "A barking dog doesn't bite." But when they came upon a barking dog, they all ran away, with the rabbi running ahead of them. His oldest disciple asked him why, in contrast to his teaching, he had run away. The rabbi answered, "I know, but does the dog

---

192 Matthew 5:22-24: "But I say unto you, that whosoever is angry with his brother without a cause shall be in danger of the judgment: and whosoever shall say to his brother, Raca, shall be in danger of the council: but whosoever shall say, Thou fool, shall be in danger of hell fire."
193 An expression of contempt.
194 See C.G. Jung, "Psychology and Religion," CW 11, par. 133.

know, too?" That is mistrust against the dark side of nature. This is why the dog might indeed bite, because we mistrust nature.[195]

Concerning the dark, one can be pretty sure (if the formulation of the question is right) that after some time a solution offers itself naturally, for example through a dream, or incidents of synchronicity, which all contribute in unexpected ways.

The problem of being too soft: Jung knows this from his own experience! Otherwise one wouldn't be a doctor. He felt the same way. For a physician it may become an absolute vice.

I asked Jung: What about becoming president of the [Swiss] Medical Association? Jung said that it was a question of responsibility toward the collective. Ask the *I Ching*! It may be the right thing, even necessary, or it may be wrong. He, for example, had consciously assumed quite a few such positions and then relinquished them again. In part they were meaningful, in part wrongly assumed responsibilities. These are collisions of duty. In those instances, the "you should" of police ordinances don't help. Therefore, to help with the decision, consult the *I Ching*.

When Jung wrote *Wandlungen und Symbole der Libido*[196], he realized that he had come to conclusions that were contrary to Freud's. Fear arose in him, that it would cost him the friendship. Mrs. Jung thought that Freud was generous enough to be able to accept his findings, but Jung, himself, wasn't so sure. He couldn't go on writing for two months, until he finally came to the decision that he had to risk sacrificing the friendship.[197] Then the inhibition lifted, and he wrote the chapter on the symbolism of sacrifice! It is very difficult to give up an entrenched mindset. It inhibits new insight. Why can one not understand? Out of fear one might understand!

[Ignaz Tauber discussed with Jung his wish to write a research paper on Egyptian mythology and asked him how he should proceed. It was a lifelong occupation; he himself had grown up in Egypt.]

---

195 See C. G. Jung's letter to Dr. B. Cohen, 28 April, 1934, in: C. G. Jung, *Letters*, vol. I.

196 C. G. Jung, *Symbols of Transformation*, CW 5.

197 See Memories, *Dreams, Reflections by C. G. Jung*, chapter V, "Sigmund Freud."

Jung: For the Greeks, the Egyptians were the wisest people. When you think of archaeology, you do not know what this is based on. The Egyptians didn't have a philosophy, no science (except for astrology), nothing. But they had mythology – that's it! Their mythology contains an incredible wealth of wisdom and depth.

Jung's practical advice was: Better than taking a sabbatical for several months is to do a retreat of a few days from time to time. Otherwise there is the pressure of "now I should be able to do it" and then you are blocked. Indeed, several friends had thought one could give it a try, but it didn't work, because, as Jung pointed out, it is an inner growth process that one cannot control.

After writing his *Answer to Job* and *Mysterium Coniunctionis*, Jung came to terms with the fact that this was "it." He didn't have any further ideas. So he only did masonry. Something new could only come from without, whereas before, he always wrote when motivated from within. Anything he wanted to write that was suggested from others either didn't work at all, or was only a wearisome "milking." But now he was able to write about an outer suggestion as if it had been ordained from within. For example, he has long had the idea about *flying saucers*, and when the artist[198] with the fireman came, he thought about it again and played with the idea of at least writing down some essential points. But only when Walther Niehus[199] told him that he had better write it down was he able to do it. He now is totally dependent on such encouragement from outside. It is Oedipus' riddle of the Sphinx: in the morning on four, at noon on two, and in the evening on three.[200]

I told Jung my dream:

When I visited you with Sabi, I tied my shoes.

---

198 Referring to the painting «Der Feuersäer» (the Fire-Sower) by Erhard Jacoby. See C. G. Jung, "Flying Saucers: A Modern Myth of Things Seen in the Skies," chapter 'Ufos in Modern Painting,' CW 10, pars. 725 ff. and plate II; see also Eva Wertenschlag, «Der Feuersäer,» *Jungiana. Beiträge zur Psychologie von C. G. Jung*, Series A, vol. 19, (Küsnacht: Verlag Stiftung für Jung'sche Psychologie, 2015), pp. 9–20.
199 Jung's son-in-law; engaged in the edition of C. G. Jung's work.
200 The baby crawls on all four; the adult stands on two legs; the old man walks with a cane.

Jung said that it means to solidify my standpoint first and then go into the world. Not to invest too much into my project on Egypt; to write only enough to bring out the *essence*. For scientific purposes there must be completeness. However, to give a paper to an educated public, no such extensive apparatus is necessary. I must restrict myself to classical examples. There is the danger of intuitive distraction, to lose one's train of thought or critical evaluation, because one is possessed by the material! I may only work the material as long as it doesn't possess me. Clear sight is from afar. This provides sureness in judgment, because one can recognize things in context. It is the backbone, the guiding line, just like the staff of Asclepius around which the snake can coil itself.

Indian mythology has a parallel. In India, Naga[201] stones are Cobra snakes with human heads. They are placed in front of the city gate; often there are fifty to sixty Naga stones. Sometimes there are single cobras with human heads – the staff of Asclepius would correspond to this – and sometimes a couple, a man and woman – corresponding to the Caduceus of Hermes. The Nagas are protective gods. Many reside under trees, *ficus indicus*, for instance in Indian villages. These gods inhabit the branches – they are chthonic demons. The basic thought here is that there is a spiral development from lower to higher regions, until they find representation in consciousness. This is the basic idea of *Kundalini* Yoga: the idea of the snake that wants to rise up toward the light is very old. Below is a tangle of darkness, above a head of light.

Jung's Egyptian gem (from which he had a signet ring made) stems from the Ophites, descendants of Egyptian-Hellenistic Gnostics. On the backside of the gem is a lion, that under Theodosius had his head scratched out because of his evil eye. A Christian Ophite had inherited the ring, and didn't want to fall under the lion's spell.

The theriomorphic symbols (of animal or half-animal form) are especially interesting. The Paleolithic Australians have ancestor spirits called *Alcheringa*: ancestors who had created the world by adapting things. Similarly, in the *Tabula Smaragdina*, Mercurius is said to have

---

201 Naga is a term for the great Cobra snake in India.

created things through adaptation, meaning an inner alignment of animals or half-animals.

[End of notes of Ignaz Tauber.]

1957 – Journal Continued

And because I simply always must "do" something, I had searched with great pain for a rice pan, in wh ch to cook the rice by steaming it, the Chinese way. I'd known that it had been Jung's wish for a long time. This rice cooker had been waiting in the attic for a while, but I simply hadn't been able to bring the whole family together, and with everyone in a good mood. Down-periods often linger far too long. Finally, on an ordinary weekday, I packed the cooker into the car and drove by myself out to Bollingen. It was late afternoon when I approached the little door of Jung's tower, unannounced, and with a hint of a bad conscience. There was absolute quiet. I certainly didn't want to disturb a nap, so I put on my bathing suit and swam into the beloved lake.

Water is so wonderfully sobering! Thereafter I was able to deliver the cooker quite matter-of-factly – in spite of the thundering "for God's sake!" when Jung got a glimpse of me, because, as it turned out, he was expecting an important visitor from abroad, to arrive in fifteen minutes. Naturally, I didn't "want" anything else and was already retreating backwards out the door when Hans[202] arrived with a telephone message that the guest had been prevented from making the flight. "You do have shameless luck!" Jung exclaimed and invited me for tea. I intended to be as "licht" as possible, like air, because I wasn't supposed to be there in the first place.

And he told me about Mrs. Jacobi's suggestion, request really, to write an essay on the conscience.[203] Initially he'd cursed and thought it presumptuous, but then he reminded himself, "You old fool! You forgot again that only fate makes demands on you, often through people." So, all morning he'd pondered the theme, realizing that it was precisely the question he had to answer at this moment – it was

---

202 Hans Kuhn, a neighboring peasant's son, who had helped Jung a lot.
203 See C. G. Jung, "A Psychological V ew of Conscience," CW 10, pars. 825 f., first edition: *Studien aus dem C. G. Jung-Institut* (Zurich, 1958).

his inner question. But a very delicate one. Saying this, he remembered a dream he just had during his nap:

> I passed by a field of potatoes and was happy to see that the potatoes did so well this year. Then I met a peacock in the middle of the field. I teased him[204] with a little whip until he became angry and attacked me. I shuddered because I suddenly realized that it was the devil. I ran away, toward home, and he after me. I was just able to slam the door shut before he could enter too. It was the home of my parents. I heard him sniff the threshold of the door and then it suddenly occurred to me that it could perhaps be the black dog of my childhood. I dared to open the door a crack and – thank God, it was him!

Jung sat there, pondering the dream for a long while, "How might I be teasing the devil? It must have to do with the essay on the conscience." The thought didn't put him at ease. Then he told me about one of his granddaughters who had wished for a copy of his *Answer to Job*, and that led us to talk about the worldview of today's youth. How wonderful that he finds the positive everywhere, even though clearly seeing the negative too.

Jung: "We old people grew up with the Christian worldview: the world was created by God and is perfect. Only *we* are bad and disrupt the perfect order. Thus, we have a bad conscience and promptly project this onto our neighbor. There must be somebody to blame, a guilty one. This is how the last wars originated. Our youth, on the other hand, think that the world is bad; it is full of treachery and malice, simply a mess! There is only one chance: the human being. Only within ourselves is there an opportunity to 'do' something – we are the great experiment! In this case our neighbor doesn't have to be the guilty one anymore; it all depends on our own heart."

Jung encouraged me to give the 1st of August speech[205] and the presentation on the tarot at the Psychology Club[206], and he expressed his wonderment and appreciation for our "Parenting School." He was

204 The peacock is of masculine gender in German.
205 August 1st is Swiss National Day.
206 She gave a lecture at the Psychology Club Zurich "Explorations on Synchronicity," 25 January,1958. (Recordings could not be found.)

so cheerful and content and, I believe, grateful that no "abyss" had been opened up! In conclusion, he told me a myth from Africa.

There is a lot I forgot about this evening; moreover, I felt that it wouldn't be right to grasp at everything with the claws of consciousness. It all had been so mild and tender. The wind quietly reconciled heaven and earth, and their children, the waves, were dancing into the future, knowing well that one could know nothing.

In the summer of this rich, impactful year, our oldest daughter Roswith gave a talk about C.G. Jung at her student association's meeting with Verena Reinhart, based foremost on his essay, *Gegenwart und Zukunft*[207], and on her personal encounters with him. It must have been a wonderful, lively evening with intense discussions into the wee hours of the morning. In the wake of it, she wrote Jung a letter, posing various questions, and he responded in spite of his immense workload:[208]

August 17, 1957

Dear Miss Roswitha,

Many thanks for your kind letter you sent me on my birthday. I have heard with great sorrow of your father's illness[209], and can only hope that it will soon take a turn for the better.

I'm very interested to hear about the success of your lecture. My little book on Job is naturally meant for older people, and especially for those who have some knowledge of my psychology. They must also have pondered a good deal on religious questions in order to understand it properly. Because there are very few people who meet these conditions, my book has been widely misunderstood. They should also know something about the unconscious. As an introduction to this I would recommend another little book of mine, „On the Psychology of the Unconscious,"[210] and, on the religious problem, "Psychology and

207 See C.G. Jung, "The Undiscovered Self (Present and Future)," CW 10, pars. 488 ff.
208 The letter is found in C.G. Jung, *Letters*, vol. 2, pp. 383 f. It is listed under "anonymous" and mistakenly entitled "To Roswitha N."
209 Kidney stones.
210 Is now to be found in C.G. Jung, *Two Essays in Analytical Psychology*, CW 7.

Religion."²¹¹ "Symbolik des Geistes" and "Von den Wurzeln des Bewusstseins"²¹² probe rather more deeply into these matters. You are undoubtedly right to tackle the problem of society first. There you learn the ways of other people and are forced to find a common basis of understanding.

The question of the young architect, as to what it might mean for God if he demands Christianity of us: First one must understand what Christianity means. This is obviously the psychology of the Christian and is a complicated phenomenon which cannot be taken for granted. And what something might mean for God we cannot know at all, because we are not God. One must always remember that God is a mystery, and everything we say about it is said and believed by human beings. We make images and concepts, and when I speak of God I always mean the image man has made of him. But no one knows what He is like, or he would be a god himself. Looking at it in one way, however, we do indeed partake of divinity, as Christ himself pointed out when he said: "Ye are gods." (John 10:34) You will find a lot about this in *Answer to Job*.

Your question why it is more difficult for us to do good than to do evil is not quite rightly put, because doing good is as a rule easier than doing evil. True, it is not always easy to do good, but the consequences of doing good are so much more pleasant than those of doing evil that if only for practical reasons one eventually learns to do good and eschew evil. Or course evil thwarts our good intentions and, to our sorrow, cannot always be avoided. The task is then to understand why this is so and how it can be endured. In the end good and evil are human judgments, and what is good for one man is evil for another. But good and evil are not thereby abolished; this conflict is always going on everywhere and is bound up with the will of God. It is really a question of recognizing God's will and wanting to do it. The other question of what meaning the Bible ascribes to society is of great importance, for the solidarity and communal life of mankind go to the roots of existence. But the question is

---

211 See C. G. Jung, Psychology and Religion: West and East, CW 11.
212 The articles in these two books are now to be found in revised form with new titles in different volumes of C. G. Jung's *Collected Works*.

complicated by the fact that the individual should also be able to maintain his independence, and this is possible only if society is accorded a relative value. Otherwise it swamps and eventually destroys the individual, and then there is no longer any society either. In other words: a genuine society must be composed of independent individuals, who can be social only up to a certain point. They alone can fulfill the divine will implanted in each of us.

The paths leading to a common truth are many. Therefore each of us has first to stand by his own truth, which is then gradually reduced to a common truth by mutual discussion. All this requires psychological understanding and empathy with the other's points of view. A common task for every group in quest of a common truth. With best greetings,

Yours sincerely,
C. G. Jung

Autumn came around, and winter followed. There was a horrible darkness, within and without. It was as if Ignaz were surrounded by a dark cloud from where thunder rolled and lightning flashed, forcing our whole family into dread and sadness. My energy was drained, but I tried, weakly, to hold my hand over the little ones and silently pray, while everything around me seemed to slowly retreat into the distance. Something froze and died. Just once, at a moment of greatest despair, I plunged into boisterous joyfulness, as fate put a delightful gift of unreasonableness into my heart. To keep it alive? Or so that suffering never ceases?

During Christmas dinner at the Club I pulled the oracle, "The Samaritan fetches water from the source. One may gain new vision by going to old sources" (after Dane Rudhyar). I thought of Jung and wrote him. There was no answer. Well then, I had to deal with it on my own and continue on my lonely path.

1958

Not much courage was needed to go ahead with my talk at the Club on the *Tarot*, on January 25. Ignaz let me go on my own, but some of our good friends joined me. How much I appreciated their warm-heartedness – if only they knew! Right before my presentation was to begin, Jung came in and slipped me a tiny piece of paper:

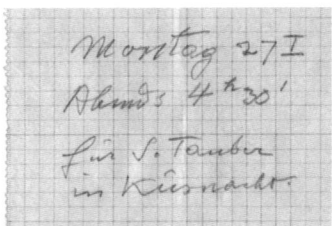

Fig. 25: Monday, Jan 27, Evening, 4:30 pm, for S. Tauber,
in Küsnacht.

I wanted to rejoice loudly – thank God a little bit of reason remained! I believe that my talk went well, and the day after next I wandered with my dog in unfriendly, rainy weather from the train station Küsnacht to Seestrasse 228. For a while I played with Felix in the yard, so he'd be quiet afterwards. Nevertheless, he greeted Jung with enthusiastic barking and by jumping up at him, but then settled quickly. Jung began immediately, as if not to waste a second, "You wrote me about your husband."

"Yes," I answered, "he believes that he's missed out on spring and his whole life …"

Jung interrupted me, "Stop – the rest that belongs to this scenario *I* am going to tell you myself: One doesn't have feelings any more. Everything is *kaput*. One has missed out, especially where sexuality is concerned. One wants to make up for it and secretly imagines who-the-devil-knows what. With one's wife it somehow doesn't work that well – and with other women one is impotent. In the end, one is virtually haunted by sexuality. People all around make one suffer. One becomes increasingly labile and completely unpredictable; one nags all day long about stuff and succumbs to outbursts of anger."

"And why should I, for the most part, be to blame?"

"Because you are the principle carrier of his anima. Against projections there is nothing one can do. This is a classical anima possession. She reigns supreme and gives him the runaround – and if this continues and he puts up with it, she will drag him into spiritual, psychic, and material death."

"Is there nothing one can do about it?"

"Of course, one can. But only if one really wants to. Most men prefer to be ordered about by their anima. Seldom are they 'fed up' and draw the consequences. If they get old at all, it's too late. One has to practice constantly."

"What and how? Could I perhaps help?"

"Yes, I believe so. Look, with my patients I proceed this way: I take this inner being to task by asking, 'What was it that you were thinking in your depression?' Or, 'Put yourself again in that bad mood: What were you saying then?' And then he says, for example, 'Everything is lost.' I continue to question him, 'Is that *your* opinion? Is everything lost for real?' And then I give him an account of his reality: How many kids he has, that they are healthy; how much money he's made; that he can have intelligent conversations with his wife, etc. I glaringly paint his reality before his eyes, so that he has to realize that it isn't congruent with what he believed a moment ago. Thus, he has to recognize that he is in the grip of a being that forces him to make false statements. That is the anima. He is in the grip of a 'woman' who asserts such nonsense. Well, what do you say to somebody like her? Is she not a vulgar woman to seize hold of him in that way? She wants to prove that she is the only one. She has an outrageous and boundless claim to power over him and says, 'You little boy, come with me!' So, that's his mother! Eventually she leads him into death. The anima in a man doesn't want to give up any illusion. And the men don't want to sober up. Just like someone with diabetes whose carbohydrate intake is forbidden or reduced, but who indulges in sugar in spite of it – well then, he'll eventually die from his sugar. If your husband was sexually deprived, then where do the five children come from? Just ask him whether it is true what he claims. He doesn't take the problem seriously enough! He simply goes along with the bad manners of his soul. You can tell him this, with regards from me, and that he should educate himself! With true self-discipline one knows that to hurt someone else means to hurt oneself, so one doesn't do it. If I take something away from someone else I take it away from myself – and I love myself far too much to do this to myself. I want to have my peace. That is wisdom.

Take your husband, if possible in the middle of his affect, into another room and start such a dialogue with this inner being, together with him. He has to imagine it. You say, 'This is a damn slut who takes your place in this manner, and you just listen to *her*. And then she has you do things that end up hurting you.' [He might say something like,] 'It serves my wife and my family right if I die, then they'll see how I worked myself to death for them!' That's being identified with the anima and sheer possession. If, in the moment, you can't talk to him, then write everything he says down on a piece of paper. Later you show it to him and start a conversation. Otherwise he doesn't believe it and says after ten minutes that he didn't say that, or at least didn't mean it."

I told him Ignaz' dream, in which

> he has to fetch his parents from a high mountain during a terrible rainstorm.

Jung commented: He should feel responsible for both parents and not simply let anything be done to him. People want an ideal, so that they don't have to do anything. With an ideal they acquire an alibi. If your husband doesn't realize this and reckons with himself in hindsight, it's no use. You should not accept his mood swings. You have to confront him, confront the being within him who ruins his life. You have to make him realize with such dialogues that his moods, disgruntled feelings and depressions are not the real thing – they are only anima deceptions!

But *you yourself* have to sacrifice any demand on your husband, otherwise you become suspect of exercising *your* power! Go dancing as much as possible, create joy in your life, and allow yourself anything within your reach. This is how you free yourself from your claims on him. If you feel resistance ("who cares?"), that's your animus! Take it as a piece of education. You can only do something like this for the sake of love.

"Do you really think that I will ever succeed, after having dreamed the following?

> Spring has arrived, but all plants are frozen and dead; only in their roots there is some sap left. And both plants in our bedroom have perished!"

Jung: "Well, then you have to tap into your unconscious. There's still some vitality left there, in the roots."

In a flat voice I heard myself say, "I want to."

He looked tired as he added, "But men rarely want to believe it. They can't accept the suffering. When they feel better, they forget the daily discipline and take it lightly. Women have a greater capacity for suffering and thus take it very seriously. In good times one has to learn to speak to one's soul and practice it daily, so one is able to do it during difficult times. Such an inner relationship that allows for a reckoning at any given time has to be crafted with much work and discipline – so one doesn't fall into one's own abyss."

Felix had settled on Jung's feet during our conversation and snuggled closely against his legs. Jung, smiling faintly, didn't let himself be distracted. There was a knock at the door and I stood up, but Felix took his time, stretching and yawning, until he was ready to go back out into the wet, soppy weather. Life never leaves you in peace for long; it always challenges – time and again.

December 18, 1958

Another year is coming to an end. This time around I have the feeling that I've aged many years. Death must be a very important goal to have us endure so much on the way toward it. After [Ignaz'] most horrendous "volcanic eruption" ever, I dreamed:

> There is a mountain covered by lava. Only a few old, tall trees are still standing. I stomp around in the lava feeling very sad. Everything seems lost …

I'm doing my daily chores as if dead, feebly thinking of my guru – but no, I must not burden him! Or might he, perhaps, have a longing for wretched humanity? After all, Ignaz was only a tool; fire and lightning come from fate. This is how far I've come in creating distance. Being able to die may well be an essential part of life. And the guru belongs to this essential life.

> Oh guru
> grow strong
> into earth and heaven –
> they receive you in love
> as their courageous man!
> And think back, perhaps,
> to whom is left:
> a small human being
> who, in happiness,
> is unhappy.

1959

On a dark evening I secretly sneak through the front door, without telling anybody. "I'm expected" is my whispered password. A small, warm light, where I find him sitting wrapped in blankets, quiet and secure in his corner as if from ages long ago. To him I flee from this world, without paper and pencil, only with flowers. I don't want to ask questions; I don't want to know anything – just sit close to him and feel his overflowing good heart. In this very spot of the earth new life awakens within me, warm and true. I sense it and I give it back to him, all of it.

Jung simply starts talking, continuing from where he has been in thought, seemingly from time eternal. In this corner we've always talked about things eternal. Today it surely is the last time – the thought keeps crossing my mind, and I'm resolved not to disturb it by bringing up anything personal. But he extracts it anyway; he brings in the present moment, the despicably human, as if there was a force streaming from it that he needs. Is it possible? I marvel, but feel it acutely: The oil that feeds the flame of eternity flows from transitory things.

Jung: "... Whoever has a claim on another cannot fulfill his own. Where sexuality is concerned, there are as many women with a passive disposition as there are those who are active. There simply are both, and one is either one or the other. It's a fact with which one has to come to terms. Human shortcomings are simply facts. Anything real in this world is better than some fantasy. Never can we have everything we want. I wanted to travel. God – how much I still would like to go on many great trips: real, far, vast travels to discover many new things! But fate put a veto in place; I was only allowed a little bit, not more.

If your husband wishes for a more sexually active wife, he should use his feeling toward himself more actively. He should give more love to his soul. This is the real demand that is put to him. He doesn't fulfill it, and so he puts it onto you. And in this respect, it is never enough. One has to take things into one's own hands, feel solely responsible and cut one's losses where one cannot have everything. We have our limits. Nobody can live it all, we are limited all around. There are people, of course, who travel and seek all their lives – but what do they have in the end? Nothing, not even an insight!

If a poisonous remark from you destroys his relationship with another woman, it wasn't a real relationship. (Evidently, it had to come out. Only you can know whether it could have been suppressed.) Then it was nothing but a fantasy, which sooner or later would have burst like a bubble anyway. A true relationship would have gained sober ground because of it. And if he, after a night with you, goes and cuts flowers in the garden for another woman, and even tells you so, it is a particularly tactless thing to do, even with the perception of inner righteousness on his part. One simply can't jump over facts by means of fantasy. After all, this is why we have facts, to awaken us to holy soberness – and he wanted to throw them to the wind.

Take care of your heart; do only half as much, and everything a bit less impulsively! If you have to write, do it. An artist doesn't ask whether it makes sense, he simply must, and he does. It emerges from the unconscious regardless of the people around, or the world, or the reasoning of consciousness. Only much later does it make sense. Most of the time what is written is not appreciated at all among experts, and is read last. This happens to me. But it is a general rule. Your husband will experience it with his research in Egyptian symbolism. But there are other values, especially those concerning one's own individuation, for which one is responsible, and should be."

Outside, lights were dancing on the dark lake, and the wind rattled the shutters. Jung mused, "Yes, the *Föhn*[213] has claimed a few people again (Wolfgang Pauli, Rudolf Jung[214]) – they were younger than me, and I'm still here, don't know why ..."

"Oh, yes, I know why!" I grumbled happily on my stool, but I couldn't really tell him, because he was smiling so mysteriously. Then

---

213 A warm wind from the South, infamous for bringing all kinds of ailments or misfortune.
214 Brother of Ernst Jung, Sabi's brother in law.

he looked at me again, "What else?" without making a move to get up. So, I told him my two most recent dreams:

> In a kind of school of life, my grade of 6 was suddenly cut in half, to 3, without giving me a chance to ask why.[215] I protested. But I was told that such was the rule in the school of life. I referred to the highest authority, Prof. Jung. They wrote to him and received a letter back, saying that I was allowed to speak, everybody was. I should give a talk on the history of the soul (connected to culture and world history).

Jung's comment was simply, "Well, then do it!"

"But how?"

"I don't know either, but you have to do it, perhaps in writing – one doesn't know."

The other dream was,

> I took my horse out of the stable into the deep snow. There was a broad, deep ditch. My dog and I were already on the other side, I don't know how, but the horse hadn't made it yet. I gave him free rein, so he could make it over in his own way. Then, with my last remaining strength, I brushed the snow off the hedge, so he could see how deep the ditch was, and hoped that he would make it.

Jung mused, "In general, the horse follows its master, so most likely it will jump across the ditch. With your instinct[216] you made it. But where the horse is concerned, there it depends on your relationship to it, how you nurture it, the whole power of your nature – it will come.

Depressions are the soul's economy. If one has overexerted oneself the soul has to contract, in order to pull up new strength from the deepest ground. One should take good care of the soul's household."

He looked pensive, and it was late. Before I left, we talked about spring; that he would like to come once again for a question and answer seminar, "out of the fullness of life," in our living room – in

---

215 "6" corresponding to the American grade "A".
216 Referring to the dog.

the spring, yes, if he still … he smiled. And smilingly we said farewell, both thinking, perhaps for the last time?

His steps died away in the empty dining room. I felt a momentary chill. Then the roaring *Föhn* carried me home to the living.

Yes, Lord, help my horse over the ditch – perhaps I should simply call him? Or perhaps I must go back myself, a whole segment of my life, in the dark, laboriously and alone. I'll mount my horse, and we'll jump over the ditch together!

A star will help!

> Give everything
> to the holy life!
> The star and the earth
> will thus forgive –

To sit on one's horse means to live fully, to be happy from top to bottom – and totally sad! Just to be fully with it, every minute. Perhaps this is why a faithful friend suddenly showed up in my life, one who had helped me as a child to jump from stone to stone across a river. Faithfulness in attitude is withstanding the fire and creates the divine. Can one know this? I'd rather feel it.

***

> Thus comes the crazy February
> Do you hear the jingle-bells?[217]

There is a reason why this Children's song is in minor mode: February is the season of flus and colds. Our kids are sick, one after the other, and when the last one is done, the first one starts over with a relapse. Ignaz, with unbearable back pain[218], drags himself to between thirty and forty patients a day, gray in the face, looking past us out of hollowed eyes. We have a felt sense: If he were to rest here with his family, he'd never get up again. During the night, emergency calls

217 Reference to the time of Lent, with its shrovetide carnivals.
218 In German, *Hexenschuss* (lumbago) – literally, and meaningfully, "a witch's shot."

Fig. 26: The horse jumping over the ditch.

alternate with nightmares. Surely, medicine men and their families are "chosen:" by god – and the devil! There's only creeping around, on high alert, like being in the jungle. Then out of the gray ether there is a phone call (one of too many): "Someone has canceled. Prof. Jung is free tomorrow at 5 pm. Can you come?" – "Yes, of course!" Do miracles have anything to do with naturalness? I'd been so sure that I'd seen him for the last time.

I found him as if resurrected in broad daylight, healthy and happy. And quite soberly he started to complain about his own biography that is to be written:

Jung: "Damn it! What was really important for my existence – encounters with personalities that were milestones for me – may not be divulged because of medical confidentiality. I've forgotten everything else. And what might otherwise interest the world in terms of names and politics I may not say either, in consideration of surviving relatives. Well then, what's left? When my book on alchemy was published, a professor from Holland wrote to me, 'Only this one particular person in the whole world could have had these dreams – was it true?' And it was! I'd been sure that I had changed and concealed almost everything beyond recognition. Biographies are hypocritical. They are here to throw dust into people's eyes. In the biography that Richard Wilhelm's wife wrote about him there is nothing of what he and I had considered the most important issues in our conversations. She simply didn't know. That's how it is. Well, now I have written about the first twenty years of my life myself, as well as I could. For the rest, there has to be a way – it's a real headache for me."

But what is happening with me? I suddenly live much more intensely than earlier. Just now, when life is supposed to recede into the distance, I begin to really love it! The *I Ching*, too, responds repeatedly with "The Marrying Maiden" and "Fellowship with Men." Why so reversed?

Then he turned his attention to me: "Before, you stood too directly under the impression of life. Like being in a battle, you had to seek new cover at any moment what with so many precipitating events. Too much was going on. There was no time for realization. Similarly, there was no awareness about the extent of the war in Germany – there, one was too close, too immediately involved. Time and distance for realization were more likely to be found in Switzerland. By the same token, a neurosis takes individuals out of daily life, so they can have a realization. Only then one gains a new, unprejudiced orientation with open eyes and inner distance to one's experiences. Only now, the ego is really present. Before that, one doesn't know who one is, so there is no true experience possible. The family most often is not a real community, but rather a *participation mystique*. (As, for example, when father or mother wants to quickly call one of their children and ends up calling all the other names, even the dog's or the cat's, or mixes them all up!) I have often observed how mothers only late in life come to truly live their own life. Only the consolidated ego can truly absorb, without having to watch out for all the various reactions. Judgment becomes more secure."

I asked, "Have not our young people already overcome the 'antichrist' and are working on a new principle? Or will the atom bomb destroy everything?"

Jung answered, "They don't ask any more, 'What is good and what is evil?' Rather, they seek to distinguish the 'right path' from the 'wrong path.' The two wavy lines of the astrological sign Aquarius ♒ are parallel, meaning that good and evil belong both to the same principle.[219] They are no longer going in opposite directions like they were in the Christian age of Pisces.[220] This is a development that arises right out of amoral paganism. The gods are favorably or unfavorably inclined, no longer good or evil. They have lost their absoluteness. We live in paganism again. Wotan was an amoral nature principle. He hung on the world tree for nine days, 'wounded with a spear, dedicated to Odin, myself to myself;'[221] and on the tree he invented the runes. (Wotanism is a shamanistic religion). Similarly, King Wen

---

219 In German, *Sinn*, as in "making sense."
220 See C.G. Jung, *Aion*, CW 9/II, par. 147; see also the picture in C.G. Jung, *Visions*, vol. 1, p. 548 and vol. 2, pp. 726 ff., where Jung points out that, in the astronomical configuration of Pisces, the two fishes are perpendicular to each other, and in the astrological sign ♓ they are directed against each other, i.e., form an opposition.
221 From Odin's self-sacrifice in the "Poem of the Runes," verse 138, translated by Carolyne Larrington, *The Poetic Edda* (Oxford: OUP, 2014). Odin is the Norse god who in Germanic mythology is known as Wotan (see Jung's essay "Wotan," CW 10, pars. 371–399).

discovered the *I Ching* in prison; he found himself in a similar situation as Wotan. Christ hung on the 'tree of the cross,' and out of this came the New Testament. In their hopeless situations, they all discovered the meaning of changing forms and a new principle of action.

The *I Ching* is based on the synchronicity principle; Yang and Yin are only relative opposites. These days, opposites are relativized once again. One must not be offended by this trend. Neither is there proof of correctness, only a 'corresponding behavior.' At times, it appears good, at others evil; one simply has to 'go with the possibility.' This is today's principle of orientation. One doesn't know much about it. Life is much too complicated for the intellect. This is why people are using the *I Ching's* synchronistic approach as a helpful tool, also dreams and dreamlike imaginations.

And then there is the behavior of animals! They guide us instinctively. My daughter recently told me an example from her vacation. She was walking with her dachshund during a thunderstorm. Suddenly, the dog ran backwards about fifty yards, its hair on end, and in the next moment lightning struck exactly at the location where the dog had stopped and retreated! Earlier in my life I had a French boxer dog that accurately captured the character of my patients. At the end of a session I asked a patient of mine, who had gone through a deep depression, what actually had helped her the most. 'Your dog,' was the answer. Every time she felt like jumping into the lake, or throwing herself under the train, my dog accompanied her and didn't leave her side until she had boarded the train. Another female patient told me about an uncanny encounter she once had while going for a walk in the little forest near a suburb of Berlin. It was after the war and it was still rather dangerous to walk by oneself. And so, when a dark-looking bicyclist passed her by, she immediately regretted not having taken her dog with her. Indeed, a bit further down the road, the bicyclist stopped, got off his bike and came towards her in a threatening demeanor. She just stared at him, paralyzed by fear. But about two meters away from her, he suddenly retreated, terror in his face, his gaze fixed at her legs. It puzzled her, but when she let her cramped-up hand sink, exhausted, her fingers touched the cool nose of a dog. A big German shepherd stood next to her – strange, she didn't see an owner. The dog had sensed the danger and had come to her rescue.

She immediately turned around and went to the train station, and the dog accompanied her. Dogs sense life-threatening dangers."

I had come burdened with my persistent worries about my husband and his research into Egyptian symbolism: Was the family too much of a hindrance? Would he be happier without a practice? Should he take a vacation? So, I asked Jung, "Did you enjoy doing scientific research, and was there a reward?"

Jung answered, "There's always ambition and a claim to power involved in a scientific project. The work is then of dubious value. But it is inevitable. A vacation should only be taken for the sake of one's health; there is no claim to power in that. Ideally, 'work' should resemble an 'active imagination,' devoid of power and ambition. Any expenditure beyond such an approach is driven by power and ambition. It then becomes about one's prestige. An effort without any reward would be disproportionate, but the true reward lies in the creative moment. Man finds true satisfaction in the moment of insight. One shouldn't wish for anything more. Such insight I savored in the moment, all by myself. The writing came afterward, out of gratitude and for other people. I had no claim to power and my only ambition was to understand.

I felt as if I was standing on an alpine meadow in bloom, alone under the sun, terribly spoiled in the happiness of so many true and lively thoughts. And suddenly I felt the presence of a dear female friend, who so arduously tried to climb out of darkness into the light. Time and again, old Saturn pulled her back into the depth of her depression. "How could she do it?"

Jung exclaimed: "Precisely, together with Saturn go into the depths! By all means, do not escape with illusions! Only at the very bottom will she experience what she is looking for. But one doesn't believe that. Many people love their depression and remain attached to it – instead of sensing that an invisible hand has placed them exactly into this situation. They let themselves be overwhelmed and don't ask, 'Why? What for? What am I to do?'"

I'll be following everything, I think almost boisterously, while taking leave from this old man who is so much more alive than the young. As a gift for my way back to my stormy everyday life, he affirms with a quiet smile, "In the spring I would quite enjoy coming to Winterthur again." His promise is resting like a little bouquet of violets in my lap, helping me through the crazy traffic between Zurich and Winterthur, in rain and blinding headlights.

***

Fig. 27: In Winterthur, June 27, 1959.
C. G. Jung, Sabi, Ignaz, and Marianne entering Tauber's house.

Fate can be benevolent; it allowed him be true to his word. He came on "Seven Sleepers Day,"[222] June 27, 1959. We invited some friends to a gathering under a motto from *Don Carlos* by Friedrich Schiller, which Jürg once gave me.

Participants were: Helen and Peter Stierlin, Ernst Baumann, Mimi and Jakob Fopp, Fries, Rupli, Arnold Renold. Sabi sends her regards to all who contributed to the good atmosphere, animating Jung to speak.

222 Originally, the Day of the Seven Sleepers is a liturgical commemoration day referring to the Christian legend of the "Seven Sleepers of Ephesus." The feast day is assigned to regionally and denominationally different dates. Later, a country lore used it for weather forecasting associated with the fat dormouse. (See also below p. 218.)

Colloquium June 27, 1959

[This colloquium has been recorded live in its entirety. The proceedings have been published in German.[223]]

On Feelings

Ignaz Tauber opened with the following address: "Professor Jung, we are so pleased and thank you from the bottom of our hearts that you are gracing us with your presence in our home again. We should already have gained wisdom through reading your books, but already Goethe said, 'What you don't feel, you won't hunt down by art.'[224] And precisely this is possible for us today when you are with us in person, that we may comprehend with our feelings as well. And this is why we have chosen as the motto for this afternoon a verse from Friedrich Schiller's *Don Carlos*:

> [...] Tell him, in manhood, he must still revere
> The dreams of early youth, nor open the heart
> Of heaven's all-tender flower to canker-worms
> Of boasted reason – nor be led astray
> When, by the wisdom of the dust, he hears
> Enthusiasm, heavenly-born, blasphemed.[225]

And so, I'd like to put the following question to you: Do you have the impression that there is, in your life, in your experiences and happenings, or in your dreams, a guideline in the sense of this motto? And, if so, do you feel led by it toward the beyond – as a human being and not as a scientist?"[226]

---

223 C.G. Jung, *Über Gefühle und den Schatten. Winterthurer Fragestunden*, (Zurich and Düsseldorf: Walter-Verlag, 1999).
224 *Faust I*, verse 534.
225 Friedrich Schiller, *Don Carlos*, Act 4, scene 21 (Marquis), verses 3526–3531.
226 According to the notes of Sabi this is *her* question.

C.G. Jung: So, this is the question that is being put to me. Well, a lot could be said about that, of course, as it is the great drawback in our culture that we are strangely incompetent in realizing our own feelings, that is, to feel the things that concern us. All too often we see people passing over events or experiences without realizing what happened to them. Because they don't realize that they have a feeling-toned reaction. For the most part they only feel what we call an affect, an emotion that has physiological side effects. Such as intensified pulse, increased breathing, physiomotor phenomena – this is what they can sense. But if it is a feeling reaction, they very often don't notice it at all, because it is not accompanied by psychophysical phenomena. In my association experiments[227] I've often seen that someone had a feeling along with a reaction, but when he was connected to an electrical circuit and the so-called psycho-galvanic phenomenon was investigated, quite possibly one might not notice a significant deflection, or none at all. At the time I conducted experiments with my original chief psychiatrist, the old Prof. Bleuler.[228] We investigated precisely the question of how feelings are distinguished from affects. When I told him something, or when I asked him a question during the experiment – one can ask questions too, one doesn't have to restrict oneself to the stimulus and response words – so when I mentioned something that we both knew to be an annoying business, then he had a clear reaction. The psycho-galvanic deflection was positive; there was an augmented stream of electricity going through the body. On that day, I heard by chance about something that had happened to Bleuler, just such an annoying matter in the asylum, and I knew that he was convinced that no one had any notion of it. Then I made an allusion to the matter from which he should have clearly noticed that I was informed. But because he was so convinced that I couldn't possibly know anything, he didn't have a deflection, only a minimal reaction. But then I told him in a way that he could see that I knew what had happened to him – and then he had a colossal deflection! So, when he is alone with himself he doesn't know what the thing is actually worth, or how much it matters to him. But if he is

227 See C.G. Jung, *Experimental Researches*, CW 2.
228 At the Burghölzli clinic (Psychiatric University Hospital Zurich). See C.G. Jung, "Tavistock Lectures. On the Theory and Practice of Analytical Psychology," CW 18, par. 49.

aware that someone else knows about it, then he has the real affect. As long as we are alone with ourselves we may swallow god knows what kinds of camels and it doesn't have an effect on us. As long as we assume that no one else is in on it, we are incapable of evaluating what a particular matter means to us. This is why I always tell people to also say something about their daily concerns. Then they realize what they are worth to them.

I always did this in my scientific work, for example. In this kind of work all sorts of thoughts go through one's mind, without really knowing what they are worth. So, then it is advantageous to speak to someone, and here – I must admit – the female gender is especially gifted. If one says something to a woman and she has an uncontrolled emotion as a consequence, then one knows the value, one knows it for oneself. To speak to men is, in this respect, not very fruitful because a man in such a case usually fails in a certain way. Probably for the following reason: "By golly, how does he know this and I didn't? So, let's not show colors." A false reaction, isn't it? Or he thinks, "How is that with me?" So, no, one doesn't say anything; one doesn't react, because one is hit somewhere. Therefore, a conversation with women is very special when it's about a cluster of insufficiently evaluated ideas. I've received reactions, for example, from female students that told me, "Ah, that hit home, that's real, now I know what it is worth," because the response of the other – a totally unprejudiced reaction – affords the realization of one's own feeling. I use to call this the "precipitating effect of feminine conversation." It really is amazing. I had the custom to send patients who needed to realize something to a woman analyst, telling them, "Why don't you tell her this story for once?" and then they suddenly had a realization.

I vividly remember a certain case: This was a philosopher, a German philosopher, who always was of a great intellectual superiority. He told me all sorts of stories, and I noticed acutely that he had no idea what he'd actually experienced, or what had happened to him. So, I told him, "Now, go to Mrs. So-and-so for a session." In the evening of the next day, the analyst in question called me and said, "What kind of a man did you send me? What's wrong with him? He is half-crazy!" I asked, "What happened?" – "Well, he started to tell me a story and got into such an emotional state that he rolled around on the floor! Is he crazy?" – "No, no, he is a German philosopher; he is not crazy." In the presence of this woman he simply realized for the first time that he had great emotion about certain things. He was hiding this from me (I saw him again later) – because he couldn't be inferior in the presence of another man. He simply couldn't be inferior to me! Whereas it didn't matter to him with a woman. This is precisely why men often show their worst side in the company of a woman. It happens frequently.

I only mention these things to demonstrate how difficult it is to have the right sensations[229], and how necessary it is to grasp and realize the right feelings, and how this is not possible when one is alone. If you jail someone on top of Mont Blanc, he cannot realize anything, because the ice and the clouds and the wind don't tell him what he is. He only knows that he is not cloud, not wind, and not snow. But when he has another human being with him, then he can realize in what kind of state he is, and in what kind of state the other person is.

And so, it is necessary that the experiences one has first go through a veritable experience process. You can have any kind of experience, but when you've experienced it alone it is as if it hasn't yet quite arrived. You have to share it with someone, and then you have a chance for a complete realization. And only then you are capable to see what feeling-toned experiences actually mean to you. One often observes that in instances where feelings are not realized, things get stuck within us and the strangest phenomena may develop, which, as a consequence, are completely incomprehensible.

I remember an English lady – she was a physician too (just to show you that this doesn't only happen to men, it can also happen to women!). She was single, would have had several opportunities to marry, but, floated over it with her studies, then the practice, and so on, without realizing what she should have done, should have realized. This I noticed, and at some point I said, "You behave exactly like one who is beloved, meaning, like a woman who knows that she is loved by a man." She was very astonished and didn't comprehend it.

229 In the spoken Swiss-German dialect, terms are often interchanged (especially between feeling and sensation, as in this case), which Jung, in his writings, strictly distinguishes. See C. G. Jung, "General Description of the Types" and "Definitions," in: *Psychological Types*, CW 6.

I continued, "Wouldn't it be possible that you once met a man whom you really loved, or of whom you were sure loved you too?" First she wouldn't have it, but then it turned out that this was indeed the case, when she was twenty years old. But because it somehow collided with medical school, she overlooked the situation, didn't want to acknowledge it. She simply didn't realize what she gave up. From there on, she was blocked, as if she'd been tabooed. No man could approach her anymore, because she should have married this first lover. When she realized that, she was astonished indeed. At the time, she was already forty-five. Later I heard that this man was a widower, and that she reconnected with him. However, it didn't quite make it to marriage – only almost.

Now, if I have to talk about myself, necessitated by your question whether I also have had experiences like that, then of course I have to say, yes, I too was once young, and there was much I didn't realize. I, too, had to learn in my own life what feelings are, and what kind of enormous importance they have.

For example, I realized only much later what it was that I'd dreamed thirty or forty years earlier. I can exactly date it historically: At about thirty-six I realized for the first time what it was that I used to do as a boy of about nine. At that moment, in fact, aged thirty-six, I read a report about prehistoric discoveries at the Burgäschisee[230]. It was about the so-called moor-settlement or swamp-settlements. They'd simply put layers of tree trunks down and erected their cabins on top. There, in front of such a cabin, one discovered a particular arrangement of stones. Each individual stone – not very big stones, about the size of a fist – was wrapped in birch bark, birch bast, and the stones were set in a regular fashion. This is a *cache*[231] of soul-stones. What this is, one knows from the still living aborigines in central Australia. They have so-called soul-stones, *churingas* – they can also be wooden –, which they receive at their male initiation. Afterwards they hide them in crevasses, hollow trees, or at the mounds of sources, and visit them once in a while, namely under very interesting circumstances: when a man feels that his libido is gone, as we say in our professional slang,

230 Lake of Burgäschi in Switzerland. See C.G. Jung, "The Visions of Zosimos," CW 13, par. 129.
231 From French, *cacher*, meaning to hide.

meaning, when his vitality diminishes; when he is lacking interest; when he "doesn't care" anymore; when he is depressed or bored, then the primitive man knows that the time has come to visit his *churingas*. Then he goes to his *cache* and brings them out. These are most often slabs of stone or wood. He lays them on his knees and starts rubbing them. He rubs them for a long time, and, thereby, the poor vital force, the diminished vital force, goes into the stone, and the good vital force that is within the stone – it is stored in the stone; it's a kind of psychic accumulator – goes into him. After that, he is well again, and the stone is buried again in its hiding place.

In the same way, our ancestors had such stone settings with precious churinga stones. A complete *cache* was found in Arlesheim[232], in those caves under the castle. They were painted on one side. One could see that they were cult objects.

When I was a boy, I had – of course without knowing what it meant – a pencil case. First I carved at one end of a ruler a little manikin with a top hat and painted it black with ink, then sawed it off and put it in my pencil case. In it, I made him a little bed and dressed him with a little coat. Then I collected flat stones at the shore of the river Rhine, painted them with watercolor, and they too belonged to this manikin. I put them into the pencil case as well. Then I locked the thing up and went up to our second-story attic. It was an old vicarage in the countryside, where we had a two-story attic. But it was strictly prohibited to go up into the second attic, because it was unsound. In spite of that, I climbed up there, onto one of the huge beams, and there I hid my box. That was my secret, and nobody knew about it. And I only went there when I was sure that no one was watching me. That was simply part of it. So, from time to time, I went up there and each time I wrote something on a little piece of paper. I don't remember what it was; that hasn't come back to me. But I wrote something, then rolled up the piece of paper into a little roll and gave it to the manikin, so it had something to read. That was his library. Each time, it was a great satisfaction that I had such a manikin that belonged to me alone, and those stones I couldn't really make heads or tails of. That went on until my eleventh year, then I completely forgot about it. In all the subsequent years I knew nothing about it anymore. And then, in my

232 Near Basel, Switzerland.

thirty-sixth year, I read about this discovery, and in that moment the whole story came back into my consciousness.[233]

This is, of course, a whole mythology. As a boy I didn't have the faintest idea of these things. I constructed this *kista* with veiled gods in it, these *cabiri*[234], with this *cache* of soul-stones and a cult around them. So, without any provocation from outside, quite naturally, like a game, it arose from within myself. So, a whole complex story simply had sunk into oblivion. Of course, I was interested in finding out under what circumstances this remembrance got so completely lost. After all, it is possible that this box is still there in its hiding place. It never came back into my mind. I absolutely can't remember having ever taken it down. It had been a *lieu de pèlerinage*[235] and enormously taboo. It was a big secret; I really don't know why. Now this was forgotten because, in my eleventh year, I had a strange experience: I was on my way to school, to the gymnasium Basel. I always walked along the banks of the river Rhine to Basel. I was alone and – suddenly I was "here!" I suddenly had the feeling that, "Now I am here!" Actually, I then had the feeling, "Yes, why here?" as if I had suddenly emerged from a wall of fog. I asked, "But what was it that had been there?" It was colossally difficult to realize that. But I had the feeling that within this wall of fog there were all sorts of objects – fathers and mothers and animals and trains and streets and wagons and other people and me. It all was sort of the same thing. These were all simply things that were moving or stood still, that simply were in there without being related to each other. But now I was! And then I knew that I was I, a human being who now can say, "This is a wagon, and not simply also just an object, but one that has wheels, and I have legs."[236]

I don't know whether I'm able to make this clear to you. It simply was the realization of an ego-consciousness. I then had an ego-consciousness. Before it was a childlike awareness of objects that were standing, or were lying around, or that walked around, as I did too. There wasn't a difference in value; I couldn't yet realize a feeling of value. Now I saw for the first time that I was – but, at that moment,

---

233 See *Memories, Dreams, Reflections* by C. G. Jung, pp. 21 f.
234 See C. G. Jung, *Symbols of Transformation*, CW 5, pars. 180–184, with figures.
235 French, a place of pilgrimage.
236 See *Memories, Dreams, Reflections* by C. G. Jung, pp. 32 f.

the whole previous history had disappeared. After that there wasn't anything anymore; the whole magic of that box had disappeared. Naturally, this was a tremendously archaic matter. It was also conditioned by my upbringing, because early on it was already evident that I was a bit critical of generally proclaimed truths. It was at that moment, that such a development evidently began.

Through the dawning of consciousness, one is pushed into a world of consciousness; one arrives at a world of consciousness where one loses the original feeling-values. One doesn't know them anymore. For me, the story with the little manikin was a highly emotional affair. And with it a whole part of my own being simply went underground, which, however, played an even more important role later when I saw what such archetypal experiences actually mean.

When one studies the anamnesis of people more carefully, one can often hear such weird things. From these, one can deduce how many feeling values got lost in the development of consciousness. The development of consciousness is a cultural process, and through the cultural process we are cut off to a high degree from the original world of senses and feelings. It is a positive loss if we no longer have this. Because then one is no longer able to correctly evaluate something analogous that happens to one again. That loss caused me, and played the role in my life, that I chose the intellect exclusively. That was my "force." I developed one-sidedly in this direction, let's say in the scientific direction, which was, of course, to my advantage. But humanly, it was to my disadvantage. It was acquired at the expense of my humanness. Because humanness lies within those things. I only tell you this as an example of how it happens. After all, you can very well imagine that in the life of this English woman of whom I told you, it was a huge loss that the matter had disappeared so completely without further ado. From that moment on, she was engaged, meaning, she simply was her whole life the fiancée of an unknown and invisible man and thus gambled that part of her life completely away.

The same happened to me. This one-sided development of consciousness was unavoidable, because, as I came to see later, I couldn't effectively realize those feeling values, those strange, archaic feeling values, at the time.

Later, when I experienced similar things, I said, "Well, yes, 10,000 years ago – or negroes in Africa – do such things. That's beside the point, that doesn't prove anything, that doesn't matter. That's old humbug!" When one devalues one's own experience – without being aware of it – in the same way, one pushes it even further from oneself. Precisely through scientific development such experiences are pushed even further away. Naturally, it took a great deal of work to dig up this continuity afterwards.

I had, for example, a dream at the age of about three. I can prove it, it's not a fantasy of mine. This was a dream that I only understood when I was in my sixties, because due to the one-sidedness of development, that whole world of experience had simply disappeared never to be seen again. It is also difficult to talk about these things, because we all are in this situation of unrealized primal experiences. And these do belong to the completeness of the personality.

Now, many of these things come up in dreams again, where one often doesn't recognize them, unless one is quasi focused on it and trained to reconstruct the context of dream contents. When one can do that, one can also find those primal relations again. But only very few can do that; hence, most people can only poorly recognize such original material. And yet it belongs to the wholeness of the personality.

I'd like to answer again the question that Dr. Tauber asked, this time in a different way, namely: Does one notice, or see, that inner conditions or realizations tend to move toward a particular goal? – Well, there I have to say, one doesn't realize it for a long time! Only after accumulating a great amount of inner experiences can one see where it's actually aimed. And even then one isn't sure, because these things have a dual aspect too. What comes from those primal times, so to speak, has a power that urges forward and holds back at the same time. One can withdraw into it. This, for example, is the case with the mentally ill, that they kind of withdraw into primal experiences; they are being drawn back. They even want to get credit for it, as if this were a special achievement. For example, they invent a special language; they have these neologisms; they express themselves in an exaggerated manner, like, for example, Heidegger – again, a German philosopher! – and don't notice that they withdraw into "power-words," into the magic words of the primitives.[237] And in that way it is lost in real life. Whereas another person would be compelled by precisely this primal power to move forward and to translate these things into actual life. Therefore, I can answer this question only partially in a positive way. It depends on the individual whether he sees what it means or not. Whether he takes the trouble to look at these things positively, or whether he is content with an impression, which then pulls him back. That can cause an equal amount of harm. This, however, most people don't realize.

In analytical practice one often has great trouble to teach people a positive regard toward this. This is exactly why I'm so critical of theologians, because they proclaim an archaic language that one could just as well dream, without pressing for an *understanding* of what is being said. If, for example, I ask any patient of mine, possibly a highly educated person, what this actually means: "Through the blood of our Lord Jesus Christ we are redeemed from our sins." What does it mean? This is a phrase that you can hear every Sunday in church. Well, what exactly does it mean in reality? What, for God's sake, does it mean? Not one of them would be able to say it, because in principal, one doesn't think about it, and that is humanity's downfall. These are, in fact, ideas that should lead further. What happens instead, however, is a sliding back into the past. One is made unconscious again. Because one doesn't know what these words mean and thus simply relies on a felt impression. "The blood of our Lord Jesus Christ" sounds so solemn, and so like Sunday, and so religious – so gloriously religious! Then one assumes to be somehow justified, and in an especially glorious state, when one can say, or sing, or pray, such a thing, even though one doesn't know what it is.

During my travels in Kenya I observed, for example, certain rituals with the Elgonyis, my black bodyguards. I asked them, "What do they mean? Why are you doing this?" They didn't know. Then I asked, "Does anyone know what you're doing here?" – "Yes, the medicine man, the N'ganga," they answered, "He knows." I went to N'ganga and asked him. He said, "Yes, yes, my father remembered still, but I don't anymore." He didn't know either, but his father, or, in the last instance, his grandfather, they still knew. But it doesn't go any further,

237 See C.G. Jung, "Paracelsus as Spiritual Phenomenon," CW 13, par. 155.

because behind grandfather comes Napoleon I, then William Tell, and then Adam, as one Swiss freshman soldier wrote in the recruiting exam. Where was I? One shouldn't tell bad jokes in between. Yes, indeed: my negroes. One of my friends said, "These people are very primitive – God, they don't even know what they do!" At that, I said, "Wait a minute, how about the Christmas tree? Do you know why we have a Christmas tree?" He didn't know either. Father had done it that way, and so had grandfather. That was all he knew. But what a Christmas tree means he didn't know. *Partout comme chez nous*[238] – we are not better. In that respect, we are just as primitive. In the same way, most all of religious language is archaic language these days. We don't know what it means. We should be clearly aware of this. And it is more to people's ruin than to their advantage, because they are in danger of slide back. One should know what it means. But in this respect one simply doesn't think. There is a huge mental laziness. It's not only with us Protestants; it's with the Catholics too.

I had an interesting experience: A professor of the Faculty of Theology in Munich came for a visit – a Jesuit, a very scholarly and very intelligent type. With visibly righteous indignation he came into my office and said, "I read your book on Job!" I said, "Well, then you'll have something to say." He responded, "Indeed. But there is only one question: How can you, as an intelligent European, and a – at least Protestant – Christian, maintain that Christ and Mary weren't real human beings?" Of course, he thought that now I'd be completely beat. Then I said, "My dear Professor, this is actually very simple, isn't it? Look, according to your own church teachings, you are born in the *peccatum originale*, that is, in the *macula peccati*, the stain of sin. I am too, as are all other people. All humans are corrupt and mortal, because the *macula peccati* burdens them. Christ and Mary don't have a *macula peccati*, and therefore they are not human beings. Period." There I witnessed for the first time a Jesuit who didn't have an answer. He didn't know what else to say. Just imagine, such a calamity! It's like asking your physician what pneumonia is and he wouldn't have an answer. Exactly like that. It's an astonishing lack of articulation, because they only take the images, the words, without realizing anything about them. They don't realize that they don't

238 French, "everywhere like at home."

understand it. They really don't know what it means. So, when you, for example – *honnête*!²³⁹ – analyze a phrase such as, "Redeemed through the blood of the Lord Jesus Christ," you arrive at astounding conclusions. But that's never done. In that respect, I received a lesson from my own father. He told me, "You think too much. You must not think, you must believe!" Then I told him, "Please, give me this faith!" He didn't have it himself, otherwise he could have given it. One can only give what one has. What one doesn't have, one cannot give. This, too, he didn't know.

So, you see, the realization of feelings, which is utterly necessary to get on with life, is a very difficult matter. In this regard, one cannot assert, or be hopeful, that these experiences unambiguously point to a goal. One has to have very big experiences, and very many, until one can say, "Most likely it goes in this or that direction." Of course, one knows that they point to something important, either in this or the other direction. Backwards, it regresses to the idea of an archaic deity. Forward, it goes toward something dark, that which we don't know yet. But comparatively, there is a big difference when regressing to an archaic mentality, where we stop thinking at all and fall for absolute suggestion. One becomes suggestible when one doesn't have conscious thoughts, only unconscious ones. Then one is enormously impressionable and falls for all sorts of stupid power words or slogans.

I believe I have now said enough about this question. Do you have more questions?

Ignaz Tauber: Anyone have a question regarding these issues?

C. G. Jung: You cannot possibly have understood everything, yes? Just be genuinely naive, otherwise you'll never realize your feelings!

---

239 French, "honestly!"

On Redemption

Ignaz Tauber: Dr. Baumann would like to ask something.

Hans Baumann: I'd be interested precisely in the problem of "redemption through the blood of Jesus Christ" in more detail. And I believe several others in the group would, too.

C. G. Jung: Yes – just realize this! What does it mean? Why should our sins be washed away through blood? What, for God's sake does this mean?

It means, for example: A human being, without sin, is being slaughtered. He is the son of a great god. He is being sent by him, but then is turned over to his enemies, without this god protectively intervening. So, this god hands over his own son to his enemies. He doesn't intervene. And then the son is cruelly executed, and the blood that pours out from him has magical powers, because it can cause the sins committed by other people to no longer exist. So how is this to be understood? In the first place like this: The sins we commit are in disobedience toward the commandments of God. In the Old Testament it is the first parents who were disobedient, and that is what became the *macula peccati origin*alis. The disobedience of the first parents has caused us to be corrupted and, as a consequence, mortal. The theme of disobedience – this highly archaic theme! – is, then, carried over into Christian dogma: Our sins consist of disobedience. About this, the world-creator is horribly angered every time – to such a degree, in fact, that he can only be appeased by having his son slaughtered. Just imagine such a bloodthirsty story! He is being reconciled through the sacrifice of Christ. So, for example, there exists a mighty tyrant, whose rage I've brought upon myself, and he is reconciled when I have my own son killed – indeed, even when I'm being led to kill my own son, as happened to Abraham. There is a Jewish commentary on this Abraham-Isaac story. There it says: When the angel brought the buck, the ram, in place of Isaac, Isaac wasn't killed. Then Yahweh said to Abraham that he could come down from the altar. It was done now, finished. But Abraham responded, no, he was going to stay up at the altar, he had something to say. Namely, *He*, Yahweh, had ordered him to kill his son Isaac, so he had almost stabbed him to death. And then Yahweh would have broken his word, because he had promised Isaac his seed. Then Yahweh said, "Yes, by god, that's true." This is why, on the Day of Reconciliation, one has to blow the *Shofar* in the Synagogue – that's the buckhorn with which the heretics are being cursed – so that *He*, Yahweh, is reminded that He almost broke his word![240] That is Jewish theology. It's the same as the story of the high priest, who once every year, on the day of the spring equinox, goes into the sanctuary. "And there," it says, "he saw the splendor of Adonai." (Adonai means Lord.) And the magnificent one spoke to him and said, "Bless me, my son." Then the high priest gave Him the blessing and added, "And may you always remember your good qualities more than your bad ones." That is the psychology of Job. From there the conflict of Job originates. It is the awareness of an original non-differentiation, one can almost say, identity of good and evil, an incomprehensible oneness of the two. They stand next to each other. For us, it means that there is an absolute ambivalence, first and foremost in Yahweh. But in the New Testament you can find the same traces, namely that the God of the New Testament is by no means a god of love; rather he is a vengeful, a terribly vengeful God, who even slaughtered his own son, in order to get out of his own anger. That's what it amounts to. Therein, quite clearly, are mirrored psychic situations in man. It is impossible for us to imagine a universal creator who would not be a pair of opposites. He must be a polarity, otherwise he would have no energy. There would be no creation of light out of darkness. If there is no darkness, neither is there light emanating out of it, and if there is no light, there is no darkness. It has to be like that. But when the two are separated, that's when matters become difficult; then there is an ambivalent image of God, which we keep hiding from ourselves. This is what theologians do.

From there arises unavoidably another observation: On the second day of creation – that was a Monday, because He started on Sunday – "There was light." On Monday the opposites were separated; the upper waters were separated from the lower ones. On the eve of *that* day, Yahweh didn't say, "And behold, it was good." He said that on all the other days, but not on that one. Now this was on the day of the woman, Luna, and on the day of the heavenly bodies. In the Middle

240 See C.G. Jung's letter to Pastor William Lachat, 27 March, 1954, CW 18, pars. 1532–1557.

Ages it was claimed that the devil was created on that day, the snake in paradise, which, mind you, existed before Adam. In the Middle Ages, it was said that this day of creation wasn't praised because it had been a somewhat unfortunate business. When I came upon this (while reading authors from the Middle Ages) I looked up the famous Genesis commentary by Origen. Indeed, there he says that God praised his creation on all of the days – but he must have kept this annoying business quiet. Something extraordinary must have happened on that day for God not to praise it.[241] That, too, was passed over. Nobody thinks about it. In the Middle Ages, such things were still sniffed out, because one thought about them. But today we think *infinitely* less about these biblical matters than one did in the Middle Ages, *infinitely* less. We do critical text analysis and such, but we don't think about things.

I wonder how many of our theologians have even a hunch about the Jewish commentaries on the Old Testament, for example about this ambivalence, or about the undeniable fact that God requests a blood sacrifice, namely, that he treated his own son in this way, and demanded the same of Abraham. There, fortunately, it didn't happen, but almost, almost! I don't know if on the Day of Reconciliation, the Shofar will actually be blown with conscious knowledge. Of course, it was blown as a call to come into the presence of Yahweh, just like when we ring the church bells. In Rothenthurm, they wrote in large letters onto the roof of the church, "Saint Anthony, pray for us!" so that he could see it from heaven.

The bell has a significance similar to the gong in the East. The gong is a metallic, far-reaching voice that is repeated by each individual when saying, "Om." That is the stroke of the gong. That is the call, the invocation. Originally, it comes from a primordial sound that I heard in Africa too, namely, "mmh." One says that instinctively for a nice view, beautiful music, a beautiful painting, a beautiful girl – one says, "mmh." I found myself with a delegation of members from the "British Association" on the Tiger Hill in Darjeeling, where we

241 See C. G. Jung, "A Psychological Approach to the Dogma of the Trinity," CW 11, par. 256; and "Psychology and Religion," CW 11, par. 104; concerning the symbolism of blood, see C. G. Jung, "Transformation Symbolism in the Mass," CW 11, chapter III, passim; and for Jung's explorations of these problems in depth, see "Answer to Job," CW 11, chapter VI.

watched the sunset over the Kanchenjunga. It was a superb spectacle. All these British naturalists said to themselves, "mmh." I couldn't
help but ask afterwards whether they knew the kind of prayer they'd
uttered. Namely an archaic prayer. At the time there were many Tibetan prayer flags around us; long bamboo sticks with tiny white flags
attached. These were decorated with block-prints that showed the
Ratna-Sambhava[242], the horse with Cintâmani[243], the priceless treasure, the unattainable treasure, and with the transcription, "om mani
padme hum." That means, "oh, the gem in the lotus."[244] Here you
have the two together. These people didn't know it, but the beauty
was so overwhelming that each one said to himself, "mmh." Now, that
is a primal sound; because it is the sound a mother says to her child
when the child doesn't want to eat, "Mmh, it tastes good, just try it,
mmh." Or if one meets up with an African negro, and the situation
isn't completely safe. One doesn't know how it's going to play out;
he doesn't trust me and I don't trust him. Then both sit on the floor,
put their weapons down and say, "Mmh, mmh, mmh," and so it goes
for a while, back and forth, "Mmh, (d)jambo, (d)jambo, (d)jambo …
mmh," and slowly one moves closer. These are soothing sounds,
recommendations, expressions of appreciation: "Mmh, this is good."
And this became an invocation. In antiquity, for example – this, too,
was ridiculed – one could always hear whistling and finger-snapping
at the Mithras temples. With this, one attracted the gods. One attracted them like dogs, like animals. One attracted them, so to speak,
through their animal attributes. So ultimately, that's where the bells
originate. Of course, there is a lot of archaic material, by which one is
simply drawn into unconsciousness.

The British scientists were a selection of famous gentlemen who
would have had a priceless opportunity to realize their feelings. But
they were so pathetic that they could only utter the primal sound,
"mmh." At last, one of them begged me to recite, for god's sake, the
sunset passage in Goethe's *Faust*. I still knew it in parts and recited
it, namely so that the feeling could be given expression. It was the

242 See C.G. Jung, "Psychological Commentary to 'The Tibetan Book of the
    Dead,'" CW 11, pars. 852 f.
243 See C.G. Jung, "The Psychology of Eastern Meditation," CW 11, par. 919.
244 See C.G. Jung, "The Type Problem in Poetry," CW 6, par. 298.

historian from Cambridge who'd asked me. I found it remarkable that he felt that something had to be said.

Anything else?

On New Symbols

Ignaz Tauber: Dr. Ernst Jung would like to ask something.

Ernst Jung: I would like to ask whether, based on your great experience with modern man, you have the impression that new symbols in religion will be formed, or could be forming. Be it within the Christian framework or something completely new. Especially with regards to the [political] split of our world, which somehow, eventually, should also lead to a *coniunctio*.

C. G. Jung: Yes, it should come to a union. Yes, this is indeed the case. One can prove this directly. In the dreams of modern man there are these mandala symbols. Though now, one doesn't have experience from earlier times. We cannot say whether these mandala symbols were already here in earlier times, or whether they appear more frequently today. I found these things mostly after the last world war, but who knew about such things before? Nobody, isn't it so? But now we have objective evidence, namely these "saucer-reports" – reports about UFOs. I wrote a little book about them.[245] This is the objective evidence that such visions occur, and that such a "lore" was invented.

Even an astronomer, the famous Fred Hoyle in Cambridge, quite naively writes a book about this motif, a novel, without the faintest idea of what he is actually writing about.[246] He describes it in the form of a sphere, a so-called *globulus*. This is a globular accumulation of matter that, over time, becomes a star through densification. It approaches the earth, though not continuing directly to the earth, but to the sun, to load up energy. This, however, darkens the sun, so that we on earth first almost burn up and then almost freeze. That's

---

245 See C. G. Jung, "Flying Saucers: A Myth of Things Seen in the Skies," CW 10, chapter V.
246 Fred Hoyle, *The Black Cloud* (1957).

the content of this novel and *le dénouement*[247]. It appears that this cloud is already developed to the point where there are intellectual processes inside. People, then, make contact – via radio-telephone – with these "currents" in the cloud. It's a fantastic idea, but it simply means that there is a globular body with super-human intelligence and of infinite duration. It has the duration of a star. So, this is the story of an astronomer.

This, then, is one of these cases; there are others, for example the story of an Englishman.[248] I don't know whether I am telling you something you already know: In a remote English village it happened that such a UFO, such a "flying saucer," landed and drew a circle around itself with a radius of about one mile. Everyone who came into contact with it from outside immediately fell into a hypnotic sleep, people and animals. Of course, car accidents occurred at these contact spots; the whole village sank into a deep sleep for twenty-four hours because of the presence of this UFO. And then, after twenty-four hours, everything awoke, perfectly normal again, as if nothing had happened, absolutely nothing. Nobody had noticed anything, and nothing was missing anywhere. After some weeks, though, it became evident that all women of that place capable of conception were pregnant. The news, of course, created a huge stir throughout this respectable village. The people waited – what else could they have done? Then they gave birth to children who were especially intelligent and nice, and who all had golden eyes. Once in school, it became evident that they were much more intelligent than the other children, and that they had a remarkable ability: It was as if they had just *one* mind together, so that only one girl and one boy needed to go to school at any given time. That was enough. The others automatically knew what the other two had learned. A special school had to be arranged for them because they had become so terribly intelligent and inquisitive. At last it dawned on the English that this simply was a superior human race, a completely new human race, that is, of superior intelligence. In the meantime, they'd also received news that it had happened in Africa too: that a Negro village had been put to

247 French, "resolution."
248 John Wyndham, *The Midwich Cuckoos*. (London and New York: Michael Joseph 1957), see C. G. Jung, "Flying Saucers: A Myth of Things Seen in the Skies," CW 10, Supplement, pars. 821–824.

sleep and afterwards had children with golden eyes, but that they were immediately killed, because this was something strange. This is how the problem was "solved" in Africa. The same happened in an Eskimo village. There, the Eskimo tribe simply left them outside. They froze, and here, too, the business was put to an end.

But in Siberia this happened under the regime of the Soviets, who took an interest, and thus isolated the village, completely sealed it off, and observed what would become of these human beings. It was found that they also had "second sight." They had telepathic abilities. In the end, this was too much for the Russians, and they shot the whole establishment down with heavy artillery, ruining everything. And the English sat there and didn't know what to do with the new race. Then there was a noble Englishman who'd earned special merits by educating those children. He had great compassion and under-standing for them. But he was of the opinion, that it's either us, or them! If they gain the upper hand, we are lost. Then we'd simply be *the poor niggers*[249] and they the real stags[250], and we'd be ruled over. So, he said, "This is impossible." – "Rule Britannia!" isn't it. He had several cases of dynamite brought to the schoolroom when they were all together, and had himself with the whole community blown up into the air. Since then, nothing else has happened. – This is such a story.

So, this means, it's a dark narrative, a "rumor," that something wants to incarnate in man. Something wants to intrude into our world system, something round, something like the sun, something golden, something superior, a wholeness, which humanity is lacking. And this is now perceived in the form of round, shining appearances. Within them there are voices, superior intelligences that claim to come from Venus, or Mars, and that look after our earthly affairs, our whole political situation. They want to give us good advice, or perhaps even help us to emigrate. After all, these are savior-ships coming from heaven to redeem us from our dullness. That's the going myth today. It is mere ignorance if we underestimate this. In America they did a "Gallup test" and found that something above forty percent of

---

249 Jung says it in English.
250 "Stag," in German "Hirsch," is a Swiss expression to denote a man who likes to show off his exceptional power or importance.

the population is convinced that these "saucers" exist, that they are around.

And if you knew the literature! I can recommend a book that is highly interesting. It's by Aimé Michel and the title is *Mystérieux corps célestes*[251]. The author himself was in aviation and is an intelligent Frenchman. He made highly interesting observations, namely that the sightings of such UFOs on any given day are all on one particular geographical line. He fixed this on a map. Highly interesting. It might signify that there is something to this. This book almost convinced me that there is some truth to these things. There has to be something physical about it. But what is being done with it, *that* is interesting for us, because a whole hope for redemption is being projected onto these things. It's not far removed from the formation of a new religion; the anticipation of redeemers from other spheres. This literature is highly interesting.

Recently there was a scandal in Basel, when someone claimed to have circled the moon eleven times, saying that the moon had water and cities "on the other side." That, of course, is total nonsense. This man is a swindler, but he has believers in Switzerland. I even know someone who, even though he's otherwise quite reasonable, is completely convinced that this is true. Of course, he, too, has this "delusion of redemption." He travels occasionally to Venus – there they have a wonderful and fabulous culture, beautiful people with blond curly hair and big blue eyes. This man has so-called "contacts." In America they say they have "contacts" with these superior beings. But this is the origin of a myth.

In the same way, the birth of Christ was announced by the wonderful conjunction of Jupiter and Saturn (that is the star of Bethlehem), which really took place. He [Christ] was also derived from the stars, so to speak. As with the epiphany of a god, he is a god who came down from Olympus, which is to say, from heaven, from a starry world, and appeared in the world. This is happening again. It happens in the same banal way as in the past, when insignificant people wandered

---

251 See also Aimé Michel, *The Truth about Flying Saucers*, (London, 1957); C. G. Jung, "Flying Saucers. A Modern Myth of Things Seen in the Skies," CW 10, par. 609, fn 4 und par. 668, fn 13. [Jung, in his library, only had the abovementioned book by Aimé Michel *Mystérieux objets célestes*, 1958.]

around and proclaimed, "Christ has appeared. He has come down to earth; he has become real." Very naive. That was the role Paul played, as you can see in his letter to the Thessalonians. He visits communities that we believed had always been Christian. These however were Jewish settlements. There he preached that the Messiah had come; that it had happened in reality; that such-and-such had happened in Jerusalem. *That* was the gospel. That is the so-called first annunciation: he had really come down to earth. In our times, the gospel is announced in such journals as the "Ebro-Bulletin"[252], or in the "Saucer Review" – and it is equally ridiculous. So, it happens in reality that such a myth comes alive.

With Buddha it's the same story. At the time one didn't know anything of Buddha; one only knew that this smart, well-meaning man was an important man. But later he became "the Great One" and more than all the gods, "the Elephant." His teaching is called "The Elephant Track." All things have a small beginning, and so it is with us now.

I wouldn't be surprised if this would lead to who-knows-where. As long as the matter is still so dark, everything can be projected onto it, of course. Which is why one would like to know what the actual reality is of these stories. But one is completely in the dark as to why one doesn't know more. I only know that a whole series of stories emerges now, after lying in the dark for years, of which one knew nothing about. These are, in part, highly interesting observations. Well then, I urgently recommend the book by Aimé Michel[253]; I can truly recommend it; it is highly interesting, because it sheds light on the possible reality. It is by far the best thing about this whole story.

What about the time?

[Break. On the audio recording, we hear people chatting.]

---

252 The Ebro Observatory in Spain published a monthly journal with articles on astrophysics, geophysics, astronomy, and meteorology.
253 Aimé Michel, *The Truth about Flying Saucers*, London, 1957. Originally published as *Lueurs sur les soucoupes volantes*, Paris, 1954, mentioned in C. G. Jung, CW 10, par. 609, fn. 4 and par. 668, fn. 13. [Jung had only the aforementioned book by Aimé Michel *Mystérieux objets célestes*, 1958, in his library].

On Projections

Ignaz Tauber: If you allow us, Herr Professor, we'd like to ask you one more question. There are two, actually, belonging together, and these are: what did you do when, at times, you ran out of vitality – when you had too much work, or suffered a depression or stroke of fate? In part you already answered when talking about these soul-stones. And the last question belongs with it: how were you able to withdraw your projections?

C. G. Jung: Yes, these two questions belong necessarily together. If one runs out of vitality, that is, participation in life, interest, energy, it is a kind of tiredness. What does one do when one is tired? One rolls up like a dog on the sofa and stays with oneself. One collects oneself, one recuperates. And if one gets into a psychic mess, one recuperates psychically by paying attention to oneself, by reflecting on things, having a good look at the problems, becoming conscious of them, and, in fact, of all that concerns oneself. Everyone who is suffering becomes selfish, egocentric. This is absolutely necessary, so that he can put himself together again. It is precisely like the Australian who seeks his *churingas* and rubs them. So, we seek a resting place, quietness, concentration, in order to help ourselves out of our difficulties. One can support this: in India, these practices are articulated, nicely described. They can "breathe themselves into being," if they want. Or they can assume a certain lotus position, which reminds one of one's own posture, the body. Just try to sit for two hours in lotus position, and you know where you are, if only for physiological reasons!

Or one satisfies some wishes that are within one's means. I had, for example, a patient who had life-threatening depressions during which she wanted to kill herself. She noticed that, if she passed by a shoe store and bought herself a pair of new shoes, things got better. With that she healed her depression, precisely because she did something for herself. It can help in many respects to do something for oneself, and, in fact, perhaps in an egotistical manner.

For this purpose, there are men who allow themselves to get drunk. And it may just be the right thing, namely because it is right to pay attention to oneself, to take oneself objectively. This way one also can free oneself from projections. What does a projection mean? A projection means, for example, that I project characteristics into someone, or find characteristics that are not there, that come from somewhere else, from myself for example. This is why I'm not sure about the evaluation of that personality. Well, what to do? One asks around what this person is like in reality. One listens to what other people say. Or one really investigates how these people are in reality and then notices, to one's own astonishment, that, perhaps, one has had a completely wrong judgment. Then one can find the reason for it. One has, for example, mistrust against someone and finds out that this is basically unjustified. Well, what to do? How can one rectify that? First of all, you know through objective investigation that this mistrust is completely inappropriate and that this person is trustworthy. But why do I project mistrust onto that person? Very simply, because something within myself is not working. It can be, for example, that I myself have misgivings and that I somehow find myself in some way untrustworthy, which, however, I wouldn't admit. I would prefer to say, "No, I'm very trustworthy." We would not appreciate if others thought of us as being untrustworthy, and so we assume that we are trustworthy. Still, we have a secret doubt about whether or not we are. Or we did something that shows that we are not quite trust-worthy. Then we are secretly pursued by a bad conscience and seek to place it somewhere, and then discover a *bête noire*[254]. We discover someone and think, "This now is the one who is not trustworthy," and with this the projection is done. Then there it is. If one can reverse this process through self-reflection, recollect oneself, get to know oneself, then one has a sure criterion; one knows the answer to, "How come you're saying bad things about this person – you know that you yourself are to blame!" But few people do this. It's about very simple things. After all, one says that everybody has his *bête noire*. There is always someone of whom one thinks, now this is a bad person, or some such thing. Then one can see that it is projected and that it might even come from oneself. Once one knows it, one can stop this nonsense.

There are, for example, men who project pure innocence onto every girl. These are the "innocents," the "forever innocent and wonderful,"

254 French, scapegoat.

who don't have any bad characteristics at all. Such people then are, of course, completely blind, that means, they are completely blind with respect to their own feelings. They don't know that they are absolutely egotistical and selfish by assuming that another is perfect. Then, of course, the girl one wants to marry has to be perfect, because one is oneself such a fabulous stag. Therefore, one can only marry a wholly perfect woman. This is a crazy demand on the other person, because one demands of the other person what oneself doesn't do. That, too, is a projection. If one thinks of someone as a lazy dog, and one isn't totally sure whether he is a lazy dog – one might even have proof that he isn't – then one has to look into oneself, whether oneself is a lazy dog. This is how it goes.

We find this everywhere in our society. Women have certain ideas about each other, and then it turns out that they themselves are like that. The same happens with men. In this regard, men are as bad as women, only their projections are aimed at different things. Just look around in the business milieu, for example: time and again you find the story of the *bête noire*. In families, too, it happens that one brother projects onto the other and doesn't see that what he criticizes is what is most faulty in himself. These are the usual things. And these, one can, of course, correct without further ado by turning within and saying to oneself, "Now, let's open *all* the drawers for once and see how things are with me." And then one discovers all sorts of things, and one sees that one doesn't need these projections any longer, that one doesn't have to project these things onto others. In this way, one can rid oneself of projections. But it isn't always a comfortable procedure; one suffers a few setbacks. One has to acknowledge that one isn't one hundred percent a fine stag. This is why the two questions go together.

One can only renew oneself if one takes charge of oneself. But people who habitually project always want to make others responsible, as if others were responsible for our own stupidities. For example, one's wife should treat one differently, because, in fact, one treats oneself stupidly. At least one's wife should do it right! And so on.

I knew of a case where the wife made the greatest scenes, even hurt her husband physically, because of thunderstorms! There is thunder and lightning, and the light flashes in her eyes, and her husband is responsible for it! She made him responsible, as if he'd been Zeus himself. If I were to introduce you to this woman you wouldn't think that she was in the least bit crazy. Quite the opposite: a highly reasonable woman. But she projected a lot; she kept blaming others, "Yes, if he or she or this or that had been different, then, of course, I'd be different." Or, "There's lightning, and, by golly, it's flashing in my eyes." A thunderstorm in the skies aims at her, because she is such a tremendously important person, and long ago has been put on Zeus' list to be aimed at, because she is such a fantastic Semele[255] or some such thing. That wouldn't be the case, if her husband weren't to blame. I asked her how her husband could be blamed and how she could make him responsible. It turned out that he was fond of thunderstorms. He loved thunderstorms! And that is his damn nastiness, that he loves what has been aimed at her and wants to kill her. This is why he is the secret ally of Zeus and Semele, who was consumed by the divine fire.

Now this is a Greek myth, played out in the life of a completely reasonable Swiss woman. She is Semele – and doesn't know it. He is, if not Zeus himself, at least a colleague of Zeus and a co-conspirator. Zeus aims, by golly, at her, because she is a goddess, a semi-goddess, a Semele, and if there is a thunderstorm, lightning would hit her. She sees clearly how lightning is flashing in her eyes, and that is a terrible impudence. Her whole reputation is being put into question, as Zeus has it in for her. And yet, it is a very fine thing when Zeus himself is interested in one's personhood. And her husband lets it all happen; he doesn't stop those thunderstorms. He is, you see, a colleague, a co-conspirator of Zeus, who wants to hand her over to Zeus. It is a whole conglomerate of "plots," of cabals. Out of this arises a very complicated play of emotions towards the husband. She doesn't know this; she has no clue. So, if she wants to liberate herself from these projections, she'd have to go to her little room in private, sit on a chair and write, "So, my husband makes thunderstorms." Then she'd say, "No, now that's too crass. My husband can't make thunderstorms. But where do these flashes in my eyes come from?" – That is the "lightning-god" who is after her. But she still doesn't realize that it is *she* who has it in for the "lightning-god." That's the tricky part.

255 The mortal mother of Dionysus, by Zeus.

These are the reflections she has to make, and when she can make such reflections, she'll come out of her projections.

The miracle is how these people come to have such archetypal ideas. But that's because we all have a collective unconscious that contains such ideas. And if something is not particularly interesting … well, one doesn't go for a walk in a golden chaise; Zeus doesn't come through the roof in the form of golden rain; and one doesn't ride a Europa bull – ah yes, then life would be beautiful – but one has to ride the streetcar in the city, and that's so boring. Then archetypal compensations come up, and people construct such ridiculous fantasies. Of course, these are very interesting for the clinician who treats them. You're apt to hear, for example, the whole Greek mythology in the Zurich dialect; it happens on street number such-and-such in Zurich, and it is Mrs. So-and-so – Mrs. Cabbage-head. It is all terribly banal, but when you look carefully, it is actually "The God and the Bayadere," or "Zeus and Semele" and so on. Under certain circumstances, this may ruin a marriage; it ruins the relationship with the children, if, for example, a woman has a Semele fantasy, which happens quite often. Then what happens to her son? In that case, he is Dionysus! Woe betide him! He is being drawn into the myth and has to embody Dionysus. If he becomes an alcoholic, the whole world will wonder why. He could well have become an alcoholic in honor of this myth.

I've seen more than one case where the mother, a most reasonable person, had all sorts of fantasies with just such Zeus characteristics. After all, you know how many love affairs Zeus had. Nothing of the sort happened in her own life; however, she had a son who then committed all these foolish things. And then his mother wondered why; she didn't know anything. Because all projections work like missiles, psychic missiles. If someone projects onto you, it is as if you were hit by a missile. The god is like something that enters into you. A man, for example, can be made completely crazy by female projections, without realizing what's happening to him. A female missile has hit him. And the other way around. This is why it is important to know what belongs to one, and what doesn't belong to one. If, therefore, the aforementioned lady, with her Semele fantasies, would have had the inclination to think whether she really was Semele, lover of Zeus, mother of a god, she'd soon be taught otherwise. But this is never thought about, only acted out, done; one lets it happen. This precisely is the danger. From there, of course, arise neuroses, this you can easily see. Just imagine a man who, for his wife, virtually represents Zeus, or perhaps just a colleague of Zeus, and who is suspected of making thunderstorms. Lord – after some time, he inevitably must have a megalomania! If he doesn't think about it, then he only feels the effect from others' reaction to him, as if he was "god-be-with-us" himself. This, of course, has an *effect*. This changes him. This is why there are many men – with the assorted corresponding women – who through marriage come into a very strange psychic disposition by way of such archetypes, which the wife brings with her. And vice versa! I always have to add that. It's not only one gender, it's the other one too. This poisons our society and our personal relationships to a high degree, because it doesn't fit. It doesn't fit with us. This is why I need to know who I am, if I want to free myself from such things. It means that I need to know that it doesn't belong to me to have such affectations. Perhaps I have such an affectation if it was shot into me, secretly shot into my back. One can ruin someone with such expectations, especially children. For example, the mother can completely ruin her son by having the wrong expectations. She can "twist" him, and this can happen with grown-ups too. This is why the analysis of projections is so important.

Of course, as a medical doctor I couldn't afford to have fun with my patients by staging Greek myths. To the contrary, I had to pay attention so that I noticed the projections. For this reason, I couldn't afford to also project. If one has a profession like I have had, then, of course, the devil only knows what is projected into one. One is the savior, and who knows what else. It's …! One finally gets sick and tired of it. But if one doesn't know this, it has devastating consequences! It is a rule that parents, be it the father or the mother, want to elicit the very thing in their children that they don't do themselves. They push their children into the life they haven't lived themselves. This is unrelentingly so. It is a mathematical formula. One can see very clearly the effect on the children. I believe that a year ago I gave you here, in this circle, an example of a family in which six daughters had to personify the anima of the father.

Group: No.

C. G. Jung: No? The father was – to use a decent expression – a bourgeois[256]. He didn't know that he also had a rabble-rouser within him. So, he had six daughters, and he was a great hater of Germans. The first daughter married a German theologian. Theologians he couldn't stand anyway. The second was engaged for years to a German theologian as well, and finally married him. The third had a long-lasting affair with a German, *à l'insu de ses parents*[257], and ended up marrying him. It was a rather scandalous story. She'd already had a certain artistic inclination. Even more so the fourth, who had strong artistic inclinations. This one teamed up with the youngest one, the fifth daughter.[258] They both lived in a bed and breakfast in Paris and went out with Corsicans; they were leading such a wild life that it almost created a scandal for this absolutely honorable family. I then had the middle daughter come to see me and told her, "You know, I heard it all – something has to be done." After all, these girls had been spoiled by the family, by the parents. She said, "It's so terrible – I don't know what to do. This doesn't work, does it?!" I said, "Yes, it is a highly alarming situation." I didn't know these people otherwise, but I knew the family as a very good family, and also as decent people. So, I said, "We have to initiate something. Go home and write to your sister that Professor Jung doesn't agree with how they carry on." Whereupon both sisters went back home. The whole thing was called off and both got married – namely because I meddled in their affairs. I took on the role of the father and said, "Under no circumstances is this going to work!" If the father had said this just once, if he'd only once wanted to know what was going on there, the whole thing would not have happened. Because then they would have realized their projections, their expectations. They were all "twisted" by the fact that their father wasn't aware of a piece of life within him, and that their mother had a field of vision as if she was eternally looking through a cigar box. She didn't react either. When I asked the daughter, "Why didn't you ever speak about this with your father or your mother?" she said, "That's impossible. You can't discuss that. Such a thing doesn't exist in our environment." That's

256 Jung uses the German *Pfahlbürger*, a mix of citizen and "Pfahlbauer", the prehistoric pile dwellers who lived in pile villages on lakes around the Alps.
257 French, without the parents' knowledge.
258 Here, Jung rectifies his misperception: there were five, not six daughters.

the right attitude for projections to flourish! These children simply had to compensate for the pitiful, narrow horizon of their mother and the even more deplorable narrowness of their father. Some of them had to marry what their father hated, what he despised, and the others what their mother hated and despised. This, then, goes with the saying: "Father's blessing builds houses for the children. But mother's curse tears them down."[259] Only here there wasn't any blessing, because there were such projections. But what family doesn't have such projections? If I hadn't intervened there, those two girls would have slipped into prostitution. As simple as that. Just imagine such a thing: two Swiss girls with Corsicans, embroiled in vendettas, tinkering with sharp knives. One would fear that they'd be murdered at some point.

Now I have to stop; now I've had enough.

Sabi Tauber: Would you like to have a glass of wine now?

C. G. Jung: No, no – now I have to travel home, on the wings of the wind, *littéralement!*[260]

Ignaz Tauber: I believe I speak on behalf of everyone when I thank you cordially for the efforts you have made to give us a sense of your knowledge and experience.

C. G. Jung: I'm always afraid that I talk too much and repeat myself. Didn't I tell you a story twice? Isn't it true, when one gets old, there comes this *loquacitas senilis.*[261] I had an uncle who said to his sons, "When you notice that it doesn't function so well anymore, please let me know. Then I'll retire." They promised, and, a few years later, they found that the time had come for the old man to retire. The oldest son went to him and said, "Father, we thought it is now time for you to retire." Whereupon the father replied, "What? Never before did I feel so alive, strong, and youthful! I've never been in such good form!" – It was already too late!

---

259 Ecclesiasticus (Book of Sirach) 3:9: "For a father's blessing strengthens the house of the children, but a mother's curse uproots their foundations."
260 "literally", Jung says it in French.
261 Senile talkativeness.

Fig. 28: C. G. Jung, June 27, 1959.

Chats on the Way Home

On the way home, he told us about the Seven Sleepers Day: If it rains that day, it'll rain for a long time thereafter.[262] The conversation revolved around northern countries, how Sweden, for example, has only had a theology for the last fifty years, Jung noted, evident in the latest sermon given by the archbishop of Stockholm (rather dull, "father as fate," nothing else). People in the north were closer to nature, Jung said, more pagan, rather less spiritual, if only because of the big, long-lasting darkness through the winter months. One knew more of almost every other nation. In Germany there has been a philosophy since Carus[263], a cultural wealth that still hasn't been completely absorbed. It takes a lot of time.

Ignaz talked about his ongoing struggle between his practice and his scientific work. Jung told him that he'd only really started to do scientific work after he'd become an invalid.[264] "I owe the best part to my practice; everything came out of it. There is meaning in having helped others. One feels justification. A scientist is always too one-sided; egotism looms large, and human satisfaction is missing."

And so, this Seven Sleepers Day came to an end.

In the legend from about the 6th century, it is said that seven young Christians fled the persecution of the emperor Decius and were walled in on Mt. Achilleus. After about two hundred years, God reawakened them, so that through the example of their fate, they could teach the emperor Theodosius the doctrine of the resurrection of the dead. The legend is not solely Christian. It also contains elements of Kabir worship in the Near East, the myth of Endymion[265],

262 A predictive lore comparable to Groundhog Day.
263 Paul Carus (1852–1919), American philosopher, born and educated in Germany.
264 Jung probably means after his heart attack, 1944.
265 Selene falls in love with Endymion, moves him into a cave and, with the help of Zeus, lets him sink into eternal sleep; thus she begets 50 daughters with him.

the nine sleepers of Sardinia[266], the Assumptio Mosis, the legend of Abimelech, et cetera.[267]

How much longer do we have to sleep? The dormouse[268] hibernates through winter for many months (and is especially active at night) – so that there always will be a new spring – and a new day.

---

266 See report in *The American Journal of Philology*, 1881, vol. 2, No. 5, p. 123.
267 See C. G. Jung, "Concerning Rebirth", CW 9/I, pars. 240 ff.
268 In popular belief, the name of the day refers to the dormouse, a rodent known as *Siebenschläfer* in German for its seven-months hibernation.

1960

On January 3, I had the following dream:

> We receive a red and golden box from Jung, with "something precious and substantial" in it. I was very happy. It wasn't anything written, no books, but I put it among his books and was really glad that it wasn't a book, but something "truly real."

A great weariness seemed to lay itself upon Jung. Only rarely did we get to see him. A brief greeting, a visit with flowers, hearing about him. These things widened the distance and prepared for the last farewell. "I wanted to go a long time ago, but you keep holding me back with ropes," he'd supposedly said.

Still, Jung celebrated his 85th birthday with visible joy. Elsi Attenhofer[269] regaled him with her play at the Grand Hotel Dolder, Zurich.

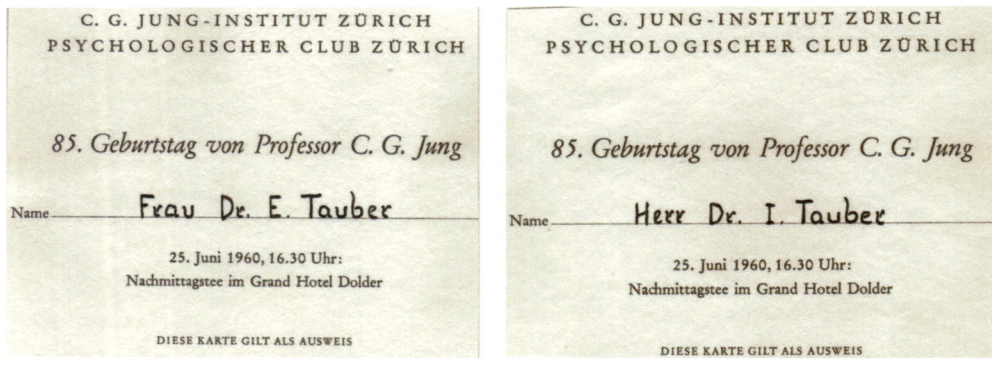

Fig. 29: Invitation to Jung's 85th birthday
for afternoon tea at the Grand Hotel Dolder.

Cornelia Brunner's birthday address spoke to our hearts and minds:

"This celebration is cause for deep gratitude, foremost because we have our dear jubilarian with us today and can celebrate with him,

269 Swiss cabaret artist and actress.

and because the fullness of days for the completion of his great work was given to him. We want to thank you that you continue to change our lives with your work. For this is the greatness of your psychology: that it seizes people and transforms their lives. What we own innately, we have received again through the insights gained from psychology. Beyond our brief, daily existence, our lives have gained meaning and significance for us and for our environment through you. You have given us the key to access the treasures of the unconscious and, with it, to the seeds of the future. With this treasure we are no longer so blindly at the mercy of fate; we can recognize the 'patterning' and learn to put ourselves in the service of inner order.

As a woman I would like to thank you especially in the name of us women. You reinstated for us the lost feminine god-image as a primal archetypal image of the feminine principle, in all of its dignity and eternal significance. Thus, we are no longer solely dependent on orienting ourselves according to the masculine moral principle. We are given the possibility to find our way back to our own feminine being with its own ethos of feeling. At the same time, you also have helped us with our spiritual development from the source of our own inner nature. Instead of the duty to believe, you have given us the possibility of direct religious experience that reaches back into the past, to the natural roots of the eternal images.

One of your most important gifts is a new valuation of the here and now. You help us to recognize and form the dormant germs of life until they become lived reality. Thereby you unite the Otherworld and This World, unconscious and consciousness – nothing is as difficult to bear as unlived life! You expect from a man that he tries out his ideas in life, and from a woman that she becomes conscious of life. It is not through flight from life, but through consciously living life that we attain spiritual meaning.

All of us received the same task from Jung: If we don't break down over our mistakes, but instead learn from them; if we can approximately fulfill the challenge that life has set for us; if we are able to build on what is given to us; if we are heard by others in small or large circles – then we all carry out Jung's mission. With Jung and through Jung a new époque has begun for us."

1961

Ein Jahr, ein Jahr
ist wiederum vorüber.
Und wenn wir oft auch Leid erfahren,
manche Stunden glücklich waren,
lasst uns singen: Bruder!
Du bist mein Kamerad,
Du bist mein Kamerad![270]

A feeling along these lines has long been nudging me to bring the "Wild Geese"[271] to Jung. Finally, I wrote him a letter, describing our "Wild Geese Club." Apparently, he found pleasure in it and wrote back at once [fig. 30].

This was the last note we received with his signature.

How overjoyed I was! Unfortunately, not all of the "Wild Geese" could (or would want to) be with the party – their loss. Present were Maria and Hans Baumann, Helen and Peter Stierlin, Alice Rüsch, Ignaz and Sabi Tauber.

270 A year, a year / Has passed again. / And though we often went through grief / There were many happy hours too. / Let us sing: brother! / You are my comrade, / You are my comrade! (Soldier's song by Kurt Onken, World War II.)

271 The origin of the name is not clear. Possible and meaningful would be the reference to Hexagram # 53 *The Evolution*, in the *I Ching*. – In any case, a quartet of women, girlfriends from gymnasium-times, had called themselves "Wild Geese." They all had become doctor's wives and mothers, when they undertook a few times a year a little trip to a chosen destination, enjoying a nice meal and perhaps a visit to an exhibit of some sort. The idea was to get away from the demanding everyday life. The wild geese, flying high up in the clean blue air, fast and free, served them as image. In later life, their husbands had joined this "Club."

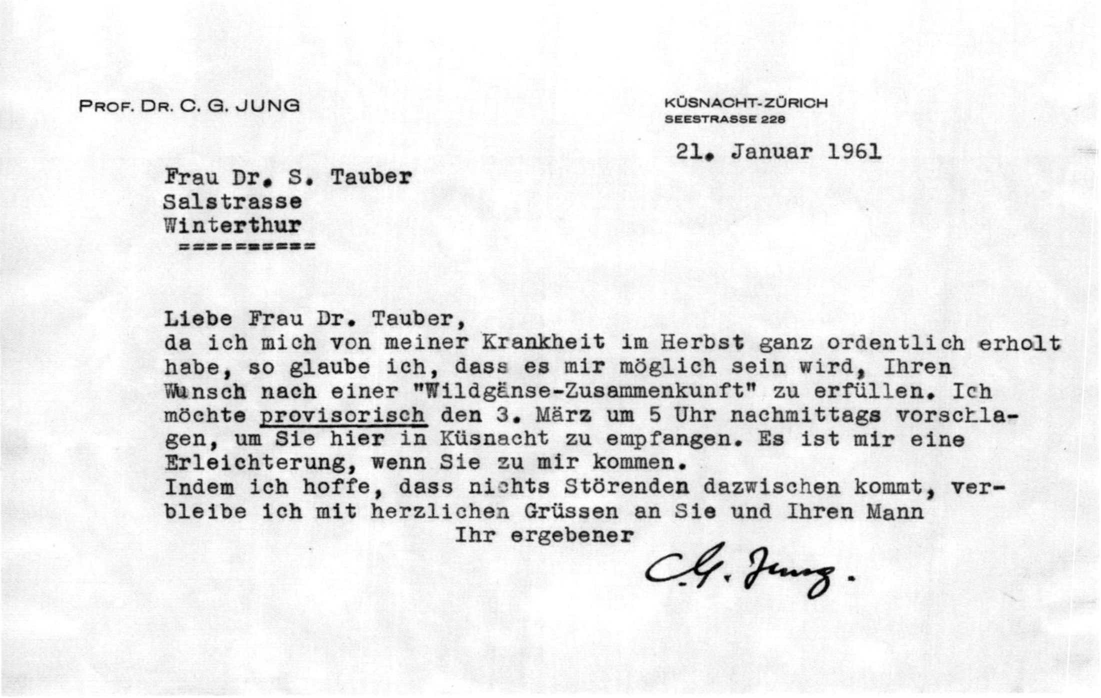

KÜSNACHT-ZÜRICH
SEESTRASSE 228

21. Januar 1961

Frau Dr. S. Tauber
Salstrasse
Winterthur
===========

Liebe Frau Dr. Tauber,
da ich mich von meiner Krankheit im Herbst ganz ordentlich erholt
habe, so glaube ich, dass es mir möglich sein wird, Ihren
Wunsch nach einer "Wildgänse-Zusammenkunft" zu erfüllen. Ich
möchte provisorisch den 3. März um 5 Uhr nachmittags vorschla-
gen, um Sie hier in Küsnacht zu empfangen. Es ist mir eine
Erleichterung, wenn Sie zu mir kommen.
Indem ich hoffe, dass nichts Störenden dazwischen kommt, ver-
bleibe ich mit herzlichen Grüssen an Sie und Ihren Mann
                    Ihr ergebener

                        C. G. Jung.

Fig. 30: Invitation to the "Wild Geese" gathering.
Letter of C. G. Jung to Sabi Tauber, January 21, 1961.

Dear Frau Dr. Tauber,
As I recovered reasonably well from my illness this past fall I believe that it will be possible for me to grant you the wish of a "Wild Geese gathering." I suggest tentatively
3 March at 5 pm, receiving you here in Küsnacht. I'm relieved if you are able to come
to my place.
Hoping that nothing will interfere, I remain with cordial regards to you and your
husband,
Your devoted
C. G. Jung

Fig. 31: C. G. Jung in the circle of the "Wild Geese" gathering.

"Wild Geese" March 3, 1961 in Küsnacht

Jung received us in his large living room, in a convivial and visibly light-hearted mood. Miss [Ruth] Bailey had prepared a sumptuous table for us. There was an ambiance of Mozart's cheerfulness, wherein the absence of Mrs. Jung provided the dark undertone. (I felt a bit ashamed when the words of Marie von Ebner-Eschenbach[272] suddenly came into my mind: "Men are leaders in all areas of life, only on the way to heaven they let women go first.") – Miss Bailey poured tea, after which Jung's subtle impatience made her disappear quickly. He wasn't interested in small talk, immediately urging us into *medias res*[273]. I was to sit on his left in the role of "interpreter," as his hearing had greatly diminished.

To begin with, Ignaz had a question about archetypes. Shortly before our meeting, we'd had a rather heated discussion as to whether instinct and archetype were opposites, or whether the archetype also contained instinct. He put it to Jung like this:

"Galilei corrected the geocentric worldview and proved the heliocentric system. Isn't your theory of the archetypes a similar discovery? It enlarged the egocentric, shortsighted attitude of man to become the right, 'deo-centric' worldview."

Jung answered, "Yes, yes, this is why his portrait is hanging there!" (pointing to the wall). "Indeed, the two are comparable."[274]

The rest of his explanation continued as follows (later reconstructed with great care):

Of course, the archetype also contains the energetic dimension. It is qualitative *and* quantitative, simply everything, the ultimate recognizable factor determining both impulse and form in organic and inorganic nature.

272 A famous German poet (1830–1916).
273 The core of the matter at hand
274 A portrait of Galileo Galilei hangs in the dining room, a copy after the original by Justus Sustermans, Uffizi Gallery, Florence.

Jung proceeded by telling us how he had come to recognize the archetype in a completely empirical manner. It isn't a well-defined entity; it cannot be seen. For example, an archetype could appear in the form of a tree, symbolizing the mother archetype, but also as a phallus, like a mushroom, standing for masculinity. It has two poles, two opposed aspects (e.g. loving mother / all-devouring mother), and as a result of that polarity it is energetically charged. Without the two poles it would have no energy.

Hans asked whether the schema of Tinbergen[275] could be associated with it, but Jung thought there was no exact correspondence.

Jung continued with his elaborations, taking only occasional breathers: how the natural sciences knew nothing about the Otherworld, the hereafter, so the only available recourse was – and he himself had learned to live accordingly – to listen to what is communicated from within, through dreams and other means.

Once he'd dreamed of a person close to him about the way she had died: she had disappeared as if through an explosion, and then transited in a mysterious way into a different state. Whereupon he asked his surrounding neighborhood whether a child had been born recently. At some point, someone brought him the news that a girl had been born to an acquainted family. "Ah – my surprise was great: if the mother only knew to whom she'd given birth!" He was careful, however, not to say anything of the sort, but soon afterward he went to visit the little girl (obviously because he wanted to welcome the reincarnated person, which, of course, he didn't mention). The Newfoundland dog of the family, otherwise remarkably child-friendly, hadn't even noticed the child until the moment of Jung's presence. Sometimes later, Jung received a letter from the mother, telling him that the dog had become very attached to the little girl since Jung's visit, as if only with his visit the child became quasi legitimate.

Often he told himself at the dinner table, "These 'my' children are, in fact, total strangers, whom fate has assigned to my house as if 'accidentally.' Who knows where they've come from and what will

275 Nicholaas Tinbergen (1907–1988), Dutch biologist, one of the founders of ethology; he proposed four complementary categories of explanation for animal behavior.

become of them." In general, he didn't talk about his research and problems during family meals.

Whenever he felt anxious about an archetype having him in its grip, he repeated to himself over and over, "I am, first of all, a captain in the Swiss army; next, I have a medical license; I am father of five children, and I live at Seestrasse 228 in Küsnacht."

Jung shared with us how he always felt "magically touched" when his mother scolded him – even as a student and grown man his heart started to pound when she summoned him. She could act completely unconsciously. As a boy he once beat up the neighbor's children and had been disciplined accordingly. When, in the aftermath, he was playing with blocks behind the sewing machine, feeling small and humiliated, he suddenly heard his mother mumbling, "It would have been better to do away with the whole brood ..." (meaning the neighbor's children). If one would have taken her to task about her pronouncement afterwards, she would have refused the accusation with outrage. Even much later, when he already had his practice in Küsnacht, she once appeared out of the blue and asked to talk to him. He immediately felt the tachycardia coming on, as ever. After her sermon he stood there feeling destroyed, but she took leave kindly, saying without any affect, "That's what I wanted to tell you, just so you know."

Women are "given" factors, like the weather. They are here; they have an effect, and one may not bemoan them when they hurt you. For better or for worse, they have form-giving significance for men. His wife, still mostly lived in the Middle Ages. Her world ended in circa 1870. For twenty-five years she worked on her book about Perceval without finishing it, because the magician Merlin remained a puzzle for her. Jung himself understood this figure only after becoming acquainted with the alchemists.

I suggested that his wife bridged the distance between him and her with her love for him.

"Only to a certain degree," he responded.

Can he be so sure!?

As an aside, Gret Baumann-Jung once had told me that Emma Jung had never understood how anyone could lose the joy of life. She herself had to go through so much terrible hardship because of her husband and all the crazy women, but she never lost her *joie de vivre*. She, Gret, could only explain it like this: Emma must have had a very "young soul," a lot of fresh, available natural energy. He, on the other hand, had a very "old soul."

Miss Bailey kept looking through the crack of the door with increasing frequency, thus reminding us to wrap it up. Jung, animated and in good spirits, would have regaled us for much longer with stories from the wellspring of his lively world. Two hours had flown by. It seemed that he, too, regretted our departure. Surely, he felt our eager participation and understanding. How often he must have felt lonely? Our gratitude and words of appreciation made for a joyful mood even as we parted. (Thank god for such rituals – otherwise humanity would, indeed, fall prey to the archetypes.)

As it happened, on this evening with the "Wild Geese Club" I saw him for the last time. *He* has taught me to form genuine relationships with eros. *He* has shown all of us the possibility of creating culture out of transference. Not the total sacrifice is required, but a transformation! Perhaps that is why the invaluable gift of our encounter with Jung was completed in this way. The circle had closed – around us.

Far off in the North our oldest daughter lived her strong-willed, young life, shaken by hefty inner storms. In her distress she asked Jung for advice. And she received one of his very last letters.[276]

Küsnacht-Zurich, May 17, 1961

Dear Fräulein Tauber,
Prof. Jung read your letter and asked me to write to you – he himself does not feel healthy enough to answer personally –, that the story of the Fall is still valid, because it is a myth, and what is said in the myth is unquestionable and always valid.
Prof. Jung then quoted: "You lead us into life, / You let the wretched man feel guilt, / And then you leave him to his pain, / For all guilt avenges itself on earth."[277]

276 Translated from German by the editors.
277 J. W. von Goethe, *Wilhelm Meister's Apprenticeship*.

He then continued: You can't create anything without guilt, and only he who pays the costs can achieve something.

With kind wishes,
Aniela Jaffé, sec.

Not the sacrifice is required, but a transformation! Not to the beyond belongs our purest love, but within our living hearts on this earth. *Hic Rhodus, hic salta!* Only then our self is redeemed from this world, to enter with its unique name into eternity – for an uncertain duration.

> You, guru, I was allowed to witness
> in real life –
> and thus build a castle for my soul.
> Windows and doors open –
> hopefulness alive –
> walls constructed in measure and plumb line
> for humanity's needs.
> Oh, please!
> Let your star
> shine from afar,
> into his middle –
> a life
> upon which you bestowed meaning.

Fig. 32: Ex Libris Sabi Tauber.

Translator's Note

As their daughter-in-law I had the privilege of getting to know Sabi and Ignaz at a more mature age, as elders. The major storms in life and in their marriage, which form much of the content of this journal, had either softened or been outgrown, as Jung would say.

Remarkably, the threads weaving my parents and my future in-laws together reached back to the mid-1930s, when they all attended medical school at the University of Zurich. There they knew each other and bonded with their respective partners. Some students were aware that a certain psychiatrist, C. G. Jung, held interesting seminars at the ETH (Swiss Federal Institute of Technology), and to go or not to go was a topic of discussion. As I've heard it, Ignaz declined, too busy earning his livelihood, and Sabi refused, at the time still dismissing psychology altogether. My mother, on the other hand, secretly attended one or the other of these seminars, as she much later told me.

My parents settled in Zurich, both of them practicing medicine while raising their family. It was a bilingual household, given that my mother had grown up in Biel, a town at the border between the German and the French speaking Switzerland. She exposed us children (of which I was the oldest) early on to the French language, which included hiring French speaking household help and even hosting a school girl from war-torn Paris for a year. Since then, my love for languages and translation was a constant.

In 1962, we moved to Winterthur when my father accepted a chief of staff position at the Canton Hospital. The parents celebrated a reacquaintance, joining the families together and subsequently nurturing their new-found friendship in various ways. Meanwhile, there was a gradual rapprochement between the Tauber's elder son, Jürg, and myself. We got married in 1966 – he, fresh out of medical school and ready for his surgical residency and I in the third year of the Romance Languages program at University Zurich.

Sabi and Ignaz had become my role models through their very way of being: their humor facing the vicissitudes of daily life and a playfulness with each other and with whatever arose from the unconscious. They introduced me to Jung's psychology with all its ramifications, including the *I Ching*, the tarot, and astrology – all of it new, mysterious, and promising. I started to record my dreams and imitated Sabi's way of painting images. I was intrigued by this different kind of translation, from night-time dream stories and images to day-time language and practice.

Since Jung's death, Sabi had intensified her studies in Eastern philosophy. She'd become an avid reader of books written by the great Chinese philosophers and Japanese Zen Buddhists. Years later, she would feel especially gratified when she discovered that her childhood nickname had a particular meaning in Japanese. As she wrote in a letter, July 18, 1985, it means "true art," in the sense of an attitude characteristic of Zen, "Where this beauty of the incomplete is related with the ancient, original-unrefined, there you find a wisp of Sabi."

Her enthusiasm and devotion inspired us young ones in turn. Indeed, aside from Jung's psychology, medicine, music and the arts, Zen practice would become part of the foundation of our marriage and family life – before and after our immigration to the United States, in 1971. As is the case for most immigrants, we preserved our native language and customs within our family. During the first seven years in New York City, I entertained a lively correspondence with those "back home," and I considered myself lucky to spend most summer vacations in Switzerland with our two, later three children.

I've given a synopsis of our life in the introduction of my book, *The Soul's Ministrations* (Chiron, 2012), leading up to the tragic moment when Jürg was diagnosed with a tumor in the brain stem and surgery was scheduled immediately.

It was May, 1984, in Chicago. Sabi and Ignaz arranged to come to our aid for much-needed physical, emotional, and spiritual support. At that occasion, Sabi brought a machine-typed copy of her journal along. "For the waiting time," (during recovery), she'd scribbled on the cover. It was a welcome gift, and ever since I've kept the manuscript like a sacred treasure.

Jürg died in November 1989, in Sacramento, leaving us bereft and at a great loss. I started analysis, unsure of the direction my life was going to take. Looking for an inspiring task that would help me overcome my grief and spiritual loneliness, I remembered Sabi's journal: Could I engage in the formidable task of translating it into English, perhaps for later publication? In her response to my letter, asking for her opinion and permission, Sabi happily agreed. I made some inroads at the time, and at the occasion of the next family visit to Switzerland Sabi and I had several conversations about it. However, once I returned to graduate school, in 1993, earning an MA in counseling and a PhD in clinical depth psychology, the project was put on hold. Regretfully, my mother-in-law didn't see it come to fruition anymore.

Two decades would pass before the time was right for me to pick up the translation of Sabi's journal again. I started from the very beginning, this time around with considerably better mastery of the English language and the necessary computer skills. Nevertheless, it remained an enduring and tearful labor of love. If, in my initial attempt, I cried over my own inability, it now was the very content, page by page, that moved me to tears. I value the journal as a unique and precious document that will significantly contribute to the Jungian literature.

Marianne Tauber
Los Angeles, May, 2021

Index of Figures

Volume 1 of this series:

Stone by Stone
Reflections on the Psychology
of C. G. Jung

Edited by Andreas Schweizer
and Regine Schweizer-Vüllers

352 pages, hardbound, illustrated in color
ISBN 978-3-85630-765-3

This volume comprises original contributions by Carl Gustav Jung and Marie-Louise von Franz, along with additional works addressing analytical psychology. It is being published in honor of the centennial existence of the Psychology Club of Zurich (1916-2016).

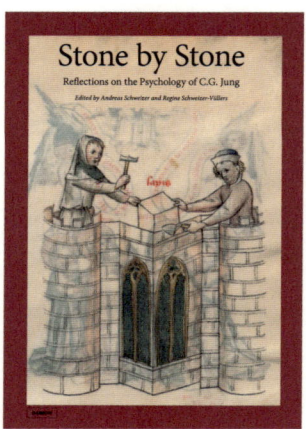

Contents:

Andreas Schweizer, *I Ching – The Book of the Play of Opposites*

Marie-Louise von Franz, *Conversation on the Psychology Club Zurich*

Marie-Louise von Franz, *The Goose Girl (Grimm's Fairy Tales, nr. 89)*

Regine Schweizer-Vüllers, *"He struck the rock and the waters did flow" – The alchemical background of the gravestone of Marie-Louise von Franz and Barbara Hannah*

Tony Woolfson, *"I came across this impressive doctrine" – Carl Gustav Jung, Gershom Scholem, and Kabbalah*

C.G. Jung, *A Discussion about Aion, Psychological Society of Basel, 1952*

Murray Stein, *Jungian Psychology and the Spirit of Protestantism*

Marianne Jehle-Wildberger, *Stations of a Difficult Friendship – Carl Gustav Jung and Adolf Keller*

Hermann Strobel, *Aloneness as Calling*

Claudine Koch-Morgenegg, *The Great Mystery – Individuation in Old Age*

Rudolf Högger, *The Treasure Vase – On the many-sided Symbolism of an Archaic God-Image from the Stone Age to the Dreams of Modern Man.*

Volume 2:

Wisdom has Built her House
Psychological Aspects of the Feminine

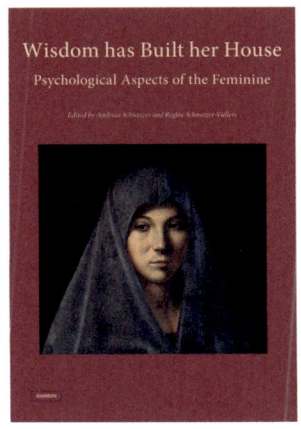

Edited by Andreas Schweizer
and Regine Schweizer-Vüllers

260 pages, hardbound, illustrated in color
ISBN 978-3-85630-776-9

For the house of wisdom that already exists in the beyond – in the unconscious – to truly manifest within an individual human being, the whole of a person is required, along with all their four psychic functions of consciousness. This encounter with wholeness – with the divine – is a shocking event that leaves both parties – the human and the divine – renewed. The cover image of this volume portrays precisely this kind of event. It was painted by a Sicilian artist, Antonello da Messina (15th century) and it depicts *L'Annunciata, The Annunciation of Mary*, the fateful moment in which Mary encounters the Archangel Gabriel and becomes aware of her destiny. The angel is not depicted; we see only Mary and the shock she experiences in her encounter with the divine.

The essays in this volume by Marie-Louise von Franz, Rivkah Schärf Kluger, Gotthilf Isler, and Laurel Howe revolve around this encounter. They detail the possible union of the opposites – the divine with the human, the feminine with the masculine, the demonic with the redemptive. Ultimately, they are all about a new god-image in which the feminine – Wisdom in its feminine form – is united with the masculine. This development has been in the making within the collective unconscious for centuries and it wants to become a reality in our time.

Contents:

English Titles from Daimon

Ruth Ammann - *The Enchantment of Gardens*
Susan R. Bach - *Life Paints its Own Span*
Diana Baynes Jansen - *Jung's Apprentice: A Biography of Helton Godwin Baynes*
John Beebe (Ed.) - *Terror, Violence and the Impulse to Destroy*
E.A. Bennet - *Meetings with Jung*
W.H. Bleek / L.C. Lloyd (Ed.) - *Specimens of Bushman Folklore*
Tess Castleman - *Threads, Knots, Tapestries*
- *Sacred Dream Circles*
Renate Daniel - *Taking the Fear out of the Night*
- *The Self: Quest for Meaning in a Changing World*
Eranos Yearbook 69 - *Eranos Reborn*
Eranos Yearbook 70 - *Love on a Fragile Thread*
Eranos Yearbook 71 - *Beyond Masters*
Eranos Yearbook 72 - *Soul between Enchantment and Disenchantment*
Eranos Yearbook 73 - *The World and its Shadow*
Michael Escamilla - *Bleuler, Jung, and the Schizophrenias*
Heinrich Karl Fierz - *Jungian Psychiatry*
John Fraim - *Battle of Symbols*
Liliane Frey-Rohn - *Friedrich Nietzsche, A Psychological Approach*
Marion Gallbach - *Learning from Dreams*
Ralph Goldstein (Ed.) - *Images, Meanings & Connections: Essays in Memory of Susan Bach*
Yael Haft - *Hands: Archetypal Chirology*
Fred Gustafson - *The Black Madonna of Einsiedeln*
Daniel Hell - *Soul-Hunger: The Feeling Human Being and the Life-Sciences*
Siegmund Hurwitz - *Lilith, the first Eve*
Aniela Jaffé - *The Myth of Meaning*
- *Was C.G. Jung a Mystic?*
- *From the Life and Work of C.G. Jung*
- *Death Dreams and Ghosts*
C.G. Jung - *The Solar Myths and Opicinus de Canistris*
Verena Kast - *A Time to Mourn*
- *Sisyphus*
Hayao Kawai - *Dreams, Myths and Fairy Tales in Japan*
James Kirsch - *The Reluctant Prophet*
Eva Langley-Dános - *Prison on Wheels: Ravensbrück to Burgau*
Rivkah Schärf Kluger - *The Gilgamesh Epic*
Yehezkel Kluger & - *RUTH in the Light of Mythology, Legend*
Nomi Kluger-Nash   *and Kabbalah*
Paul Kugler (Ed.) - *Jungian Perspectives on Clinical Supervision*
Paul Kugler - *The Alchemy of Discourse*
Rafael López-Pedraza - *Cultural Anxiety*
- *Hermes and his Children*
Alan McGlashan - *The Savage and Beautiful Country*
- *Gravity & Levity*
Gregory McNamee (Ed.) - *The Girl Who Made Stars: Bushman Folklore*
- *The North Wind and the Sun & Other Fables of Aesop*
Gitta Mallasz / Hanna Dallos - *Talking with Angels*
C.A. Meier - *Healing Dream and Ritual*
- *A Testament to the Wilderness*
- *Personality: The Individuation Process*
Haruki Murakami - *Haruki Murakami Goes to Meet Hayao Kawai*
Eva Pattis Zoja (Ed.) - *Sandplay Therapy*

English Titles from Daimon

Our books are available from your bookstore or from our distributors:

Baker & Taylor	Gazelle Book Services Ltd.
30 Amberwood Parkway	White Cross Mills, High Town
Ashland OH 44805, USA	Lancaster LA1 4XS, UK
Phone: 419-281-5100	Tel: +44 1524 528500
Fax: 419-281-0200	Email: sales@gazellebookservices.co.uk
www.btpubservices.com	www.gazellebookservices.co.uk

Daimon Verlag - Hauptstrasse 85 - CH-8840 Einsiedeln - Switzerland
Phone: (41)(55) 412 2266
Email: info@daimon.ch
Visit our website: **www.daimon.ch** or write for our complete catalog